'This excellent book should never need to have been written. The fact that it has been written is a shocking indictment of the dissembling sophistry and opaqueness of health service gatekeeping in NHS continuing healthcare over the last 20 years or more. A copy should be essential reading for the Secretary of State for Health and all health service managers and social workers involved in CHC decision-making. It is my hope this book will put the woeful application of CHC decision-making back under the spotlight and into the national conversation, and arm those representing those entitled to CHC with the arguments to ensure that NHS clinical commissioning groups no longer manage to deprive entitled people of their right to free CHC and in many cases force them into inappropriate means-tested social care or place undue pressure onto their carers.'

– *Simon Bull C.Q.S.W., Assistant Borough Solicitor, Bracknell Council*

'This book provides a fantastic overview of NHS continuing healthcare and is written to give people the information they need. It is incredibly helpful for people who want to learn more about CHC and equip themselves for the often-laborious process of applying for it.'

– *Alzheimer's Society*

by the same author

Safeguarding Adults and the Law, Third Edition
An A–Z of Law and Practice
ISBN 978 1 78592 225 1
eISBN 978 1 78450 499 1

Care Act 2014
An A–Z of Law and Practice
ISBN 978 1 84905 559 8
eISBN 978 0 85700 991 3

How We Treat the Sick
Neglect and Abuse in Our Health Services
ISBN 978 1 84905 160 6
eISBN 978 0 85700 355 3

Community Care Practice and the Law
Fourth Edition
ISBN 978 1 84310 691 3
eISBN 978 1 84642 859 3

Betraying the NHS
Health Abandoned
ISBN 978 1 84310 482 7
eISBN 978 1 84642 569 1

NHS Continuing Healthcare

An A–Z of Law, Practice, Funding Decisions and Challenges

Michael Mandelstam

Jessica Kingsley Publishers
London and Philadelphia

First published in 2020
by Jessica Kingsley Publishers
73 Collier Street
London N1 9BE, UK
and
400 Market Street, Suite 400
Philadelphia, PA 19106, USA

www.jkp.com

Copyright © Michael Mandelstam 2020

All rights reserved. No part of this publication may be reproduced in any material form (including photocopying, storing in any medium by electronic means or transmitting) without the written permission of the copyright owner except in accordance with the provisions of the law or under terms of a licence issued in the UK by the Copyright Licensing Agency Ltd. www.cla.co.uk or in overseas territories by the relevant reproduction rights organisation, for details see www.ifrro.org. Applications for the copyright owner's written permission to reproduce any part of this publication should be addressed to the publisher.

Warning: The doing of an unauthorised act in relation to a copyright work may result in both a civil claim for damages and criminal prosecution.

Library of Congress Cataloging in Publication Data
A CIP catalog record for this book is available from the Library of Congress

British Library Cataloguing in Publication Data
A CIP catalogue record for this book is available from the British Library

ISBN 978 1 78775 162 0
eISBN 978 1 78775 163 7

Printed and bound in Great Britain

Acknowledgements

Thanks are due as follows.

As ever to the staff at the public library in Sudbury, Suffolk for their unstinting and professional help. And to the office of the Public Service Ombudsman in Wales for supplying at short notice reports of a number of ombudsman cases.

To Peter Clifford and Nigel Bennett, with their trained eyes, for looking over the sense of the book. And to Hugh Mandelstam with an untrained eye (equally as useful) for doing the same.

Harking back many years, also to Bernie Crean and Simon Bull with whom I had many lengthy conversations about NHS Continuing Healthcare.

I would emphasise, however, that all expressed views, mistakes and any other infelicities are entirely my own.

Lastly, of course, I would like to thank all the staff at Jessica Kingsley Publishers. In particular Stephen Jones for talking through, and supporting the idea of, the book. And Victoria Peters for her unfailing efficiency and patience.

Contents

Note on terminology 11

Preface 13

1. Introduction 15
2. Basic rules and common pitfalls 19
3. Background, explanation and evidence of a dysfunctional system . . . 29
4. A–Z list 69
   - **A.** Accommodation and NHS Continuing Healthcare — 70
     - Adaptations, see *Home adaptations* — 71
     - Advocacy and NHS Continuing Healthcare — 71
     - Aids to daily living, see *Equipment* — 73
     - Altered states of consciousness, see *Decision Support Tool* — 73
     - Appropriate clinician (end of life) — 73
     - Assessment — 74
   - **B.** Breathing, see *Decision Support Tool* — 76
   - **C.** Care Act 2014 — 77
     - Carers — 80
     - Case management — 83
     - Challenging behaviour — 83
     - Challenging decisions — 85
     - Charging for services, see *Means-testing* — 85
     - Checklist — 85
     - Children — 91
     - Clinical commissioning groups — 91
     - Cognition, see *Decision Support Tool* — 100
     - Commissioning support units — 100

	Communication, see *Decision Support Tool*	101
	Competence, see *Expertise of assessors, and knowledge of the patient*	101
	Complexity	101
	Consent	102
	Consultation in decision-making	103
	Continence, see *Decision Support Tool*	104
	Continuity of care	104
	Cooperation	106
	Coordinator	107
	Cost-effectiveness	107
	Coughlan case	111
D.	Decision-making process	113
	Decision Support Tool	114
	Delay	122
	Deprivation of liberty	125
	Diagnosis	126
	Direct payments	126
	Discrimination	127
	Dispute resolution between NHS and social services	127
	Disputes between a person and the NHS	130
	Domains of need, see *Decision Support Tool*	134
	Double scoring	134
	Dowry payments, see *Learning disability*	135
	Drug therapies and medication, see *Decision Support Tool*	135
E.	Education, health and care plans	136
	Eligibility	138
	End of life, see *Fast Track Pathway Tool*	138
	Equipment	138
	Evidence of need	139
	Expertise of assessors, and knowledge of the patient	141
F.	Family involvement, see *Person and family involvement*	144
	Fast Track Pathway Tool (end of life)	144
	Final decisions about CHC eligibility, see *Clinical commissioning groups*	151
	Funded nursing care	151
G.	Gap between health and social care	156
	Grogan case	157
	Guidance	157
H.	Health care needs	159
	Health Service Ombudsman	161
	Health services generally	162
	Home adaptations	163
	Hospices	164
	Hospital discharge	164

I.	Incidental or ancillary or of a nature beyond social services	169
	Independent review panels	173
	Indicative cases	177
	Informal carers, see *Carers*	189
	Input (of care)	189
	Intensity	189
	Interim provision of care during assessment and decision	190
J.	Joint funding	192
	Joint working	194
	Judicial review	194
L.	Learning disability	198
	Legal cases, see *Indicative cases*	199
	Legal framework	199
	Legal remedies, see *Disputes between a person and the NHS*	200
	Local authorities, see *Social services*	200
	Local Government and Social Care Ombudsman	200
M.	Means-testing	203
	Meeting need	203
	Mental capacity	204
	Mental Health Act 1983, see *Mental health aftercare*	204
	Mental health aftercare	204
	Mobility, see *Decision Support Tool*	206
	Multi-disciplinary team	206
N.	National Framework on NHS Continuing Healthcare	210
	National Health Service Act 2006	211
	Nature	215
	NHS-employed staff	216
	NHS England	217
	Northern Ireland	218
	Nurse assessors	218
	Nutrition, see *Decision Support Tool*	223
P.	Panels	224
	Paying privately, see *Private top-up care*	224
	People's own homes	224
	Person and family involvement	225
	Personal health budgets	228
	Personal injury compensation	229
	Pointon case	229
	Predictable unpredictability	229
	Primary decision maker	230
	Primary health need	231
	Private top-up care	232

	Process, see *Decision-making process*	233
	Professional judgement	234
	Prohibitions	234
	Psychological and emotional needs, see *Decision Support Tool*	234
	Public Service Ombudsman for Wales	235
Q.	Quality of care, see *Nature*	236
	Quantity of care, see *Incidental or ancillary or of a nature beyond social services*	236
R.	Referral for NHS Continuing Healthcare	237
	Registered nursing	240
	Rehabilitation and recovery	240
	Reimbursement	241
	Remedies, see *Disputes between a person and the NHS*	242
	Resources	242
	Respite care	243
	Responsible commissioner, see *Clinical commissioning groups*	243
	Review of decision about CHC, see *Disputes between a person and the NHS*	243
	Reviewing a care package	244
S.	Safeguarding	247
	Scotland	247
	Screening, see *Checklist*	248
	Section 117, Mental Health Act, see *Mental health aftercare*	248
	Setting	248
	Skin, see *Decision Support Tool*	250
	Social care	250
	Social services	250
	Specialist staff	251
T.	Timescales, see *Delay*	253
	Topping up, see *Private top-up care*	253
	Training	253
	Transition	254
U.	Unpredictability	256
V.	Wales	259
	Well-managed needs	259
	Withdrawal of care	264

Note on terminology

General terminology

The term 'local authority' is used synonymously with the term 'social services'.

The Department of Health was renamed, in 2018, the Department of Health and Social Care.

The Local Government Ombudsman was renamed, in 2017, the Local Government and Social Care Ombudsman.

Acronyms

Acronyms frequently used include:

CCG: NHS clinical commissioning group

CHC: NHS Continuing Healthcare

DH: Department of Health

DHSC: Department of Health and Social Care

DST: Decision Support Tool

HSO: Parliamentary and Health Service Ombudsman

LGO: Local Government Ombudsman

LGSCO: Local Government and Social Care Ombudsman

NHS: National Health Service

PSOW: Public Service Ombudsman for Wales

References

The following shortened references are used in the footnotes:

Checklist 2018: refers to Department of Health and Social Care. *NHS Continuing Healthcare Checklist*. London: DH, 2018.

Decision Support Tool 2018: refers to Department of Health and Social Care. *NHS Continuing Healthcare Decision Support Tool*. London: DH, 2018.

Fast Track Pathway Tool 2018: refers to Department of Health and Social Care. *Fast Track Pathway Tool for NHS Continuing Healthcare*. London: DH, 2018.

National Framework 2018: refers to Department of Health of Health and Social Care. *National Framework for NHS Continuing Healthcare*. London: DH, 2018.

National Framework Practice Guidance 2018: is contained within Department of Health of Health and Social Care. *National Framework for NHS Continuing Healthcare*. London: DH, 2018.

NHS Responsibilities Regulations 2012: refers to *NHS Commissioning Board and Clinical Commissioning Groups (Responsibilities and Standing Rules) Regulations 2012*.

Preface

I grew up believing in at least three things. *First*, in the National Health Service. It was, if not in the blood, then the family. And that, when we were in most need, it would within reason be there for us all. *Second*, that the NHS helped people free of charge, as section 1 of the National Health Service Act 2006 states, irrespective of their financial position in life. *Third*, that in general and in a democracy, transparency about vital public services is of paramount importance.

I now find myself writing about something which is significantly undermining these three beliefs: the policy and practice of NHS Continuing Healthcare.

It has become clear that the NHS is no longer there for certain categories of NHS patient, not because they do not have health care needs, or are in less need than other patients – but perversely and precisely because they have *greater* levels of need. Yet, by sleight of hand and by stealth, they have been, and continue to be, rebranded as having primarily social care needs, which have to be paid for either by those chronically sick and ill people themselves, if they have savings and property of their own, or otherwise by local councils. It also increases the risk, self-evidently, of a person's health care needs being downplayed clinically, of being regarded as 'social' not 'health', and therefore not being met adequately.

This state of affairs offends also against the second belief (and legal rule) that people's health care needs must be met free of charge.

The third belief, in transparency, has been eroded because for several decades past, central government – aided by senior civil servants and a caste of regional and local NHS management – have refused to engage in an honest public debate, let alone a meaningful one, about NHS Continuing Healthcare. This refusal constitutes an unmistakable political failure. Made up of confusing and flawed rules, which seem anyway regularly to be disregarded in practice, the system has remained impenetrable to most patients and their families, as well as to a large majority of the health and social care practitioners meant to be applying it.

The need for transparency is paramount because, without it, the key issue can never be acknowledged, discussed and resolved. If politicians and the Department of Health and Social Care wish to exclude from ongoing NHS care those with high levels of chronic health care needs, then let them say so, and let us at least debate and vote on the issue. We would all know where we stood.

Simply then, I write the book for two reasons: in the main, to explain the rules so that patients, families and practitioners can better understand and challenge decisions. But, also, in Chapter 3, why this can be difficult to do, and why the system needs to change if fair and lawful decision-making is ever consistently to be achieved.

Chapter 1

Introduction

November 2013: an article appeared in the newspaper. It was about a gregarious 86-year-old man who, when he wasn't pruning his roses, was at church meetings. He had been driving, cycling and swimming into his mid-80s. In the distant past he had lied about his age to join the army, served with the Argyll and Sutherland Highlanders for seven years and been in Palestine on a peacekeeping mission after the end of the Second World War. He later worked as a council gardener for more than 30 years. And then, in 2013, he suffered a major stroke, was admitted to hospital and then discharged to a nursing home.

He was left unable to swallow, so a percutaneous endoscopic gastrostomy (PEG) had been attached to his stomach for medication and nourishment. His speech was so poor it was impossible for him to communicate pain or any basic needs. When assessed, he could move his left arm and leg only; slight improvement in his right leg had now actually increased the risk of falling. He could not stand. He had contracted methicillin-resistant Staphylococcus aureus (MRSA) in hospital. It was hard to tell how much he understood of what was going on around him. He was doubly incontinent.

He was then assessed as to whether he had a 'primary health need'. If so, he would be eligible for NHS Continuing Healthcare (CHC) and the nursing home placement he required would be funded by the NHS. This would be on the basis that he had predominantly health care needs, something which was self-evident.

To the astonishment of his son, the NHS, in the form of the North East Essex Clinical Commissioning Group, took a different view, concluding that his father had predominantly social care needs. This meant that he would have to pay for his own care, since he owned a bungalow (the family home) and had savings, for which he had worked hard all his life. This would be until most of his money was used up and home sold, and the local authority would eventually have to step in, as a last resort, to pay for his care as social care.

When his son was trying to explain to his father in simple terms that the NHS didn't think he was ill enough to help, 'He opened his blue eyes wide, looked straight at me and, I'm pretty sure, mumbled: "Bloody cheek."' The newspaper's request for an explanation from the NHS was met by the dead hand of bureaucracy: 'We can confirm we fund all cases that meet eligibility for CHC [Continuing Healthcare] funding. It is a statutory requirement.'[1]

ONE STORY, one might say, and so what? There are always hard cases, things that sound a bit odd, go a bit wrong. But what if that hard case is in fact one of many, is in fact the norm? What if the above case is typical; how are we to explain it, and why is it important to do so? The answer lies in a system boasting a number of unpalatable characteristics.

First, the outcomes it delivers in practice are wholly counter-intuitive to the person in the street as well as to the professional practitioner. Unsurprisingly so, since the greater a person's continuing health care needs are, the less likely it is that they will be met by the NHS.

Second, this outcome differs from most rationing of health services, which does not deny the existence of a health need but means merely that there may be a wait. Alternatively, the need maybe cannot be met at all because of limited resources – for example, when a person is deemed to be a low priority for cataract or orthopaedic surgery. Or when a particular type of treatment for an illness is deemed too expensive for the NHS to offer.

By contrast, in the context of NHS Continuing Healthcare, a person's multiple, ongoing health care needs are instead simply redefined as social care. This is rationing of a quite different order; in effect it is a reclassification of something in order to spirit it away. Adverse and unfair consequences include confusion for patients, families and practitioners; they are also financial since people have to pay for social care, in contrast to health care which is free of charge. People may be required to sell their home and use up their savings – for both of which they may have worked hard all their lives.

A further ramification is that if we pretend that health care needs are social care needs, there is sometimes a risk that the type of care provided will not be clinically appropriate.

Third, this counter-intuitive state of affairs is made worse because the underlying policy driving NHS Continuing Healthcare has never been

---

1 Beales, M. 'Continuing healthcare: a severe stroke, yet Ted Beales still doesn't qualify.' *The Guardian*, 9 November 2013.

explained to the public in any meaningful way. Central government has avoided doing so because of the political sensitivities involved: it doesn't want to own up. Yet the NHS has been called the nearest thing we have to a national religion.[1] It is of central political importance in general elections and featured prominently in the 2016 referendum about Brexit. Therefore, it would appear all the more reprehensible that a deceit, at the heart of the NHS, should remain unspoken and unacknowledged.

Fourth, the rules, when we manage to find and decipher them, within legal regulations and central government guidance, are awash with vague terms. This matters because it is these terms which determine people's 'eligibility' – that is, their right to NHS Continuing Healthcare. Words such as 'incidental', 'ancillary', 'nature', 'totality', 'complexity', 'intensity' and 'unpredictability' are sufficiently nebulous to allow endless argument between the NHS, local authorities, practitioners, patients and families. To muddy the waters further, there are disparities between the guidance, legislation and case law as well as internal inconsistencies in the guidance.

Fifth, once identified, these confusing rules must be applied by local NHS bodies, presently called NHS clinical commissioning groups (CCGs). Evidence suggests, however, that sometimes at least they pay little attention to the rules; that decision-making can approach the arbitrary and anarchic; and that such undermining of the rules may at times have been encouraged and prompted by NHS England (and by its predecessors).

Lastly, the reason for all of the above is simple: NHS Continuing Healthcare policy is about money and who will be paying – or who won't – for people's ongoing, complex health care needs.

The result is also predictably simple. To the neutral onlooker, shambolic rules and characteristics, both absurd and sometimes surreal, stand out. To patients and families caught in its toils, the system delivers distress and unfairness. Whilst practitioners and managers working in the NHS and social services find themselves locked into unproductive, perpetual conflict, which consumes time, energy and financial resources.

THIS BOOK THEREFORE sets out to achieve the following.

First and primarily, to provide a practical guide to the rules[2] for health and social care practitioners, patients, families, health and social care

---

1　Lawson, N. *The view from No. 11: memoirs of a Tory radical.* London: Bantam Press, 1992.
2　The book confines itself to England: the situation in Scotland is now significantly different; Wales is similar to England; and in Northern Ireland the concept of NHS Continuing Healthcare is tenuous. However, short summaries are given in the A–Z section of this book (see Chapter 4) in relation to these other parts of the United Kingdom.

management, voluntary organisations and others. For those unfamiliar with the rules, a summary is provided in Chapter 2.

The A–Z section of this book (see Chapter 4) provides more detail drawn from legislation, guidance, legal case law and ombudsman cases. It does not just set out the rules but considers their merits and shortcomings, their application in practice and what to consider when judging if they have been applied correctly. The rules may be flawed but there is no other option but to try to use them as far as possible to achieve fair decisions.

Secondarily but also crucially, Chapter 3 charts the background to NHS Continuing Healthcare over the last three decades. The present position cannot be understood without this.

Chapter 2

Basic rules and common pitfalls

This chapter sets out the basic rules underpinning NHS Continuing Healthcare (CHC) decisions made by NHS clinical commissioning groups (CCGs) and refers to some of the pitfalls to be wary of. Further detail is contained in Chapter 4.

Challenging decisions made by the NHS on the basis of the outline of the rules below is something which may need to be done, whether by the patient themselves, their family or indeed by the local authority (which must try to ensure it does not unlawfully provide services which the NHS has a duty to provide).

Normally the best way of questioning a decision is to focus on the *decision-making process*, and the presence and quality of evidence, explanation and reasoning, rather than a direct attack on the *final decision* about eligibility for CHC. This is why at least the basic elements of the decision-making process need to be understood. Options for challenging decisions are indicated in Chapter 4: see **Disputes between a person and the NHS**.

The following outline is drawn from relevant legal regulations,[1] the Care Act 2014 and from guidance published by the Department of Health and Social Care. The guidance includes National Framework guidance, a Checklist, a Decision Support Tool and a Fast Track Pathway Tool – as republished and amended in 2018. They are available online.[2]

---

1 NHS Commissioning Board and Clinical Commissioning Groups (Responsibilities and Standing Rules) Regulations 2012.
2 All are published by the Department of Health and Social Care. The *National Framework for NHS Continuing Healthcare*, the *Checklist*, the *Fast Track Pathway Tool* and the *Decision Support Tool* are available at: *www.gov.uk/government/collections/nhs-continuing-healthcare-and-nhs-funded-nursing-care*, accessed on 23 September 2019.

The outline below covers the main rules used to decide whether a person has a 'primary health need' and so is legally eligible for CHC. The main rules are as follows, starting at the foot of what could be viewed as a decision-making pyramid.

Primary health need and CHC eligibility – following steps in order

- Referral to the NHS clinical commissioning group
- Checklist (screening tool)
- Decision Support Tool (main assessment tool, multi-disciplinary team)
- Nature, intensity, complexity, unpredictability (decision about these characteristics)
- Quantity and quality of care (decision about these, measured by using the legal terms 'incidental', 'ancillary', 'nature')
- Primary health need (final decision).

Alternative end of life route to primary health need and CHC eligibility

- Fast Track Pathway Tool (completed by appropriate clinician, based on a person having a rapidly deteriorating condition which may be approaching a terminal phase).

Funded nursing care (FNC) – when a person in a nursing home is not eligible for CHC

- Small contribution by the NHS to nursing home fees, if a decision has first been taken that a person is not eligible for CHC.

Legal and ombudsman cases

- Decision-making about CHC eligibility must be informed by relevant legal and ombudsman cases. In particular, indicative cases in which patients were found to have been eligible for CHC.

Primary health need represents the summit of the decision-making process. It is a legal term. Regulations state that the purpose of an eligibility assessment for CHC is to determine whether a person has a primary health need. If so, then they are eligible for CHC, which is defined as a package of care arranged and funded solely by the NHS.[1]

---

1   NHS Responsibilities Regulations 2012, rr.20, 21(5), (6), (7).

The word 'solely' means that the NHS alone has the duty, so joint funding is not possible. The Care Act 2014 reinforces this, prohibiting social services from providing, under the 2014 Act, anything that the NHS is required to provide, thus precluding social services from arranging or funding CHC.

Eligibility means that 'the NHS will be responsible for providing for all of that individual's assessed health and associated social care needs, including accommodation, if that is part of the overall need'.[1] This could be in any setting, hospital, care home, hospice or a person's own home.

The person will benefit from the health services themselves, which may not otherwise be available through the local authority, by way of social care, in the same quality or quantity, and benefit financially as well. This is because under section 1 of the National Health Service Act 2006, health care provision must, by definition, be free of charge.

If the person is not eligible for CHC, then they may have to pay very significant costs for what will be deemed social care needs, by using their savings and selling their home. If they have no, or few, financial resources of their own, or when those resources are depleted, local social services authorities must step in to fund the care.

GETTING THINGS STARTED: initial referral to the NHS could be made by anybody but there is a specific duty as well. Under the Care Act 2014, when a local social services authority is assessing a person's social care needs, it must make a referral to the NHS if it appears that the person may have CHC needs.[2] This is a low threshold duty – there just needs to be an appearance of possible need; likelihood or certainty of eligibility for CHC is not required.

Local authorities do not, for various reasons, always comply with this duty, with the result that a person may be denied the opportunity of a CHC assessment. So, patients and families may sometimes need to remind and urge the local authority to make a referral by submitting a Checklist to the CCG. On receipt, the CCG should normally make a final decision about CHC eligibility within 28 days (see below).

THE CHECKLIST in most cases (not end of life: see below) is the first step towards possible eligibility for CHC. It is a screening tool that is completed to give the NHS an idea of whether to complete a fuller assessment. It is published as guidance by the Department of Health and Social Care and, if a screening tool is to be used at all, regulations state that it must be the Checklist and no other.

---

1 National Framework 2018, para 54.
2 Care and Support (Assessment) Regulations 2014, r.7.

The Checklist is the gateway to that fuller assessment, which involves use and completion of the Decision Support Tool (DST: see below). Therefore, patients, families and practitioners need to try to ensure that it is completed appropriately. Once the Checklist is received by the CCG, an overall decision about CHC eligibility should normally be made within 28 days.

The Checklist is meant to set a low threshold only, meaning it should not be used stringently to exclude people from fuller assessment. It can be completed by a range of health and social care practitioners. Extensive evidence about the person's condition is not required. For a resident of a nursing home, the Checklist must be considered before an assessment for funded nursing care (FNC: see below) takes place.

Practices of CCGs which may sometimes undermine the rules in guidance and regulations – and therefore may be challengeable – include:

- using other screening tools instead
- not completing a Checklist for hospital patients who are returning to their own homes (CHC eligibility is not dependent on setting)
- making arbitrary decisions not to complete a Checklist at all
- giving no reasons or evidence at all for completing a negative Checklist
- not involving families and not listening to the evidence they put forward
- demanding excessive evidence at the Checklist stage
- over-restricting the classes of practitioner from whom they will accept Checklists (thus choking off their flow)
- exceeding, routinely, the timescale of 28 days for making decisions about eligibility following receipt of the Checklist
- in respect of nursing home placements, assessing for FNC before considering completion of a Checklist (and a DST): this is the wrong way around, is unlawful and can profoundly affect the outcome. See ***Checklist***.

THE DECISION SUPPORT TOOL (DST) comes next if a person gets through the Checklist stage. The DST, published by the Department of Health and Social Care, involves fuller assessment; regulations state that it must be used.

For patients, families and practitioners, it is crucial to know about the DST and to try to ensure that it is completed accurately and fully. The DST looks more closely, via a multi-disciplinary team, at the person's needs. It is used to score those needs in terms of a number of 'domains' (e.g. behaviour, cognition, continence, communication).

The DST states that if a person is scored sufficiently highly, it is more likely that they will get through the next stage (see immediately below) and be eligible for CHC. Even if they have not scored so highly, they may still be eligible, because the DST scoring is indicative only and not decisive.

The DST should not be used prescriptively or slavishly, is not meant to supplant professional judgement, cannot directly determine eligibility for CHC and, crucially, is subordinate to law, since it is merely guidance.

In other words, the DST is an assist to deciding about a primary health need; any final decision must be consistent with the test set out in legislation concerning quality and quantity of care (see below), and should have taken account of relevant legal and ombudsman case law. This last point is particularly important because the scoring system set out in the DST can sometimes result in people being excluded from eligibility, even though under the regulations and legal case law, there would be a strong argument for a finding of eligibility.

Practices of CCGs which can sometimes undermine the rules in guidance and regulations about the DST – and which are therefore challengeable – may include:

- not using a multi-disciplinary team at all or in any meaningful sense
- not involving practitioners knowledgeable about either the health condition or patient or both
- not involving families, not listening to the evidence they are putting forward, sometimes undermining them, sometimes even intimidating them
- downplaying evidence of need
- doing assessments for funding nursing care (FNC) first, and never getting around to completing a Checklist (and then DST) at all – this is the wrong way around and can profoundly and unlawfully affect the outcome
- applying the DST differently (and arguably in discriminatory fashion) to people with learning disabilities
- routinely rejecting the recommendations of the multi-disciplinary team and even rescoring the DST themselves

- using the DST prescriptively and to determine eligibility directly, without reference to, and consistency with, both regulations and legal and ombudsman cases. See *Decision Support Tool*.

NATURE, INTENSITY, COMPLEXITY, UNPREDICTABILITY. Guidance states that the DST functions as a tool, an indicator, to determine overall whether the *nature, intensity, complexity or unpredictability* of a person's needs are such as to indicate a primary health need and therefore eligibility for CHC.

According to the guidance any single one (not necessarily all) of these four characteristics may be sufficient to demonstrate that the quantity or the quality of care required is such as to point to eligibility for CHC. The guidance indicates that the higher the score on the DST, the more straightforward this decision will be.

Although referred to in the guidance, these four terms do not occur in legislation. They represent a further tool, a help, for deciding the legal question about quantity or quality of care (see below). Therefore, they remain subordinate to that legal question and to the relevant legal (and ombudsman) case law.

Practices of CCGs which can undermine both law and guidance – and which are therefore challengeable – can include:

- insisting that all four characteristics be present (not appreciating that these four characteristics are conjoined by the word 'or', not 'and')

- stating that unpredictability must always be an ingredient

- stating, sometimes apparently absurdly, that once unpredictability is identified it becomes 'predictably unpredictable' and so is not unpredictable at all

- not involving families and not listening to the evidence they are putting forward, about how their relative's multiple needs interact and lead to complexity or intensity of need

- stating that, because family carers do not keep formal care records, there is insufficient evidence of the patient's needs to suggest CHC eligibility (but without the CCG itself making an effort to gain that evidence as part of the assessment it is under a duty to conduct). See *Nature*, *Intensity*, *Complexity* and *Unpredictability*.

QUALITY AND QUANTITY OF CARE comes next and this question is of greater legal significance than the steps immediately above.

The decision about nature, intensity, complexity or unpredictability – the characteristics set out in guidance – is meant to lead to a judgement about the quantity and quality of health and nursing care required. Another way of referring to quantity and quality would be to consider the scale and type of care required.

The quantity test is referred to in legal case law and in regulations, in difficult but all-important language. It is about whether the health and nursing services a person needs are, *in their totality*, 'merely incidental or ancillary' in relation to (a) the provision of accommodation (care home placement) being arranged by social services, or (b) to anything else social services is doing for the person under the Care Act 2014.

The words 'incidental or ancillary' suggest something minor or peripheral. If the health and nursing services are merely that, then social services can legally provide them (assuming that the services are also of a nature falling within social services' legal remit); otherwise, the NHS must, under regulations, decide that a person has a primary health need.

The quality test is referred to in legal case law and legislation by the word 'nature'. It is about whether the health and nursing services required are, in their totality, of a nature beyond that which a local authority, whose primary responsibility it is to provide social services, could be expected legally to provide.

In other words, taking the quality and quantity tests together, the issue is whether the health or nursing services required, taken as a whole, are beyond the legal remit of social services. If so, the NHS must, under regulations, decide that a person has a primary health need and is therefore eligible for CHC.

Practices of CCGs which can undermine the rules in law and guidance – and are therefore challengeable – include:

- failing to refer to the quality and quantity test at all and to the primary heath need test

- failing to take account of the *Coughlan* legal case[1] from which these questions derive

- using the Decision Support Tool prescriptively and narrowly, without wider consideration of the true legal test of eligibility. See **Incidental or ancillary or of a nature beyond social services** and **Nature**.

---

1   *R(Coughlan) v North and East Devon Health Authority* [2001] Q.B. 213.

Finally, if the health and nursing services required in their totality are either more than just incidental or ancillary (as described above) or are, in any case, of a nature beyond what is expected of social services, then the CCG must decide that the person has a primary health need. In this case it must also decide that the person is eligible for NHS Continuing Healthcare.

END OF LIFE, nonetheless, commands a different route. The decision-making process described above – the Checklist, Decision Support Tool, quality/quantity test – is bypassed.

Instead, if a registered medical doctor or nurse responsible for the diagnosis, treatment or care of a patient completes the Fast Track Pathway Tool (FTPT), then the patient will be eligible for CHC. This tool is another piece of Department of Health and Social Care guidance, use of which is prescribed in regulations.

Completion of the FTPT is to confirm that the patient has a primary health need arising from a rapidly deteriorating condition and that the condition may be entering a terminal phase. Once it is completed, the CCG must decide that the person is eligible for NHS Continuing Healthcare and arrange provision without delay. If a person nearing the end of their life does not qualify via the FTPT, they may nonetheless still do so via the Checklist and Decision Support Tool process.

Practices of CCGs which can undermine the rules in law and guidance – and which are therefore challengeable – include:

- not using an appropriate nurse or doctor to complete the Tool
- refusing to accept the Tool even though the legal requirements in the regulations have been adhered to
- imposing rigid timescales of prognosis of death to govern eligibility; this is inconsistent with both regulations and guidance
- delaying provision until the person has died. See ***Fast Track Pathway Tool***.

FUNDED NURSING CARE represents a further piece of the jigsaw. It applies if a person fails to qualify for NHS Continuing Healthcare but is in a nursing home, in which case they will normally qualify for funded nursing care (FNC).

FNC involves the CCG paying a weekly amount, £165.56 at the time of writing, to the nursing home to cover the registered nursing care that the resident needs. This amount should then reduce either what a resident is paying to the home as a self-funding resident or what the local authority is paying to the care home.

Assessment for funded nursing care can legally take place only after consideration has been given to whether a CHC assessment is required, using the rules above. This is significant because the needs of some residents could be met by registered nursing care alone but they may have needs equivalent to those in the *Coughlan* case, or in other indicative legal or ombudsman cases (see below). So, if the assessments are done in the wrong order, with FNC coming first, there is a risk of people being wrongly denied eligibility for CHC.

Practices of CCGs which can undermine the rules in law and guidance – and are therefore challengeable – include:

- considering and assessing for FNC first, before CHC has been considered

- not understanding that even a need for registered nursing care alone can still mean that a person is legally eligible for CHC

- awarding FNC to people with nursing needs on a par with those of patients in several indicative legal or ombudsman cases in which CHC eligibility was found, including the all-important *Coughlan* legal case

- ignoring the quality/quantity (incidental, ancillary or nature) test. See **Funded nursing care**.

LEGAL AND OMBUDSMAN CASES should be considered when the rules above are applied. Guidance makes clear that, when taking a decision as to whether somebody has a primary health need and is therefore eligible for CHC, the CCG should take account of indicative legal or ombudsman cases – that is, those cases which indicated that the patient involved was eligible for CHC. It would then be expected that eligibility would be awarded to other patients with similar or equivalent needs. This said, every case is individual, and must be carefully assessed on its own merits.

A broad-brush representation of the patients in these cases would be people with multiple, significant health care conditions requiring ongoing care. Importantly, some of these patients may not score so highly on the DST (see above) but could in law still be eligible – which is why DST scoring is not meant to be decisive. And, as already noted above, even if a person's needs can be met by registered nursing care alone in a nursing home, they might still be eligible for CHC – if their needs are equivalent to those of patients in indicative cases.

Yet CCGs sometimes make decisions seemingly with either no reference to (or knowledge of) these indicative cases, or even with an apparent determination to ignore them, contrary to law and guidance. This could therefore be another potential ground of challenge, not least because the courts have pointed out that nursing home residents, with needs at a level equivalent to Pamela Coughlan's in the pivotal *Coughlan* case, should be found to be eligible for CHC.[1] See **Indicative cases**.

---

1   *R(Grogan) v Bexley NHS Care Trust* [2006] EWHC 44 (Admin), para 51.

Chapter 3

Background, explanation and evidence of a dysfunctional system

In order to understand NHS Continuing Healthcare (CHC) in the present, the recent past needs to be outlined, if only to explain why it is so difficult to understand and to challenge decisions.

Most rules in health care, social care and welfare generally tend inevitably to contain blemishes and elements of uncertainty or ambiguity, but there is usually some sort of sound core. In the case of CHC, this is not the case. The evidence set out in this chapter reveals a long-standing dysfunctional system compounded by a lack of transparency. For the last 30 years at least, successive governments have brought about, presided over and perpetuated this state of affairs.

The *existence* of this dysfunctional system is no accident. It consists of an underlying and concealed policy, unknown and unannounced to the wider public. This has been to rebrand, by stealth, people's continuing health care needs and to deem them instead to be social care in nature. By so doing, those people are moved away from free NHS care to means-tested social care for which they have to pay.

The *consequence* of such dysfunctionality includes confusion, unfairness, upset, distress, loss of trust, detriment to people's welfare and also to their finances. And it has involved, as well, a generation of health and social care practitioners caught in the crossfire of a three-way conflict between patients and their families, local NHS commissioning bodies and local social services authorities as to who should pay for the care of people with complex, ongoing health needs.

WE CAN START IN THE EARLY 1990S. Unease was surfacing about the degree to which the NHS had surreptitiously been shedding beds from its hospitals. These included long-stay beds occupied by older people, typically with co-morbidities, sometimes with dementia and challenging behaviour.[1] This reduced provision also affected other, younger adults, sometimes with multiple needs following illness, disease or accident.

This development was coupled typically with a reluctance or blunt refusal of the NHS to fund the care of such patients, outside of hospital, in nursing homes. Any objection was not to some of the long-stay wards being closed; they were no idyll of health care.[2] Rather, it was that the loss of NHS-funded care was subject to neither public consultation nor debate.

Some basic health or nursing needs would still be met in the community by the NHS free of charge, but ongoing care needs and accommodation (e.g. a care home) would normally be provided as social care and be subject to a financial means-test. People would have to pay for their care. Effectively, means-tested social care as a category was being expanded to include what once was non-means-tested health care. The Department of Health, from the outset, drove and oversaw this stratagem but made no murmur in public. Of transparent policy, legislation or guidance there was no sight.

And there the matter might have rested, had it not been for interventions, from the early 1990s onward, by, amongst others, the Health Service Ombudsman, the law courts, charities and Parliamentary committees.

SCRATCHING THE SURFACE OF NHS CONTINUING HEALTHCARE was something the Health Service Ombudsman had already begun by the early 1990s, finding that the NHS was failing to provide a service it had a duty to provide in its refusal to fund Continuing Healthcare outside of hospitals.[3]

By 1992, the Department of Health had published vague guidance about NHS input into residential and nursing homes, entitled *Local authority contracts for residential and nursing home care: NHS related aspects*. It referred to a distinction between what it called specialist and general nursing, the former being the remit of the NHS, but not the latter.[4] This distinction was

---

1 Barker, K. (Chair). *A new settlement for health and social care: interim report*. London: The King's Fund, 2014, pp.13, 16–19.
2 Robb, B. *Sans everything*. London: Nelson, 1967.
3 HSO, W.478/89–90. In: Health Service Commissioner. HC 482. *2nd report 1990–1991*. London: HMSO, 1991. And: *North Worcestershire Health Authority* (E.264/94–95). In: Health Service Commissioner. HC 11. *Selected investigations completed April to September 1995*. London: HMSO, 1995.
4 HSG(92)50. *Local authority contracts for residential and nursing home care: NHS related aspects*. London: Department of Health (NHS Management Executive), 1992.

subsequently developed by health authorities as a criterion in their local policies to indicate eligibility for continuing care, a distinction labelled by the Court of Appeal seven years later as 'elusive'.[1]

By 1994, the ombudsman had published a significant, stand-alone and hard-hitting report, encapsulating the emerging concerns. Leeds Health Authority had refused to fund the care of a man who was doubly incontinent, could not eat or drink without assistance, could not communicate, and had a kidney tumour, cataracts in both eyes and occasional epileptic fits. He required substantial nursing care. The Health Service Ombudsman found a failure in service, citing the duty in section 3 of the National Health Service Act 1977 to provide aftercare following discharge from acute hospital care. The decision to refuse NHS funding had been unreasonable.[2]

1995 GUIDANCE FAILED TO IMPROVE THE SYSTEM. Published by the Department of Health following the *Leeds* case, it was entitled *NHS responsibilities for meeting continuing health care needs*. It laid claim to 'greater openness and consistency', the sort of aspiration, or perhaps mantra, to be much repeated over the coming years, and it left to local health authorities the responsibility for developing local eligibility criteria.

The guidance otherwise gave a brief steer only towards what constituted eligibility for full NHS funding. It referred to ongoing, regular and specialist medical supervision needed because of the complexity, intensity, nature or unpredictability of a person's medical, nursing or other clinical needs. However, it appeared to restrict application of these criteria to 'inpatient care', suggesting therefore hospital care only; this lack of clarity about care outside of hospital would be noted four years later by the Court of Appeal.[3]

> **1995 guidance: limited possibility of continuing care outside of hospital.** The guidance did state, in passing, that eligibility could exist outside of hospital if the person was expected to die in the very near future, or if they required rehabilitation or recovery arranged and funded by the NHS to minimise the risk of a failed hospital discharge.
>
> A further proviso was added that if a person met the eligibility criteria for

---

1 *R(Coughlan) v North and East Devon Health Authority* [2001] Q.B. 213, para 13.
2 *Leeds Health Authority* (E.62/93–94). In: Health Service Commissioner. *Failure to provide long term NHS care for brain damaged patient*. London: HMSO, 1994.
3 *R(Coughlan) v North and East Devon Health Authority* [2001] Q.B. 213, para 41.

> continuing NHS inpatient care, but no hospital bed was available, then the health authority should fund a bed elsewhere. But, overall, the clear steer of the guidance was that although the NHS would certainly provide some community health services to people not in hospital, it would not be funding and arranging their overall care.[1]

The 1995 guidance would fail to live up to its own puffery. In 1995 and 1996 the Health Service Ombudsman was continuing to lay bare restrictive policies being operated by the local health authorities.

> **1995 and 1996: continuing faults within the NHS.** The ombudsman made a series of adverse findings against the NHS – for example, a policy of not contracting for continuing care nursing home beds, even though the authority's hospital beds were inadequate to meet continuing care needs;[2] simply not funding continuing care beds in either hospitals or nursing homes;[3] not informing patients and their families about continuing care;[4] quite improperly, through impermissible means-testing, making even partial continuing care funding dependent on whether the patient received income support;[5] or prejudging people's continuing care status and simply not telling them anything about the process.[6]

POLITICAL CHANGE, 1997. In this year, Tony Blair stated at the Labour Party Conference, 'I don't want [our children] brought up in a country where the only way pensioners can get long-term care is by selling their home.'[7] The misleading nature of this statement soon became apparent. Within two years,

---

1 Department of Health. *NHS responsibilities for meeting continuing health care needs*. HSG(95)8. London: DH, 1995, Annex paras 21–22.
2 *North Worcestershire Health Authority* (E.264/94–95). In: Health Service Commissioner. HC 11. *Selected investigations completed April to September 1995*. London: HMSO, 1995.
3 *Avon Health Authority 1996* (E.615/94–95). In: Health Service Commissioner. *Investigations of complaints about long term NHS care*. London: HMSO, 1996.
4 *East Kent Health Authority 1996* (E.685/94–95). In: Health Service Commissioner. *Investigations of complaints about long term NHS care*. London: HMSO, 1996.
5 *North Cheshire Health Authority 1996* (E.672/94–95). In: Health Service Commissioner. *Investigations of complaints about long term NHS care*. London: HMSO, 1996.
6 *Buckinghamshire Health Authority 1996* (E.118/94–95). In: Health Service Commissioner. *Investigations of complaints about long term NHS care*. London: HMSO, 1996.
7 Gheera, M. *Key issues for the new Parliament: funding social care*. House of Commons Library Research. London: HC, 2010.

his government would downplay, and effectively subvert, the implications of the landmark 1999 *Coughlan* legal case (see below).

This case had spelt out the rights of patients to non-means-tested NHS Continuing Healthcare and effectively set a relatively low threshold for eligibility. Following the judgment, the Secretary of State for Health immediately issued a statement, arguably highly misleading and turning the implications of the case upside down.[1] In hindsight, his comments were predictive of the Department of Health's apparent determination in the following two decades, and thus continuing today, to diminish and dilute in practice the implications of this legal judgment.

The Labour government would also go on even to fail to adopt the key recommendation of its own Royal Commission's report of 1999, which was to make personal social care free of charge. Its adoption would have lent credibility to the 1997 commitment. It would have lessened the impact of people being wrongly deprived of NHS Continuing Healthcare status, since at least they would not then have had to pay for the resulting 'social care'.[2]

BARELY A WHISPER ABOUT NHS CONTINUING HEALTHCARE. It would transpire that not confessing to the underlying policy was to be by no means the preserve of one particular government or political party. A long-term trend was set in 1997.

For instance, in 2013, Nick Clegg as Deputy Prime Minister announced the Coalition government's determination to limit how much people would have to pay for social care in their lifetime. Yet there was no mention of NHS Continuing Healthcare and what was meant by 'social care' as opposed to 'health care'.[3] Similarly, in 2014, Labour's proposal (as Parliamentary Opposition) was criticised as a 'death tax', which would have involved exacting a further, inheritance, tax when people died by taking a percentage of their estate to pay for social care.[4]

In any case, the Coalition government never did deliver even on its limited aims relating to social care, losing power before it could do so. Following the Conservative Party's election victory under David Cameron

---

1 BBC News. 'Health patients face bill for long-term care,' 16 July 1999. Accessed on 26 June 2019 at: http://news.bbc.co.uk/1/hi/health/371855.stm
2 Sutherland, S. (Chairman). *Royal Commission on Long Term Care: with respect to old age*. London: Stationery Office, 1999. And: Secretary of State for Health. *The NHS Plan: the government's response to the Royal Commission on Long Term Care*. Cm 4818–II. London: TSO, 2000, p.8.
3 Clegg, N. 'Nick Clegg: how we'll change unfair care system for pensioners.' *Daily Telegraph*, 10 February 2013.
4 Elliott, F. 'Labour resurrects "death tax" plans.' *The Times*, 30 July 2014.

in 2015, its manifesto promise, about capping how much people paid for social care, was discarded.[1] More precisely, the relevant provisions of the Care Act 2014, which were due to be brought into force in April 2016, were put on ice where they remain.[2]

Theresa May, as Prime Minister, then proposed in her election campaign of 2017 to alter even these unimplemented legal provisions, although she would rapidly execute a U-turn.[3] By 2019, a Green Paper about social care had been delayed for over two years.[4] In July of that year, Boris Johnson, newly elected Prime Minister, stated that he would fix the crisis in social care once and for all.[5] Within a mere four months, he too turned tail; his election manifesto omitted any concrete policy on the issue.[6]

Yet, to repeat, within all of the above discussion of social care and how it would be paid for, there was still little or no mention of the far more fundamental issue of clarifying what social care (as opposed to health care) actually was in the first place. There is, after all, little point talking about how much people should pay for something if nobody knows what that something is.

Such dissembling leads to confusion and upset. And the issue of how care would be paid for would not apply only to a financially well-heeled, upper stratum of society. It would affect, for instance, people who had saved assiduously all their life, albeit on low wages, or those who had managed to buy a council house and become a property owner, as noted in a BBC *Panorama* programme.[7]

The real question here was, and is, not about the place of property in society, and how ideally care costs should be met and be shared between the individual and the state. It is about answering that question in a transparent and fair manner, whatever that answer may be, rather than resorting to opacity and concealment, always remembering it was politicians in 1975

---

1   Conservative Party. *Strong leadership, a clear economic plan, a brighter more secure future.* Conservative Party Manifesto. London: CP, 2015, p.65.
2   Bingham, J. 'Care system "crumbling" after broken promise on fees cap – inquiry chair.' *Daily Telegraph*, 7 November 2015.
3   Henwood, M. 'What do the election manifestos pledge for social care?' *The Guardian*, 24 May 2017.
4   Jarrett, T. *Social care: forthcoming Green Paper (England)*. House of Commons Library Briefing Paper. London: HCL, 2019, p.5.
5   '"Action this day" as Boris Johnson raises hopes on social care reform – Yorkshire Post says.' *Yorkshire Post*, 27 July 2019.
6   Smyth, C. 'Migrants key to fixing social care.' *The Times*, 28 November 2019.
7   BBC *Panorama*. 'The national homes swindle.' Broadcast 5 March 2006. Transcript accessed on 27 June 2019 at: http://news.bbc.co.uk/1/shared/spl/hi/programmes/panorama/transcripts/national_homes_transcript.txt

who spoke of a property-owning democracy[1] and who followed this up in 1991 with the notion of wealth cascading down the generations.[2]

PAMELA COUGHLAN, 1999: the *Coughlan* case was a Court of Appeal judgment which opened up, legally and to the Department of Health's discomfiture, the controversy of NHS Continuing Healthcare.

In a landmark judgment, the court criticised the 1995 guidance, finding aspects of it unclear and some of the earlier 1992 guidance elusive. It stated that the local authority should be responsible for paying for nursing home placements, but only if the nursing services required were incidental or ancillary (about the quantity of care) to the provision of the accommodation, or of a nature (about the quality/type of care) which fell within what social services was expected to provide. Otherwise, the resident would be eligible for NHS Continuing Healthcare status.[1]

At the time of this case, local authorities were not legally barred, as they now are, from funding registered nursing care. Yet the court ruled that Pamela Coughlan's needs in any case far exceeded the social services legal remit. This means that her needs would have exceeded what is now called funded nursing care (FNC) in nursing homes – i.e. the small element of the overall nursing home or care home fee paid by the NHS when a person is not eligible for NHS Continuing Healthcare. (This is because FNC includes legally what social services used, at the time of the *Coughlan* case, to be able to fund.)

Pamela Coughlan had multiple but generally stable needs, requiring registered nursing, not in principle dissimilar to significant numbers of residents in nursing homes. Thus, the Court of Appeal had in effect set what was arguably a relatively low threshold for eligibility for NHS Continuing Healthcare.

Therefore, the implications of the case were, or should have been, that in practice significant numbers of residents of nursing homes, with multiple health conditions, equivalent to (not necessarily the same as) those of Pamela Coughlan, would be eligible for NHS Continuing Healthcare, simply because they were in those nursing homes with needs for nursing and other health services, which were not merely minor, peripheral or incidental, and which were not social care in nature. See **Indicative cases**.

---

1   Moore, R. 'Margaret Thatcher began Britain's obsession with property. It's time to end it.' *The Guardian*, 6 April 2014.
2   Singh, S. 'Why the cascade of wealth has dried up.' *The Independent*, 16 February 1996.
1   *R(Coughlan) v North and East Devon Health Authority* [2001] Q.B. 213, paras 13, 40.

The *Coughlan* case continues to be of central legal importance. The principles enunciated have found their way into NHS regulations, and 2018 guidance emphasises its significance.[1] NHS clinical commissioning groups should consider it when they take decisions about NHS Continuing Healthcare, but it is not clear in practice how assiduous they are in doing so.

DUCKING AND DIVING TO AVOID THE IMPLICATIONS OF THE COUGHLAN CASE was a reaction of the NHS identified in due course by the Health Service Ombudsman. Following the case, the Department of Health issued interim guidance in August 1999, which promised final guidance later that year.[2] Instead, publication was delayed for two years.

During this period, the Health Service Ombudsman came across evidence that the Department of Health discouraged the NHS from reviewing its practices and complying with the law established in *Coughlan*. For instance, one letter sent by a regional office of the Department could justifiably have been interpreted as a 'mandate to do the bare minimum'.[3]

In the same vein, at one meeting with such a regional office, a health authority in Suffolk was told to 'duck and dive' for a while.[4] Call it what you will – ducking or diving, delaying or dodging – this did not suggest a warm embrace of the Court of Appeal's ruling or of law in general. It set a pattern which was to endure as Pamela Coughlan herself observed in 2014, 15 years later. She had thought her legal victory would mean that patients, already distressed and unhappy at having such significant health care needs, would no longer be caught in the middle of conflicts about funding. How wrong she was.[5]

At last, in belated response to the *Coughlan* case, the Department of Health issued its revised guidance in 2001. This continued to leave local eligibility criteria to be developed by health authorities, inviting in practice continuing inconsistency.

The guidance did, however, like its 1995 predecessor, state that those authorities should at least 'pay attention' to certain principles, informing eligibility, when formulating their local criteria. Some of these principles did relate to the *Coughlan* case, including reference to the legal limits of

---

1   NHS Responsibilities Regulations 2012, r.21. National Framework Guidance 2018, paras 11, 157.
2   HSC 1999/180; LAC(99)30. Department of Health. *Ex parte Coughlan: follow up action*. London: DH, 1999.
3   Health Service Ombudsman. *NHS funding for long term care*. London: TSO, 2003, para 21.
4   *Suffolk Health Authority 2003* (E.2339/01–02). In: Health Service Ombudsman. HC 787. *Selected investigations completed December 2002–March 2003*. London: TSO, 2003.
5   Deith, J. 'Continuing healthcare: the secret fund.' BBC Radio 4 *File on Four*, 23 November 2014. Accessed on 18 July 2019 at: www.bbc.co.uk/programmes/b04p86c4

social services provision, and also to the point that the care setting did not determine eligibility for NHS Continuing Healthcare.

> **2001 guidance: key points.** The guidance stated that health authorities should pay attention to the following in relation to deciding eligibility. *First*, to the legal rule that health authorities should not require social services to provide services beyond their legal remit (given the emphasis on this in the *Coughlan* case). *Second*, to the nature or complexity or intensity or unpredictability of the individual's health care needs (and any combination of these needs) requiring regular supervision by a member of the NHS multi-disciplinary team, such as the consultant, palliative care, therapy or other NHS member of the team. *Third*, to whether a patient's needs required routine use of specialist health care equipment under supervision of NHS staff. *Fourth*, to the individual having a rapidly deteriorating or unstable medical, physical or mental health condition and requiring regular supervision by a member of the NHS multi-disciplinary team, such as the consultant, palliative care, therapy or other NHS member of the team. *Fifth*, to the individual being in the final stages of a terminal illness and likely to die in the near future. *Sixth*, to the point that care or supervision from a registered nurse and/or a GP would not be, by itself, sufficient reason to receive NHS Continuing Healthcare. *Seventh*, to the rule that the location of care would not be the sole or main determinant of eligibility: it could be provided in an NHS hospital, a nursing home, hospice or the individual's own home.[1]

The approach of this guidance, an approach which would be repeated in the future, was to refer to, but dilute, the *Coughlan* case. It failed to spell out, in practical terms and with practical examples, the relatively low threshold for eligibility that the case had set – examples that could have demystified the Court of Appeal's vague terms 'incidental', 'ancillary' and 'nature'. And the guidance retained terms such as 'complexity', 'intensity', 'unpredictability', terms which were not part of the legal test set out in the *Coughlan* case. They were imprecise terms capable of fuelling much dispute and, arguably, of 'perpetuating a myth' about the eligibility rules, in conflict with *Coughlan*.[2]

---

1 Department of Health. HSC 2001/15. *Continuing Care: NHS and Local Councils' responsibilities.* London: DH, 2001, Annex C.
2 Nicola Mackintosh, solicitor quoted in: BBC *Panorama*. 'The national homes swindle: a growing scandal.' Broadcast 23 July 2006. Transcript accessed on 27 June 2019 at: http://news.bbc.co.uk/1/hi/programmes/panorama/5216252.stm

FUNDED NURSING CARE made its entrance in 2001 by means of section 49 of the Health and Social Care Act 2001. It was referred to loosely as 'free nursing care' and more specifically at the time as a 'Registered Nursing Care Contribution' of a person's care (RNCC), broken up into three bands of need and corresponding financial value. In 2007, it became known as funded nursing care (FNC) with just one band of need.

In essence, it was (and is) a relatively small NHS financial contribution, at the time of writing paid at a flat rate of about £165.00 per week, to nursing home fees, if a person does not otherwise have full funding through NHS Continuing Healthcare.

Local authorities could up to this time, in line with the *Coughlan* judgment itself, still fund health or nursing services if they were merely incidental or ancillary (peripheral) to a person's placement in a nursing home, and if they were of a nature (quality or type) that social services could be expected to provide. But in future, with this new legislation, such services could no longer include the provision of registered nursing care. Instead, that element would have to be funded by the NHS.

Emerging practice soon suggested that many residents awarded RNCC (and later FNC) should arguably instead have been fully funded under NHS Continuing Healthcare, to the extent that their nursing needs were equivalent to those identified in the *Coughlan* case.

It was no coincidence, therefore, that by 2006 the courts had identified how easily these new rules about RNCC could be misapplied so as to deny people, wrongly, eligibility for NHS Continuing Healthcare, not least because of the three RNCC eligibility bands – the highest had set a threshold greater than the *Coughlan* case had set[1] – effectively and directly undermining the legal judgment.

Generally, the guidance did not spell out sufficiently clearly the legal basis and extent of RNCC and then FNC. And arguably still, today, it does not do so.[2] Even if the guidance had been clearer in its explanation, there is no reason to suppose that in practice it would have been followed, given the apparent determination to restrict the numbers of people eligible for NHS Continuing Healthcare.

In summary, the introduction of RNCC (now FNC) was arguably a mischievous response to the *Coughlan* case, designed to eviscerate it. By sleight of hand, the Department of Health attempted to water down, to a

---

1   *R(Grogan) v Bexley NHS Care Trust* [2006] EWHC 44 (Admin), paras 50, 59, 67, 71.
2   National Framework 2018, paras 246–251. And: Department of Health and Social Care. *NHS Funded Nursing Care practice guidance*. London: DH, 2018.

small financial contribution, what should have been full NHS funding in nursing homes for at least a significant number of people. Some felt this was misleading; others were more direct. Claire Rayner, health campaigner, commented that the government had said that people's nursing care would be free of charge in future, but they were 'lying'.[1]

OUT OF HOSPITAL became a more sweeping policy still from the early 2000s onward, moving beyond the large-scale closure of the long-stay geriatric NHS beds which had been taking place from the 1980s. Swift and more widespread shutdown of hospital beds was taking place, for example, on elderly care and rehabilitation wards, as well as in community hospitals.

Between 1997 and 2007, 32,000 NHS beds were lost despite the NHS Plan in 2000 stating that 7000 new beds were needed by 2010.[2] From 2010 to 2016, a further 52,000 were lost.[3]

Overall, taking a 30-year view, between 1987 and 2017, the King's Fund reported that NHS beds, general and acute, had reduced in number from 299,000 to 142,000. This was part of a widespread trend, in other countries as well, owing to reduced lengths of hospital stay generally (e.g. because of more day surgery). Nonetheless, it was taken to an extreme in the United Kingdom which had been left with 'fewer acute beds relative to its population than almost any other comparable health system'.

The consequence was that hospitals were left with too few beds. The report went on to note that, by 2017, 'overnight general and acute bed occupancy averaged 90.3 per cent, and regularly exceeded 95 per cent in winter, well above the level many consider safe'. Yet still more closures were planned in order to save money, something the report considered 'unrealistic'.[4]

This would mean ever more patients with complex health care needs in the community, rather than in hospital. The theory was that NHS community health services would meet their ongoing care needs. The reality was that this group of patients would find themselves pressed tight against the border crossing between health and social care. There, denied NHS Continuing Healthcare funding, they would be pushed unceremoniously across that

---

1 Rayner, C. 'Claire Rayner: I'm leaving the Labour Party after 50 faithful years.' *The Independent*, 26 September 2001.
2 Donnelly, L. 'NHS hospitals lose 32,000 beds in a decade.' *Daily Telegraph*, 24 May 2008. Department of Health. *Implementing the NHS Plan: developing services following the National Beds Inquiry*. Health Service Circular 2001/03. London: DH, 2001, para 7.
3 British Medical Association. *State of the health system: beds in the NHS: England*. London: BMA, 2017.
4 Ewbank, L., Thompson, J. and McKenna, H. *NHS hospital bed numbers: past, present, future*. London: King's Fund, 2017, p.1.

border, not only at risk of sometimes going without clinically required health care, but also having to pay for what was now being called social care.

OLDER PEOPLE ABANDONED is a wider conclusion that could reasonably be drawn. The denial of eligibility for NHS Continuing Healthcare for (mainly) older people with complex needs in the community – and thrusting them into the arms of means-tested social care – was, and continues to be, part of a bigger picture.

For instance, the closure of so many hospital beds would mean that there was sometimes even a doubt, without exaggeration, of whether some of those older patients would ever make it out of hospital alive, in which case the question of NHS Continuing Healthcare for these patients would be moot and not arise. This was because of the clinical consequences of crowded hospitals, ill-equipped to meet the complex needs of patients with co-morbidities.

> **Neglect and many deaths.** At Stoke Mandeville NHS Trust, Maidstone and Tunbridge Wells NHS Trust and the Mid Staffordshire NHS Foundation Trust, poor care and neglect were responsible for many hundreds of avoidable deaths, and misery for many others.[1] The casualties were, in the main, older inpatients with complex needs.
>
> This legacy continues; today, hospitals remain short of acute beds. The evidence is that if hospital bed occupation exceeds 85 per cent, then safe care is jeopardised; then, and now, many hospitals operate near 100 per cent bed occupancy.[2] The implications for older people continue to be delayed admission (a trolley on a corridor), admission to an inappropriate ward, lack of basic care, treatment and rehabilitation, infection, development of other problems (including pressure sores, malnutrition, poor medication management, falls) – and premature discharge from hospital.[3]

---

1   Healthcare Commission. *Investigation into outbreaks of* Clostridium difficile *at Stoke Mandeville Hospital, Buckinghamshire Hospitals NHS Trust, July 2006*. London: HC, 2006. And: Healthcare Commission. *Investigation into outbreaks of* Clostridium difficile *at Maidstone and Tunbridge Wells NHS Trust, October 2007*. London: HC, 2007. And: Francis, R. (Chair). *Independent Inquiry into care provided by Mid Staffordshire NHS Foundation Trust January 2005–March 2009*. London: The Stationery Office, 2010.
2   British Medical Association. *State of the health system: beds in the NHS: England*. London: BMA, 2017. (Including literature review on safe bed levels.)
3   See e.g. Appleby, J. *Winter beds pressures*. London: Nuffield Trust, 2016.

The loss of hospital beds is clinically counter-indicated but has continued; the Department of Health's own older people's 'tsar', Professor David Oliver, stated that the NHS was systematically failing older people in hospital and that the notion of large reductions in older people needing to attend hospital was 'absolute la la land'.[1]

Even when older people with complex needs do emerge from hospital, they may not have received adequate diagnosis, or may even have received a pseudo diagnosis of 'acopia'. This sometimes stems from a form of therapeutic nihilism, a reluctance to get to grips clinically with a patient's needs. It may be accentuated by negative attitudes towards the elderly – not helped by hospital targets and treatment pathways which are inconsistent with appropriate treatment of the elderly with multiple health conditions.[2] A diagnosis of 'frailty' is now replacing the idea of acopia; but this term, too, in order to be useful rather than negative, requires proper diagnosis and consideration of the multiple health conditions that may be underpinning it.[3]

Premature discharge of people from hospital is also a consequence of overcrowding,[4] with serious implications.[5] This is aided by reference to older people as bed blockers, frequent flyers, delayed transfers of care (DTOC) cases or, more recently, as the 'super stranded' to be avoided at all costs. Such terms can, if care is not taken, too easily vilify and reduce needy patients to merely inconvenient bed occupants and unwanted statistics.

Likewise, older people may not receive the hospital-based rehabilitation they require, leaving them with decreased physical (and mental) functionality, greater disability and at more risk of being deemed to need means-tested social care.

---

1   Winnett, R. 'Nursing home health care "worse than in jail".' *Daily Telegraph*, 25 November 2012. And: Calkin, S. 'Plan to keep elderly out of hospital is "la la land".' *Health Service Journal*, 14 March 2013.

2   See variously: Francis, R. (Chair). *Independent Inquiry into care provided by Mid Staffordshire NHS Foundation Trust January 2005–March 2009*. London: The Stationery Office, 2010, p.400. And: Cornwell, J. *The care of frail older people with complex needs: time for a revolution*. Sir Roger Banister Health Summit, Leeds Castle. London: King's Fund, 2012, pp.1–3. And: O'Connor, R. and Neumann, V. 'Payment by results or payment by outcome? The history of measuring medicine.' *Journal of the Royal Society of Medicine 99*, 2006, 226–231. And: Philp, I. *A new ambition for old age: next steps in implementing the National Service Framework for older people, a report from Professor Ian Philp, National Director for Older People*. London: Department of Health, 2006, p.4. And: Oliver, D. '"Acopia" and "social admission" are not diagnoses: why older people deserve better.' *Journal of the Royal Society of Medicine 101*, 2008; 168–174. And: Falconer, M. 'Out with "the old", elderly, and aged.' *British Medical Journal*, 8 February 2007.

3   Oliver, D. 'David Oliver: frailty in acute care.' *British Medical Journal*, 29 September 2016.

4   Appleby, J. *Winter beds pressures*. London: Nuffield Trust, 2016.

5   Health Service Ombudsman. *A report of investigations into unsafe discharge from hospital*. London: HSO, 2016, p.2.

> **Decrease in rehabilitation: hoping older people will disappear from the system.** This trend was predicted accurately by two eminent geriatricians in 2001. They foresaw that the (then) new policy of 'intermediate care' in the community was part of a long-standing political and managerial agenda to keep old people out of hospital and would result in diminished health-based rehabilitation for the elderly. This was in the hope that 'somehow they would disappear from the system'. It was convenient for the caste of management to confuse convalescence out of hospital with a need for rehabilitation within.
>
> They foresaw also increased, premature discharge of people from hospital and a bypassing of the 'skilled diagnostic evaluation that the complexities of disease and disability in old age require'. But, they noted, nobody was owning up about what was happening.[1]

All this suggests a pattern of the NHS 'wishing away' older people with high levels of ongoing needs, not just in relation to NHS Continuing Healthcare, but more generally.

PERSISTENT OMBUDSMEN, independent investigators of complaints, can, as we have already seen, be a thorn in the side of the Department of Health and the NHS, when occasion demands. If the Department had thought that its 2001 guidance would calm the choppy waters, a 2003 special report from the Health Service Ombudsman dashed its hopes. Scarcely could it have been more critical of, and unwelcome to, central government.

The ombudsman found that the guidance was not only as unclear as its 1995 predecessor (which itself had been criticised by the Court of Appeal in 1999), but in fact was 'weaker' still. This meant it was even harder to judge, using the new guidance, whether local NHS criteria were in line with it. The ombudsman stated that any such system should be 'fair and logical and should be transparent in respect of the entitlement of individuals'. Yet from what she had seen, 'the national policy and guidance that has been in place over recent years does not pass that test'.

The ombudsman recommended reimbursement of nursing home fees to all those service users who had as far back as 1996 themselves paid, wrongly, for their care.[2] The Department of Health instructed the NHS to comply

---

1 Grimley Evans, J. and Tallis, R. 'A new beginning for care for elderly people? Not if the psychopathology of this new national framework gets in the way.' *British Medical Journal*, 7 April 2001, pp.807–808.
2 Health Service Ombudsman. *NHS funding for long term care*. London: TSO, 2003, paras 28, 31, 39.

with this recommendation by conducting retrospective reviews, which resulted ultimately in large sums of money being repaid (see below).

THE *POINTON* CASE in 2004 represented another significant Health Service Ombudsman report shedding light on NHS Continuing Healthcare. The ombudsman published an investigation into the care of a man with advanced Alzheimer's disease in his own home. Cases hitherto had centred on care homes and care being provided by paid staff rather than family members.

The ombudsman found, however, that NHS Continuing Healthcare eligibility was precluded neither by the person being in their own home, nor by the fact that they were being cared for primarily by an informal carer, in this case the man's wife.[1] See ***Indicative cases***.

The year's end, in December 2004, saw the Health Service Ombudsman continue her critical analysis of the system, casting doubt on the process of retrospective reviews and reimbursement (see above) and making the following recommendations for action to be taken by the Department of Health.

> **Health Service Ombudsman recommendation, 2004.** The ombudsman recommended (a) the establishment of clear, national minimum eligibility criteria which would be understandable by health professionals, patients and carers; (b) the development of a set of accredited assessment tools and good practice guidance to support the criteria; (c) supporting training and development to expand local capacity and thus ensure that continuing care cases were assessed and decided properly and promptly; (d) clarification of standards for record keeping and documentation; (e) seeking assurance that the retrospective reviews had covered all those who might be affected; and (f) monitoring the progress of retrospective reviews.[2]

At the same time an independent review, commissioned by the Department of Health and published in December 2004, made a number of findings similar to those made by the Health Service Ombudsman about reviews and financial restitution.[3]

---

1 *Cambridgeshire Health Authority* (E.22/02–03). In: Health Service Ombudsman. HC 704. *Selected investigations completed October 2003–March 2004*. London: TSO, 2004.
2 Health Service Ombudsman. HC 144. *NHS funding for long term care: follow up report*. London: HSO, 2004.
3 Henwood, M. *Continuing health care: review, revision and restitution, summary of an independent research review*. London: Department of Health, 2004.

Stung, the Department of Health announced that it would commission a 'new national framework' on continuing care. This may have represented a climb down in practice, but the Department still would not concede the principle. It maintained, despite a wealth of evidence to the contrary, that the existing criteria were 'fair and legal'.[1] It would, in any event, take nearly three years for the Department to bring such a framework into force, in October 2007.

If 2003 and 2004 represent perhaps a peak of ombudsman activity, the ombudsmen over the next 15 years would continue to be involved heavily with NHS Continuing Healthcare, receiving in 2018, for example, 496 complaints about it, of which 196 were investigated[2] (constituting a significant proportion of a total of 1722 complaints against the NHS investigated in 2018–2019).[3]

HEALTH COMMITTEES of the House of Commons, like ombudsmen, can exert pressure, or at least try to, on central government. And in 2005, the Health Committee did just this, by exposing the shambolic nature of NHS Continuing Healthcare policy and practice. It reported that the system was 'beset with complexity', had been contentious for over a decade, was a postcode lottery, and that the system should have built-in incentives to promote people's rehabilitation and independence.[4]

In a fierce report it related how ten years after a predecessor Health Committee had raised concerns, people still found themselves 'subject to a bewildering funding system which is little understood even by those who administer it, and which few patients or carers would describe as fair, or as guaranteeing their security and dignity'. Criticisms made included the following.

> **Confusion, inconsistency, opacity, complexity, assessing patients to identify funding rather than their needs, frustration for professionals, artificial distinction between health and social care.** The Committee highlighted the

---

1 Department of Health. *New national framework on continuing care.* Department of Health press release (Stephen Ladyman). London: DH, 2004.
2 Phillips, N. (Victoria Derbyshire programme). 'Our life savings are spent on care that should be free.' *BBC News*, 11 June 2019. Accessed on 18 July 2019 at: www.bbc.co.uk/news/health-48555199
3 Parliamentary and Health Service Ombudsman. *The Ombudsman's Annual Report and Accounts 2018–2019.* London: PHSO, 2019, p.35.
4 House of Commons Health Committee. *NHS continuing care.* HC 399–1. London: TSO, 2005, Summary.

> administrative and financial costs of the 'confusion, inconsistency and opacity surrounding the system' arising from the 'artificial distinction between health and social care', and that many people over the previous 20–30 years were now in fee-paying care homes or in the community, rather than being cared for free of charge in long-stay hospital beds. This had led to a highly complex funding system in which assessments might be more about identifying the funder than about the needs of the patient.
>
> The Committee noted that when asked to define the division between health and social care, the Secretary of Health had previously stated that he could not do so. (Today, the National Framework still states, with no hint of apology, that there is no definition that the government can provide;[1] even though it is, and always has been, within central government's gift to supply just such a definition for legal and administrative purposes.)
>
> The continuing problems were resulting in 'frustration for health and social care professionals, and suboptimal care and financial hardship for some of our most vulnerable populations'. It 'strongly recommend[ed] that the Government remove once and for all the wholly artificial distinction between a universal and free health care service operating alongside a means-tested and charged for system of social care'.[2]

The government's response to the Committee was dismissive, noting that removing the artificial distinction between health and social care would amount to a fundamental and costly restructuring of the welfare state, which it already had ruled out.[3] This was less than frank. In reality, central government was already deep into the business of restructuring the welfare state – by shifting free health care to means-tested social care. It was not about to admit this.

GROGAN WAS THE NEXT MAJOR LEGAL CASE, in 2006. Notwithstanding the 2004 contention by the Department of Health that its revised guidance of 2001 was fair and lawful, the courts now subjected it to a further buffeting.

The judge referred to concerns, confusion, deficiencies and lack of clarity; the guidance was, in the judge's view, 'far from being as clear as it might have been' and was not sensible, not helpful and could usefully be rewritten.

---

1 National Framework 2018, para 50.
2 House of Commons Health Committee. *NHS continuing care*. HC 399–1. London: TSO, 2005, paras 2, 13, 24, 25, 26, 27, 29, 30, 40, 43, 49.
3 Secretary of State for Health. *Response to Health Select Committee Report on Continuing Care*. London: TSO, 2005, p.4.

Perhaps more troubling to the government was the court's clear statement that patients with a level of need equivalent to that of Pamela Coughlan should be eligible for full funding in the form of NHS Continuing Healthcare – and just not be awarded (what today would be called) funded nursing care (FNC) in a nursing home.[1] This meant that, in principle, many nursing home residents might be entitled to full NHS funding, not just to the financially modest nursing contribution represented by FNC.

The *Haringey* case had in 2005 preceded the *Grogan* case. It, too, was significant, emphasising the legal limits of social services provision and that local authority social services were therefore not to be regarded simply as a default provider of any health service the NHS chose not to provide.[2]

Also, in 2006, a King's Fund report pinpointed inequity, stealth and the essentially political dimension of NHS Continuing Healthcare policy.

> **King's Fund report: withdrawal by stealth of NHS care, inequity, injustice.** This report noted that a much wider debate was required about the distinction between health and social care needs, especially given the substantial grey zone between the two. There was an underlying sense of injustice, because some people qualified for free NHS care whilst others had to pay for social are without relevant categories of need being clearly distinguishable, in which case the legitimacy of operating two separate systems would continue to come under scrutiny and to face increasingly adversarial and judicial challenge.
>
> Change in the future had to be on the basis of public debate and clear policy decisions, something which had hitherto been absent. Continuing care policy had been 'developed by default and…the withdrawal of the NHS took place by stealth'.[3] This concise characterisation remains as valid today as it was in 2006.

BBC TELEVISION *PANORAMA* programmes over the years have creditably probed the health and social care system, including NHS Continuing Healthcare. Notably, in 2006, this was not just once but twice, because the first programme triggered an unprecedented reaction and angry protests

---

1 *R(Grogan) v Bexley NHS Care Trust* [2006] EWHC 44 (Admin), paras 27, 62, 64, 66, 67.
2 *R(T) v London Borough of Haringey* [2005] EWHC 2235 (Admin), para 70.
3 Henwood, M. *Wanless review: NHS Continuing Healthcare in England.* London: King's Fund, 2006, pp.11, 13.

about unjust, cruel and unfair decisions, thereby warranting the second, a few months later. It was a growing scandal, a 'national homes swindle'.[1]

One particular trend the *Panorama* investigation revealed was how, entirely paradoxically, as a person's health care condition deteriorated, they would be at risk of losing NHS funding.

One of the programmes noted presciently that nothing seemed likely to change. Pamela Coughlan herself (see above) stated that there was a huge fraud being perpetrated with nobody able to do anything about it. Her solicitor stated that everybody was colluding with this; practitioners on the ground were being pressurised by health authorities and the government was giving out a 'wrong version' of the legal position.[2]

A House of Commons Health Committee Chairman, David Hinchcliffe, conceded the lack of transparency which was due to the political unacceptability of owning up to what was happening. The programme concluded that the NHS lived by its own rules, not necessarily the law.[3]

2007 – A LANDMARK, or so it should have been, in the sense of finally mending NHS Continuing Healthcare, including faults relating to fairness, consistency, transparency, logic and compliance with the law, in particular compliance with the *Coughlan* and *Grogan* legal judgments outlined above. Nearly three years after the commitment to new guidance given in December 2004, it finally arrived in October 2007 in the form of a *National Framework for NHS Continuing Healthcare*, published by the Department of Health.

Accompanying it were a Decision Support Tool (DST) for assessment, a Checklist for screening purposes, and a Fast Track Pathway Tool for end of life. All this guidance would be revised in 2009 and then reissued in both 2012 and 2018, but in essence the 2007 versions formed the basis of what is extant guidance today. Their stated intention was to create in effect national eligibility criteria, replacing the local eligibility criteria operated by strategic health authorities, and to improve consistency in, and understanding of, decision-making.[4]

---

1 BBC *Panorama*. 'The national homes swindle: a growing scandal.' Broadcast 23 July 2006. Transcript accessed on 27 June 2019 at: http://news.bbc.co.uk/1/hi/programmes/panorama/5216252.stm
2 BBC *Panorama*. 'The national homes swindle.' Broadcast 5 March 2006. Transcript accessed on 27 June 2019 at: http://news.bbc.co.uk/1/shared/spl/hi/programmes/panorama/transcripts/national_homes_transcript.txt
3 BBC *Panorama*. 'The national homes swindle.' Broadcast 5 March 2006. Transcript accessed on 27 June 2019 at: http://news.bbc.co.uk/1/shared/spl/hi/programmes/panorama/transcripts/national_homes_transcript.txt
4 Department of Health. *National Framework on NHS Continuing Healthcare*. London: DH, 2009 (revised 2007 guidance), paras 10–12.

In 2012, regulations were passed, setting out the bare bones of the assessment process for NHS Continuing Healthcare, enshrining the *Coughlan* legal case in legislation, and mandating use of all of the above guidance, thus elevating its legal relevance.[1]

However, the skeletal nature of the regulations meant that the real detail remained in guidance only, which is much easier to circumvent. This became apparent in late 2019, in the *Gossip* case (see below).

THE NATIONAL FRAMEWORK. The Framework guidance sets out in principle much which is consistent with the *Coughlan*, *Grogan* and *Pointon* cases. Furthermore, it created a more prescriptively national approach, so as to limit, in principle at least (see below), local variations and extremes. Consequently, one expert view is that it is generally excellent.[2]

On another appraisal, it is not quite what it seems. Certainly, it appears on one level to reflect, and pay lip service to, the *Coughlan* and *Grogan* legal cases. But arguably it fails to spell out sufficiently clearly their implications and the relatively low eligibility threshold established. And, most importantly, it fails adequately to explain clearly the legal position occupied by (what is now) funded nursing care (FNC).

Furthermore, an integral adjunct to the Framework is the Decision Support Tool, an instrument for gathering information about the patient's needs. This might have been unexceptional as a means of collecting and organising clinical information about a patient – except for the 'scoring' system it contains.

Prescriptive application of this scoring system generally results in the bar for NHS Continuing Healthcare being set considerably higher than did the Court of Appeal in the *Coughlan* case. This means, for example, that patients with similar needs to Pamela Coughlan are unlikely in practice to be found eligible for CHC, even though legally they clearly should be, and more generally, the quantity and quality of care test, used in the *Coughlan* case, not being applied.

True, the Tool states that it should not be used prescriptively or supplant professional judgement, and that it should be applied consistently with the *Coughlan* case. However, financially pressed NHS clinical commissioning groups generally need no second asking to apply it restrictively.

The Decision Support Tool, in particular the scoring system, could therefore be regarded as a Trojan Horse insinuated by the Department of

---

1 NHS Responsibilities Regulations 2012.
2 Clements, L. *et al. Community care and the law.* 7th edition. London: Legal Action Group, 2019, p.496.

Health into the decision-making process, with a view to undermining the implications of the *Coughlan* and *Grogan* cases (see above).

The 2007 guidance also heralded the end of the Registered Nursing Care Contribution (RNCC), which had been identified in the *Grogan* case as sowing seeds of confusion by setting a high threshold of eligibility, which had threatened, unlawfully, to displace the *Coughlan* case. RNCC was now replaced by funded nursing care (FNC; see above); but it was almost as if the Decision Support Tool was designed to pick up where the RNCC had left off, in terms of muddying the waters. See ***Decision Support Tool***.

TENS OF MILLIONS OF POUNDS IN REPAYMENT: the new 2007 guidance notwithstanding, the Health Service Ombudsman in that same year returned to the fray by criticising the Department of Health's guidance about financial restitution for people who had wrongly been forced to pay for their care.[1] In response, the Department reissued the relevant guidance.[2]

By 2008, the Department of Health confirmed that over £180 million, perhaps in excess of £200 million, had been repaid to thousands of elderly people who had wrongly been charged for what should have been free NHS Continuing Healthcare. The average repayment was reported as amounting to some £90,000 per person.[3]

LEGAL CLARIFICATION FINALLY? Introduced in 2013, before becoming the Care Act in 2014, the Care and Support Bill proposed a wide-ranging reframing of adult social care legislation, superseding the old National Assistance Act 1948 as the bedrock of adult social care.

It represented an opportunity to clarify the boundary between health care and social care, between the National Health Service Act 2006 and the Care Act 2014, not least because section 22 of the Care Act refers to this very divide by prohibiting social services fundamentally from doing anything the NHS is required to do and, in any case, from arranging or providing registered nursing care.

Concerns were raised by the Parliamentary Joint Committee on the Draft Care and Support Bill about the need for clarity. Consistent with its long-standing determination to keep NHS Continuing Healthcare policy out of the public eye, the Department of Health batted away the concerns,[4]

---

1   Health Service Ombudsman. *Retrospective continuing care funding and redress.* HC 386. London: TSO, 2007.
2   Department of Health. *NHS Continuing Healthcare: continuing care redress.* London: DH, 2007.
3   Womack, S. 'Elderly care blunders cost NHS £180m.' *Daily Telegraph*, 13 February 2008.
4   Secretary of State for Health. *Care Bill explained including a response to consultation and pre-legislative scrutiny on the Draft Care and Support Bill.* London: TSO, 2013, paras 77, 78.

meaning that the hazy boundary between social care and health care (in particular NHS Continuing Healthcare) – which had existed before the Care Act and had given rise to so many problems – would remain. Deliberately so.

In that same year of 2013, the All Party Parliamentary Group on Parkinson's published a report of its inquiry into an obviously 'ailing system'.

> **All Parliamentary Group on Parkinson's: an ailing system, poor assessments, complexity, delay, people dying while waiting, lack of transparency.** The Group's findings included the following: due to a lengthy process, people with Parkinson's were dying whilst awaiting a decision about NHS Continuing Healthcare; 59 per cent of assessments did not involve a professional with specialist expertise or knowledge in the condition, leading to inaccurate and incorrect decisions on funding; all of the health and social care professionals spoken to admitted the system was so complex that they followed the correct process with difficulty.
>
> In addition, 40 per cent of people going through the process reported experiencing a lack of empathy and transparency from professionals; 24 per cent of people with Parkinson's were continually reviewed and reassessed, despite having a progressive condition; in 21 per cent of cases, there were clear examples of existing national guidance not being followed either in the length of assessment or in how the decision is made, with no repercussions for breaching these guidelines; lack of local performance data meant monitoring, enforcement and corrective action were absent.[1]

STEALTH, LOTTERY, BEWILDERMENT: these were words used by the King's Fund in 2014, in line with its 2006 report (see above). Hardly a ringing endorsement of the effect of the National Framework guidance issued seven years previously and designed to achieve fairness, consistency and transparency.[2]

In a final report about the health and social care system generally, the King's Fund concluded that the fault lines between health and social care were illustrated most acutely in the battles over NHS Continuing Healthcare, which had 'parallels with winning, or not winning, a lottery', creating along

---

1 All Party Parliamentary Group on Parkinson's. *Failing to care: NHS continuing care in England.* London: Parkinson's UK, 2013.
2 Department of Health. *National Framework for NHS Continuing Healthcare.* London: DH, 2007, paras 4, 35.

the way much friction between the NHS and local authorities, as well as significant bureaucracy.[1]

The main report followed an interim one, which had considered NHS Continuing Healthcare in more depth. One of its findings was particularly striking and goes to the heart of the matter: the greater your ongoing health needs, the less likely it was (and is) that the NHS will take responsibility for your care.

> **King's Fund: health care denied to those in the very greatest need.** The report noted that NHS Continuing Healthcare was essentially for people who needed nursing support, whose conditions were not 'curable', but who still had significant health conditions and needs. It remained 'one of the most acute illustrations of the problems of alignment in the current system. The different funding streams mean health and social care each have an interest in pushing the funding problem on to the other.'
> Consequently, the report stated that:
>
> At a time when the health and social care systems ought to be converging to meet the needs of frail older people and those with multiple conditions, they are in fact diverging, with social care becoming a residual service only for those with the very greatest needs.[2]

The interim report generally pinpointed the lack of logic and of transparency, the malleable boundary between health and social care, and the changes that had taken place without debate, decision or scrutiny.

> **King's Fund: unfairness, bewilderment, lack of logic and transparency – and a policy of stealth without debate, decision or scrutiny.** The interim report pointed out simply but in some depth the lack of alignment in the entitlements, funding and organisations involved in health and social care, singling out NHS Continuing Healthcare as the epitome of arbitrary and unfair distinctions.
> For instance, it reported how patients and their families were 'puzzled, indeed bewildered, as to why dementia is viewed largely as a social care

---

1 Barker, K. (Chair). *A new settlement for health and social care: final report*. London: The King's Fund, 2014, pp.2–3.
2 Barker, K. (Chair). *A new settlement for health and social care: interim report*. London: The King's Fund, 2014, pp.13, 16–19.

> problem, and thus is heavily means tested, when its impact can be at least as devastating as cancer'.
>
> It noted that it was incredibly hard to draw a distinction between what is health care and what is social care around the end of life, with little logical division between what was means tested under social care and what was free at the point of use as health care. It highlighted that NHS sources of finance, and entitlements to free care, had also moved more than is generally appreciated and that the boundary between health and social care had been far more malleable than commonly understood.
>
> The report traced how, from the 1980s on, long-stay beds in the 'back-wards' of NHS hospitals had rapidly declined as tens of thousands of patients 'were transferred from free NHS care into means-tested nursing and residential homes. This was a large-scale switch from free NHS care to means-tested social care, affecting those tens of thousands of people.'
>
> The standards in nursing homes might have been higher than the NHS beds they replaced, but the change was never announced by the government. It was carried out by 'stealth... A change that took place in an unplanned way without explicit debate, decision, or much scrutiny.'

Such stealth implies secrecy, as BBC Radio 4's *File on 4* observed in *Continuing healthcare: the secret fund*, broadcast in the same year, 2014.

> **The secret fund: confrontation, arbitrary decision-making, downplaying needs, eligibility decisions based on financial considerations and not clinical needs.** The programme found confrontational and adversarial attitudes on the part of NHS decision-makers, denial of NHS Continuing Healthcare to people with very high needs, downplaying those needs in assessment, arbitrary decision-making, dubious decision-making based on financial considerations rather than clinical needs, likewise reviewing and removing people from eligibility in proportion to the pressure on the local budget, reliance on patients and families not understanding the rules, the difficulty of challenging decisions.[1]

INCONSISTENCY, CONFUSION, INTIMIDATION were among the conclusions of the Continuing Healthcare Alliance (a group of charities) in

---

1 Deith, J. 'Continuing healthcare: the secret fund.' BBC Radio 4 *File on 4*, 23 November 2014. Accessed on 18 July 2019 at: www.bbc.co.uk/programmes/b04p86c4

2016 when it published a survey and overview report about NHS Continuing Healthcare, as if, after all these years, yet another report were needed. It was.

> **Continuing Care Alliance: poor quality assessments, inconsistency in withdrawal of care as needs worsen, delay, interference by panels in decisions, confusion, intimidation.** In summary: 40 per cent of professionals reported inconsistency of decision-making in multi-disciplinary teams; 66 per cent of survey respondents felt that professionals involved in assessment did not possess any in-depth knowledge – or knew very little – about the health condition of the person being assessed. Eighty per cent of professionals said the Decision Support Tool (DST) was not fit for purpose, or there was room for improvement.
>
> Those with well-managed needs were often assessed as being ineligible despite having needs that should have qualified, with denial or withdrawal of care leading to a worsening of their needs.
>
> Forty-two per cent of survey respondents who had applied for NHS CHC had waited more than 28 days (the deadline set by the National Framework) to receive their final decision regarding eligibility; 35 per cent of survey respondents said they had been told by the multi-disciplinary team that eligibility would be recommended, only to have that decision rejected by the review panel (even though such interference by a panel should have been happening only exceptionally).
>
> In addition, the report referred to the system remaining complicated, confusing and intimidating for individuals and families. More than half (54%) of survey respondents said they were not provided with enough information or advocacy; of professional survey respondents, 39 per cent said they found the NHS CHC assessment process complicated; and 78 per cent believed the system was difficult or very difficult for patients and their families to navigate.[1]

AND SO TO THE MORE RECENT PAST AND TO THE PRESENT. One might have been forgiven for thinking that, with so much evidence of enduring dysfunctionality, the system would long since have been overhauled. Quite the opposite.

In 2017, there occurred a particular incident, which might appear, at first glance, to be simple oversight. Things can go wrong in the best of systems.

---

1   Continuing Care Alliance. *Continuing to care: is NHS Continuing Healthcare supporting the people who need it in England?* London: CCA, 2016, pp.4, 6.

However, in the context of the lack of enthusiasm within the NHS for Continuing Healthcare – and for older people with complex needs more generally – it could be seen as all too characteristic.

In summary, three NHS clinical commissioning groups admitted that 300 referrals for NHS Continuing Healthcare had been ignored for months – ignored by the Arden and Greater East Midlands Commissioning Support Unit (CSU), an organisation to which the CCGs had delegated NHS Continuing Healthcare responsibilities. The referrals had been sent to the right email address, but this email address had been left 'unmanned' for months. This had resulted 'in delays in packages of care being allocated and queries not being dealt with in a timely manner'. Evidence that this was no isolated failing was that the CSU had in addition also continued to fail to meet any of its key performance measures for NHS Continuing Healthcare.[1]

Consigning patients to a digital never-never land is an all too convenient way of allowing drift and of saving money. A symbol perhaps of what Professors Tallis and Grimley Evans had been getting at 16 years earlier when portraying the wish of NHS management to make older people with complex needs somehow disappear from the system.[2]

AUDITING OF THE STATISTICS and of their implications was undertaken in 2017 by the National Audit Office (NAO). The scrutiny was unfavourable and triggered a follow-up report in 2018 from the Public Accounts Committee of the House of Commons. The NAO pulled together various key statistics on matters such as declining numbers of eligible people, delays in assessment, lack of monitoring and highly variable rates of eligibility from one area to another (indicating a postcode lottery).

> **National Audit Office: use of the Checklist and decreasing eligibility.** For the year 2015–2016, 160,000 people in total in England were receiving CHC funding. During that year, of 124,000 people screened with the Checklist, 77,000 went on to a full assessment; of those, just 22,000 were CHC-eligible. NHS England commented in response that the system, at the Checklist screening stage, was raising expectations unduly and was poor use of time for assessment staff and that work would be carried out to raise the Checklist threshold.

---

1 Heather, B. 'CSU blunder leads to hundreds of missed Continuing Healthcare alerts.' *Health Service Journal*, 20 September 2017.
2 Grimley Evans, J. and Tallis, R. 'A new beginning for care for elderly people? Not if the psychopathology of this new national framework gets in the way.' *British Medical Journal*, 7 April 2001, pp.807–808.

> Indeed, between 2011–2012 and 2015–2016, there was a fall from 34 per cent to 29 per cent in the estimated proportion of people referred for a full assessment that resulted in that person being assessed as eligible for CHC.

NHS England did not, however, suggest to the NAO that the discrepancy between positive Checklists and negative Decision Support Tools might be the result of poor full assessments, faulty decision-making by CCGs, and prescriptive use of the high and legally dubious threshold posed by the Decision Support Tool scoring system.

Nor did NHS England volunteer the information, further undermining the statistics, that the number of people having CHC awarded, but then having it rapidly removed through (dubious) review, seemed to be drastically increasing. It has been reported that the number of patients losing eligibility in England, between 2013 and 2016, rose sharply by 272 per cent; in Great Yarmouth and Waveney CCG, the number of people losing CHC rose by 468 per cent between 2013 and 2016. Typically, the patients being reviewed and losing eligibility were not improving or getting better, but were those with ongoing, multiple health care needs, such as an elderly woman who was unable to talk, walk, barely stand, was doubly incontinent and able to take liquids only.[1]

In relation to raising the threshold of the Checklist, this was republished a year later, with the very same low threshold, contrary to NHS England's assertion made to the NAO. Instead, NHS England's efforts seemed to be directed at the piloting in hospitals of a legally questionable alternative screening tool. To all appearances, this was a back-door way of undermining the Checklist and a breach of legal regulations.[2]

> **National Audit Office: end of life eligibility increasing.** Of 83,000 Fast Track Pathway Tools completed, 79,000 resulted in eligibility, a considerable contrast to the Checklist and Decision Support Tool (DST) route.

---

1   Lythe, R. 'The dementia sufferers stripped of funding and turfed out of care homes: how health experts cruelly change their minds on who's in need – with devastating consequences.' *This is Money*, 13 February 2018. Accessed on 30 August 2019 at: www.thisismoney.co.uk/money/pensions/article-5388221/Alzheimers-suffers-stripped-vital-care-funding.html
2   West Norfolk Clinical Commissioning Group. *West Norfolk Continuing Health Care innovation summary evaluation report*. King's Lynn: WNCCG, 2016, pp.18–19. And: Brennan, S. CCG accused of using flawed test to cut spending on elderly. *Health Service Journal*, 3 January 2019.

The reasons for these figures were not fully explored by the NAO. However, comments or questions could be as follows.

The Fast Track Pathway is considerably simpler than the Checklist/DST route, meaning that there is in principle less room for manoeuvre and avoidance of responsibility by CCGs. In addition, being end of life, it will not result in ongoing funding for any significant length of time, which means that financially it is more sustainable. In any case, whilst eligibility may be decided – and therefore recorded for statistical purposes – provision may in practice be delayed and indeed never made before the person dies.[1] Thus, a CCG could evade expenditure, even after a formal decision of eligibility.

The NAO recorded further findings, including the continuing huge variation between CCGs, in terms of the number of people eligible for NHS Continuing Healthcare. The statistics mocked the claim, a decade before in 2007, that the National Framework and accompanying tools would tackle the 'postcode lottery' of eligibility.

> **National Audit Office: delay, postcode variation, financial savings demanded arbitrarily by NHS England.** Nearly 25,000 people waited for longer than 28 days (the timescale set out in the National Framework), from the completed Checklist to the decision about eligibility, representing nearly a third of those progressing to full assessment with the Decision Support Tool.
>
> Eligibility varied hugely from one CCG to another, ranging from 28 to 356 people eligible per 50,000 population. Even excluding the outlying 5 per cent of CCGs with the lowest and highest percentages, the proportion of people referred and subsequently found to be eligible varied from 41 per cent to 86 per cent. Monitoring and quality assurance, to ensure that CCGs were performing consistently (and indeed lawfully), were limited. And closely linked to this, there was a shortage of data.
>
> The expected spend on CHC by 2020–2021 is £5247 million, up from £3607 million in 2015–2016. However, by 2020–2021, NHS England is expecting CCGs to save £855 million on CHC and funded nursing care (FNC). The savings are to be made by reducing the administrative assessment costs, reducing

---

1   Brennan, S. 'Report: "Patients dying in hospital waiting for community care."' *Health Service Journal*, 20 March 2019. And: Marie Curie. *Making every moment count: the state of Fast Track Continuing Healthcare in England*. London: Marie Curie, 2017, p.8.

BACKGROUND, EXPLANATION AND EVIDENCE OF A DYSFUNCTIONAL SYSTEM

> the cost of care, ensuring more consistency across CCGs, and assessing more people after, rather than before, hospital discharge.[1]

COMPROMISED CARE, DELAY, INACTION, INCONSISTENCY AND FINANCIAL CUTS: all afflicted NHS Continuing Healthcare, and with no explanation as to how any such cuts were to be achieved, at least lawfully. Drawing just such conclusions in 2018, and following the National Audit Office report, came a still more searching examination by the Public Accounts Committee.

The Committee confirmed that people were waiting too long for decisions about eligibility, that they were not being given relevant information, that the system was difficult to navigate, and that there was inconsistency between CCGs, poor training of staff, additional and arbitrary local rules applied by CCGs which might be unlawful, lack of data and inadequate oversight by NHS England.

> **Public Accounts Committee: reduction in eligibility; financial savings demanded with no explanation as to how they could be lawfully achieved.** The Committee was concerned that between 2011–2012 and 2015–2016, the proportion of people assessed as eligible for standard NHS Continuing Healthcare (following full assessment using the Decision Support Tool) had reduced from 34 per cent to 29 per cent. For 2016–2017, there had been a further drop of 6 per cent.
>
> NHS England claimed that this reduction was because assessors were probably becoming better at an early stage (the Checklist) at making accurate judgements about whether people were likely to be eligible and to need a full assessment. However, were this the case, reasoned the Committee, it would have expected logically that the proportion of those eligible at the full assessment (DST) stage would have increased.
>
> In addition, there was a lack of explanation as to how £855 million of savings, demanded by NHS England, could be made without altering the eligibility criteria to ensure that fewer people would qualify. The risk would be that vulnerable people might not have their needs met, as well as this being unlawful.[2]

---

1 National Audit Office. *Investigation into NHS Continuing Healthcare funding.* London: NAO, 2017, pp.4–5, 37.
2 House of Commons Public Accounts Committee. *NHS Continuing Healthcare funding.* London: TSO, 2018, pp.5–9, 13.

NHS England conjured up little answer to the Committee. Its claim that the savings could be made by reducing administrative costs was undermined by the Committee, which pointed out that CCGs spent annually only £149 million in total on such administrative activity. It was therefore unclear how efficiency savings on these matters could come close to the savings required.[1]

In plain words, NHS England's financial demands would inevitably lead to CCGs being forced to take ever more shortcuts, some legally questionable.

In just this vein, the King's Fund in 2019 noted the reduction in the number of people eligible for NHS Continuing Healthcare. The reasons were opaque and disputed, it reported, but campaign groups believed that the main reason was 'a determined effort by many CCGs to reduce their costs by in practice setting the eligibility bar higher than previously'.[2]

Meanwhile, in July 2019, the Economic Affairs Committee of the House of Lords felt moved to publish a highly critical report, which up to a point did at least refer to the arbitrary health and social care divide but still failed to call out NHS Continuing Healthcare by name.

> **A national scandal: arbitrariness of deciding whether needs are health or social care.** The report referred to an ongoing national scandal, decades of failed reviews and reforms, lack of public understanding, political expedience preferred to essential decision-making, over-severe under-funding, unfairness – and the severe impact (including on their own health) on families trying to provide the care themselves. It noted the arbitrariness involved in whether a person's health care needs would be funded by the NHS or be classified as social care, for which people have to pay.[3]

GOSSIP CASE: UNDERMINING THE NATIONAL FRAMEWORK? It has already been noted above that the bulk of rules about how to assess for CHC have remained in guidance rather than law, since the relevant legal regulations of 2012 are sparing in detail. This situation can be compared with adult social care law; the Care Act 2014 and associated legal regulations set out detailed and binding rules about assessment of people's needs and eligibility.

---

1 House of Commons Public Accounts Committee. *NHS Continuing Healthcare funding*. London: TSO, 2018, p.7.
2 Bottery, S., Ward, D. and Fenney, D. *Social care 360*. London: The King's Fund, 2019, p.54.
3 Economic Affairs Committee. *Social care funding: time to end a national scandal*. London: House of Lords, 2019, pp.3–7, 12.

The consequences of leaving within guidance the essential rules about CHC became apparent in the *Gossip* case of late 2019. The CCG concerned departed, in a number of respects and seemingly at will, from the National Framework guidance, and disregarded the *Coughlan* case, the seminal Court of Appeal judgment.

Declining to interfere, the court noted the immense discretion afforded by the regulations; a discretion which, in the court's approach, could not be restricted by the greater prescription to be found in the guidance. The court, though confirming that the guidance could not be ignored, proceeded to demand minimal explanation from the CCG about why it had not followed the guidance, as well as not considered the *Coughlan* case. In so finding, the court seemed to reduce the National Framework to little more than a paper tiger and to side-line the *Coughlan* judgment altogether.

The *Gossip* case essentially provided the CCG with significant immunity from judicial interference, a virtual free hand – not only in relation to the professional and clinical judgements being made about people's CHC needs, but also in respect of the application of the procedural rules delineated at some length in the guidance.[1] The case suggests a judicial turning away, a washing of hands, much as did the *St Helens* judgment of 2008 (although that case did not consider the National Framework).[2] This is perhaps not entirely surprising in the context of an obtuse, entangled, politically sensitive system, almost designed to be judiciary-resistant. The high-water mark of judicial scrutiny of the CHC system – represented by the *Coughlan*, *Grogan* and *Haringey* cases already mentioned above – appears to be an increasingly distant memory.

CCGs will be encouraged by the *Gossip* case to exercise in future still more discretion, imagination and manipulation, in order to mould CHC decisions to fit within the financial resources available at any given time. Thereby, they will erode further the notion that CHC is an entitlement based on objective eligibility – but by no means concede that this is what they are doing.

The undermining, to such an extent, of both the statutory guidance and the *Coughlan* case is, arguably at least, a judicial aberration. Nonetheless, unless successfully appealed, or otherwise overturned in any other future cases, the *Gossip* case looks set to make it considerably harder than it already is for patients, families and local authorities to challenge CHC decisions being made by the NHS.

---

1 *R(Gossip) v NHS Surrey Downs Clinical Commissioning Group* [2019] EWHC 3411 (Admin), paras 3, 76, 77, 93, 97, 119, 120.
2 *St Helens Borough Council v Manchester Primary Care Trust* [2008] EWCA Civ 931.

TOP DOWN, AS THEY SAY, IS HOW THE ROT CAN SET IN. In trying to summarise the above body of evidence, it is therefore at the top that we can start. Here we find prime ministers who, having declared that people should not have to sell their homes to pay for care, proceed to strain political sinews in order to achieve the precise opposite, and Secretaries of State for Health who make misleading statements about the effect of NHS Continuing Healthcare legal cases.

A rung down, one observes the Department of Health and Social Care. Apparent passivity has characterised its actions. Time after time it has claimed to be operating a fair and transparent policy about NHS Continuing Healthcare. Repeatedly it has faced criticism from virtually every conceivable quarter. Repeatedly it has been forced to act by replacing guidance and even passing legal regulations. And it has even left at the ship's prow the Court of Appeal's 1999 *Coughlan* case, the legal figurehead giving direction.

However, passivity is probably a mistaken perception; passive aggression might be more accurate. This is because whilst the Department of Health and Social Care gives the impression of being blown along the surface by persistent censure, the underlying and unspoken policy has remained steadfastly the same. The Department issues handsome statements about fairness and law, and even publishes national guidance meant to reflect the legal rules. Yet, at the same time, the guidance has been drafted so as to preserve ambivalence and uncertainty within the system, leaving the *Coughlan* case still at the prow, but arguably weather beaten, dilapidated and often ignored in practice.

In any case, the Department has remained largely content for its executive arm (now NHS England, formerly strategic and regional health authorities), together with NHS clinical commissioning groups at local level, to go their own way and sometimes to undermine what legal rules there are, as well as some of the Department's own guidance.

NHS England and its regional predecessors: in the shadows. Regional offices of the Department of Health, most recently in the form of NHS England, may tell local health bodies (currently in the form of CCGs) to duck and dive, avoiding the implications of legal case law, as already noted above.[1]

As far back as the 1999 *Coughlan* legal case, it was noted that a decision taken by the local health authority appeared to have been based on behind-

---

1   *Suffolk Health Authority 2003* (E.2339/01–02). In: Health Service Ombudsman. HC 787. *Selected investigations completed December 2002–March 2003*. London: TSO, 2003.

BACKGROUND, EXPLANATION AND EVIDENCE OF A DYSFUNCTIONAL SYSTEM

the-scenes guidance provided by the regional NHS Executive, unaccountably, unrecorded and not even reflecting the Department of Health's official published guidance at the time.[1]

More recently, NHS England has supported pilot projects seemingly inconsistent with the law, involving a screening tool for NHS Continuing Healthcare, alternative to the one prescribed in regulations.[2] In the shadows, NHS England applies financial pressure to CCGs: a recipe for the latter to take legal shortcuts and to exploit loopholes in the rules and, where there are none, to create them.

NHS England also continues to defend harsh and exacting decision-making, resulting in elderly people with multiple health needs being rejected for CHC, whilst denying any impropriety or unlawfulness. It has not only done so as a matter of course, but in a reprehensible and divisive manner, for example claiming that taxpayers 'rightly expect care to be taken before public money is handed out'. This particular statement is objectionable; it is akin to setting one group of elderly, vulnerable patients with high levels of health care needs against another group (i.e. the rest of the population).

NHS England's apparent approach can be both deadpan and misleading. For instance, it stated in 2019 how a majority of people put through CHC assessment turn out not to be eligible, not mentioning that at least one plausible reason for this, so evidence would suggest, is because unlawful decisions are sometimes being taken. Likewise, it has stated that there is greater consistency in assessment and eligibility outcomes across England despite the statistics showing huge variation.[3] For instance, between April and June 2019, Luton CCG funded CHC for 11.3 patients per 50,000 population, Salford CCG for 231 patients.[4]

Interrogated formally by the House of Commons Public Accounts Committee on just such matters, NHS England did not perform well in providing logical, coherent answers (see above).

---

1 *R(Coughlan) v North and East Devon Health Authority* [2001] Q.B. 213, paras 13–14.
2 West Norfolk Clinical Commissioning Group. *West Norfolk Continuing Health Care innovation summary evaluation report*. King's Lynn: WNCCG, 2016, pp.18–19. And: Brennan, S. 'CCG accused of using flawed test to cut spending on elderly.' *Health Service Journal*, 3 January 2019.
3 Taylor, J. and Rigby, N. '"Medical opinions ignored" by NHS payment assessor, workers say.' *BBC News* (BBC East), 10 September 2017. Accessed on 17 July 2019 at: www.bbc.co.uk/news/uk-england-41187615
4 NHS England. 'CHC and FNC – Quarterly Data Q1 2019–20.' Accessed on 31 August 2019 at: www.england.nhs.uk/statistics/statistical-work-areas/nhs-chc-fnc Also: Spencer, B. 'Thousands of dementia patients are being denied NHS funding for care home fees through postcode lottery.' *Daily Mail*, 8 August 2019.

CLINICAL COMMISSIONING GROUPS (CCGS): operating at local level, these are the all-important commissioners of health care provision to local populations. In the case of NHS Continuing Healthcare, however, they have been gifted a poisoned chalice by the Department of Health and Social Care and by NHS England.

From above come financial pressures which almost inevitably, and in general, carry a risk of legal and procedural shortcuts being taken in decision-making, shortcuts which the confusing rules, to all appearances, rules seem designed to facilitate.

Worse, the patients involved comprise the very group of people whose ongoing healthcare needs the NHS, as an organisation, does not welcome in or out of hospital. They are not a political priority, so the incentive for CCGs to follow what rules there are is minimal. Were they to do so, thereby increasing expenditure, they would risk being penalised by NHS England and the Department of Health and Social Care for mismanagement of their budgets.

This leads to CCGs being placed in an unenviable position and owed a degree of sympathy. It has been observed that being a continuing care assessor or panel member is tough, given the emotionally charged and financially critical nature of the decisions being taken – and that stereotypes of uncaring bureaucrats, motivated only by making financial savings, are probably unfair.[1] However, such sympathy is understandably in short supply from those patients and families caught in an impenetrable system and in a web of poor decision-making. This is made all the worse when we observe CCGs stating impassively that they are applying conscientiously the national rules without a hint of candour about just how flimsy, malleable and unfair those rules are.

They may be breached through poor assessments, assessors familiar with neither the patient nor the health condition being assessed, failure to take account of all the evidence, use of Decision Support Tool prescriptively, the ignoring of legal and ombudsman case law, panels making unreasoned and arbitrary decisions in breach of guidance, delays – and through families and practitioners being kept in relative ignorance of the rules.

In addition, CCGs sometimes misuse the process of review, ruthlessly, by trying to remove eligibility from people whose needs are only getting worse and, cynically, by varying the intensity and unreasonableness of those reviews with the financial pressures being placed upon them by NHS England. And yet they deny it all. Such misuse, when it occurs, resembles an unofficial

---

1 Oliver, D. 'David Oliver: NHS continuing care confusion.' *British Medical Journal*, 24 July 2019.

time limit (typically three months) imposed on the provision and funding of health care out of hospital – irrespective of level of need. The following example emerged from a 2014 *File on 4* investigation.

> **CCG denying connection between reviews used to remove people from CHC eligibility – and its need to save millions of pounds from its CHC budget.** A CCG, with low rates of approving CHC provision, stated in another area with low rates of approval for CHC that this was not connected to its having to cut its CHC budget from nearly £14 million to £4.5 million. The local Health Scrutiny Committee launched an investigation and concluded in a report that the reviews of people already on CHC were financially driven, simply a way of withdrawing CHC funding.
>
> The CCG denied that there was a connection between financial pressures and this approach, and stood by the correctness of its decision to withdraw funding from a woman who fell down the stairs, broke her neck and had no movement from the chest down. The CCG continued to defend its decision even when an Independent Review Panel overturned it.[1]

We should be far from startled, therefore, when patients and families, in the midst of high levels of chronic illness and disability, face an additional potential threat to their health and financial welfare. They can suddenly find themselves subject to the application – sometimes unlawfully, sometimes adversarially – of a set of hitherto hidden rules. Or when people become distressed and lose trust in the NHS, talk of 'outrageous theft', of being 'hoodwinked' and of deviousness – and believe that the NHS is acting contrary to the health and welfare interests of patients.[2]

Such a belief would not be undermined by a 2019 report that senior 'NHS officials', responsible for considering (and rejecting) CHC applications, were in a private capacity approaching families and offering to try to get negative decisions reversed – but only in return for fees of £300 to £400 per day. The report indicated with some understatement that, where this took

---

1   Deith, J. 'Continuing healthcare: the secret fund.' BBC Radio 4 *File on 4*, 23 November 2014. Accessed on 18 July 2019 at: www.bbc.co.uk/programmes/b04p86c4
2   BBC *Panorama*. 'The national homes swindle.' Broadcast 5 March 2006. Transcript accessed on 27 June 2019 at: http://news.bbc.co.uk/1/shared/spl/hi/programmes/panorama/transcripts/national_homes_transcript.txt

place within the same area in which the official worked, there would be an apparent conflict of interest.[1]

Nor should we be surprised when health and social care practitioners become uneasy at the game they are being asked to play – and at the time and resources being expended on disputes with each other, with families and between the NHS and social services at management level. This is a far cry from getting on with the job of focusing on the meeting of people's needs.

ON THE FRONT LINE, as it were, is a group of nurses, often known as nurse assessors, appointed specifically by CCGs to assess people's eligibility for NHS Continuing Healthcare.

Sometimes, these practitioners are placed in a difficult position and are used by CCGs effectively to fulfil a function of financial gatekeeping involving practices inconsistent with regulations and despite guidance emphasising that assessment and decision-making are meant to be about a person's clinical needs and not money. The reality may come across as quite the opposite, as one report found in relation to the role of assessors.

> **Assessment: not about what people need, but about who is going to pay.** The report stated that 'many of the individual submissions [sic] who had this experience raised concerns that the first priority when discussing care was who was going to pay for it, rather than what the individual actually needed and felt this demonstrated a lack of empathy with their situations'.[2]

They are placed in a difficult position also because the judgements having to be made – that health care needs are not in fact health care needs but are social care instead – are artificial. They may seem to make little professional sense and to be divorced from common sense, as one General Secretary of the Royal College of Nursing observed.[3]

There is evidence, in addition, suggesting that sometimes the pressures placed upon some assessors can result in what are perceived to be dismissive,

---

1   Barnes, S. and Rayner, G. Hancock investigates care fund 'consultants'. And Editorial: Labyrinthine care. *Daily Telegraph*, 31 December 2019, pp.6, 17.
2   All Party Parliamentary Group on Parkinson's. *Failing to care: NHS continuing care in England*. London: Parkinson's UK, 2013, p.22.
3   BBC *Panorama*. 'The national homes swindle.' Broadcast 5 March 2006. Transcript accessed on 27 June 2019 at: http://news.bbc.co.uk/1/shared/spl/hi/programmes/panorama/transcripts/national_homes_transcript.txt

bullying and unsympathetic approaches to extremely vulnerable people, ill and the least able to fight, as the solicitor in the *Coughlan* case described.[1]

In similar vein, a Parkinson's nurse, involved in CHC assessments, concluded that the process of assessment for NHS Continuing Healthcare could be intimidating, humiliating, unfriendly, exhausting, degrading, aggressive, frustrating and adversarial.[2] Likewise, health workers may report bullying at meetings and attempts to ridicule those with differing professional opinions.[3]

It is of note, in relation to this last point, that some nurse assessors themselves were reported to agree with this description of the process of assessment, reinforcing the point that they may find themselves effectively shoe-horned by CCGs into awkward and unwanted situations and decisions.

Overall, it seems that within CCGs, a fortress-like mentality can sometimes prevail. Nurse assessors are deployed, and sometimes seemingly misused, by CCGs as defenders on the outer walls whilst, as a fall back, decision-making panels sit within the inner bailey of the castle to repel patients who make it that far. This sort of siege mentality can lead to what has been characterised within NHS Continuing Healthcare as a culture of 'entrenched ineligibility'.[4]

Unsurprisingly, therefore, it sometimes seems that when people are found to be eligible for NHS Continuing Healthcare, it is almost in spite of, rather than because of, the system. Yet there is one further apparent perversity. Peculiarly, the Department of Health and Social Care, together with NHS England and CCGs, need to ensure that at least some, albeit a minimum number, of patients qualify. NHS Continuing Healthcare must be protected from extinction. Otherwise, the concealed policy of excluding from ongoing NHS care certain categories of patient with high levels of need would be at greater risk of exposure, something which, above all, the Department of Health and NHS England wish to avoid. So, appearances must be preserved, the fig leaf kept in place.

---

1 BBC *Panorama*. 'The national homes swindle.' Broadcast 5 March 2006. Transcript accessed on 27 June 2019 at: http://news.bbc.co.uk/1/shared/spl/hi/programmes/panorama/transcripts/national_homes_transcript.txt
2 All Party Parliamentary Group on Parkinson's. *Failing to care: NHS continuing care in England.* London: Parkinson's UK, 2013, p.14.
3 Taylor, J. and Rigby, N. '"Medical opinions ignored" by NHS payment assessor, workers say.' *BBC News* (BBC East), 10 September 2017. Accessed on 17 July 2019 at: www.bbc.co.uk/news/uk-england-41187615
4 Clements, L. *et al. Community care and the law.* 7th edition. London: Legal Action Group, 2019, p.496.

LOCAL AUTHORITIES, one might have thought, would be the ones that could come to the rescue, taking extensive steps to challenge questionable NHS decision-making, both on their own account and that of service users, and relieving patients and families of pursuing arduous challenges against the NHS.

Local social services authorities do not have the legal power to make eligibility decisions but remain pivotal in respect of NHS Continuing Healthcare. They have a duty to refer people to the NHS and a duty to participate in assessments, and they are prohibited from meeting Continuing Healthcare needs. They are also obligated to have a dispute resolution process in order to challenge the NHS.

However, in practice, local authorities have not in general relieved the pressure on patients, families and practitioners. They have been caught between a rock and a hard place and may fail to challenge the NHS at all or adequately – even in obvious circumstances. This can be for various reasons.

First, there is a political imperative to work cooperatively with the NHS. *Second*, there is a difficulty in robustly challenging the NHS without taking an unduly adversarial approach. *Third*, the stamina, skill and political will required to challenge persistently is considerable. *Fourth*, there is a tendency organisationally to focus on the money involved, not the law, thus querying decisions solely on the basis of the cost of a care package rather than its legal foundation. *Fifth*, and most unfortunately, if a person has financial resources of their own, the local authority has less incentive to challenge the NHS because, even if the person is denied eligibility for NHS Continuing Healthcare, they will have to pay for their own care and, therefore, not be a drain on the local authority's finances.

SURVEYING THE EVIDENCE of this chapter, we find a remarkably consistent and long-lived policy, stretching back three decades. It is about removing from free NHS care certain categories of patient with high levels of ongoing, uncurable health needs and shifting them over to means-tested social care through the porous border, deliberately left open, between health and social care.

This has been a policy sustained by secrecy. It forms part of a wider disinclination by central government, and therefore in practice by the NHS, to provide for such patients, for example adequate hospital diagnosis, treatment, rehabilitation and discharge.

Were it any other health care stratagem, such firmness of purpose on the part of the Department for Health and Social Care (formerly the Department of Health), through political thick, thin and change, might be admirable. Unfortunately, however, this particular policy has been furtive in nature and harmful in effect. Its obscurity is maintained by the confusing and uncertain rules which are to be found on the surface in regulations and guidance, and by local practice which, too often, undermines even these defective rules.

All the more noteworthy is that this concealed policy has been pursued doggedly in defiance of all obstacles: legal case law, ombudsman investigations, government guidance, severe criticism from House of Commons select committees, respected health think tanks, alliances of charities – to name but some.

It is abundantly clear that the reason for enduring stealth is that otherwise, flushed out, any government of the day would either have to accept the NHS remaining responsible for people with severe, if incurable, health care needs – or risk a political backlash for removing health care from them. This explains, but in no way justifies, what has happened.

It is not the purpose of this chapter to propose a solution to the Gordian knot of NHS Continuing Healthcare. Instead it merely suggests that the prerequisite of any solution lies in openness, so that we can all better understand the position, talk about it and vote on it, as you do in a democratic society so that an understandable, fair and transparent policy can emerge. This very point, in the form of a question, was put simply and succinctly by a BBC *Panorama* programme in 2006. It noted that it was as 'plain as a pikestaff' that people were being provided with health care disguised as means-tested social care, and that the clear, underlying policy was that elderly, long-term sick people should pay for the cost of their ongoing health care, in which case why, in the cause of straightforwardness, simply not say so?[1]

Unfortunately, dispiritingly and 14 years later, the same question remains.

---

1   BBC *Panorama*. 'The national homes swindle: a growing scandal.' Broadcast 23 July 2006. Transcript accessed on 27 June 2019 at: http://news.bbc.co.uk/1/hi/programmes/panorama/5216252.stm

Chapter 4

A–Z list

A

Accommodation and NHS Continuing Healthcare

It is not always made clear to patients, families and practitioners that NHS Continuing Healthcare (CHC) eligibility can apply within a range of settings.

Health services in general, including those to meet CHC needs, are arranged by NHS clinical commissioning groups (CCGs) under section 3 of the National Health Service Act 2006. Section 3 refers to the provision of hospital accommodation, but also to any other accommodation needed 'for the purpose of any service provided' under the Act.

Current guidance states that CHC can be provided in any setting, including but not limited to a person's home, a care home or hospice.[1] In the last two of these settings the NHS is providing the accommodation in terms of paying (an independent provider) for it, unless the care home or hospice is owned by the NHS, in which case the provision would be direct.

The guidance does not refer to hospital accommodation; this is clearly not because a person's CHC needs legally could not be met in hospital, but simply because current policy is to ensure that hospital stays are short. Indeed, previous guidance did refer to hospitals as one of the settings in which CHC needs could be met.[2]

On occasion, the question arises about whether the NHS might in some circumstances have to provide or pay for ordinary private accommodation – i.e. a roof over a person's head – in order to enable the meeting of that person's CHC needs, and without which those needs could not be met.

> **Provision of ordinary accommodation to meet CHC needs?** In the *Whapples* case, the CCG conceded that it had the legal power to do so – but then successfully argued that it was not necessary for it, in the particular circumstances, to provide or pay for a new flat for the person (in order for care to be successfully provided for her).

---

1   National Framework 2018, para 63.
2   HSC 2001/015. *Continuing care: NHS and local councils' responsibilities*. London: DH, 2001, para 5.

> However, the court doubted, without ruling on the issue, the correctness of the CCG's concession, that it had legal power under section 3 of the National Health Service Act 2006 to provide or pay for ordinary accommodation. Issues to consider would be whether such provision of ordinary accommodation could come under the phrase, in section 3, 'other accommodation for the purpose of any service provided under this Act'.
>
> A second issue would be that the meaning of the word 'hospital', also in section 3, has been given a wide meaning in old case law, to include, for example, a care home with nursing.[1] Both considerations would be relevant to deciding whether section 3 can underpin provision of ordinary accommodation.[2]

Adaptations, see *Home adaptations*

Advocacy and NHS Continuing Healthcare

Advocacy aims at a person being able to participate and engage – or at least be represented and supported – in assessments by statutory services, such as the NHS or local authorities. Given how difficult NHS Continuing Healthcare (CHC) is to understand, and the risks of inadequate and sometimes poor decision-making, advocacy takes on added significance.

Particular duties apply to the appointment of advocates under both the Care Act 2014 (adult social care) and also under the Mental Capacity Act 2005. For a duty to arise, certain conditions must be met under these two pieces of legislation.

However, in the case of CHC, Department of Health and Social Care guidance states that even when there is no duty to appoint an advocate under either piece of legislation, local authorities and NHS clinical commissioning groups (CCGs) should anyway consider appointing advocates.

- **Advocacy: mental capacity and relevance to NHS Continuing Healthcare.** The Mental Capacity Act contains specific and detailed rules about the appointment of independent mental capacity advocates (IMCAs) in a number of different circumstances, including the provision (and review) of accommodation, by way of care home or hospital provision, or serious medical treatment – if it has been

---

1 *Minister of Health v General Committee of the Royal Midland Counties Home for Incurables at Leamington Spa* [1954] 1 Ch 530.
2 *R(Whapples) v Birmingham Crosscity Clinical Commissioning Group* [2015] EWCA Civ 435, paras 23, 29, 45, 48.

established, under the 2005 Act, that the person lacks the relevant mental capacity.

This means that if a person qualifies for CHC, and the placement is going to be in hospital or a care home, they will be entitled to an IMCA if they lack the relevant capacity and do not have an appropriate family member or friend to support them in their best interests.[1]

Changes to rules about deprivation of liberty will mean that people (including those with CHC status) will be entitled in some circumstances to IMCAs in other contexts as well, including their own homes or supported living.[2]

- **Advocacy: Care Act 2014 and relevance to NHS Continuing Healthcare.** The Care Act 2014 contains specific and detailed rules about the appointment of independent advocates (IAs), including for assessment, care and support planning, revising plans and safeguarding, in relation to adult social care.

  In summary, the duty to appoint depends on whether the local authority considers the person would have substantial difficulty (not lack of mental capacity) in understanding these processes and on the absence of an appropriate family member or friend to help them.

  These rules do not apply directly to assessment and decisions about CHC, which take place under the NHS legislation, not the Care Act. However, a Care Act advocate may sometimes be involved for the following reasons.

  First, before CHC status is established, local authorities may be assessing a person under the Care Act, not least to establish whether or not the needs are predominantly social care or health care in nature.

  Second, part of that duty under the Care Act is to make a referral to the NHS if, during a Care Act assessment, it appears to the local authority that the person may be eligible for CHC.[3]

  Third, there is an exception anyway to these main rules – namely, that even if there is an appropriate family member or friend, an advocate must be appointed under the Care Act if the person lacks the relevant mental capacity, may be placed by the NHS in a hospital for more than four weeks or in a care home for more than eight, and

---

1   See e.g. National Framework 2018, para 306 for a summary.
2   Mental Capacity (Amendment) Act 2019.
3   Care and Support (Assessment) Regulations 2014, r.7.

the local authority believes it is in the person's best interests for the advocate to be appointed.[1]

Thus, Care Act advocacy is at least partly relevant, in some circumstances, to assessments for CHC.

- **Advocacy: for CHC even in the absence of a duty.** The National Framework guidance states that even if a person does not meet the criteria for an IMCA under the Mental Capacity Act, CCGs and the local authorities should nevertheless consider jointly commissioning advocates to help people with the CHC process.[2]

Likewise, further statutory guidance states that CHC 'processes and arrangements have historically been difficult for individuals, their carers, family or friends, to understand and be involved in'. Therefore, even if the person does not lack capacity – or would not have substantial difficulty under the Care Act in understanding the process – and even if there is an appropriate family member or friend to support the person, local authorities and CCGs should still 'consider the benefits of providing access to independent advice or independent advocacy'.[3]

Aids to daily living, see *Equipment*

Altered states of consciousness, see *Decision Support Tool*

Appropriate clinician (end of life)

'Appropriate clinician' is the term used in regulations to define who is responsible for completing the Fast Track Pathway Tool by stating that a person is nearing the end of life and is therefore eligible for NHS Continuing Healthcare. The appropriate clinician must be a doctor or nurse responsible for the diagnosis, treatment or care of the person under the National Health Service Act 2006. This doctor or nurse is therefore the key decision-maker. For details of how eligibility is established, see ***Fast Track Pathway Tool***.[4]

---

1 SI 2014/2824. Care and Support (Independent Advocacy Support) Regulations 2014, r.4.
2 National Framework 2018, para 307.
3 Department of Health. *Care and support statutory guidance*. London: DH, 2016, para 7.22.
4 NHS Responsibilities Regulations 2012, r.21.

Assessment

In order for a person to get NHS Continuing Healthcare (CHC), an assessment must take place according to a set of rules contained in regulations and guidance. Despite these rules, a number of factors can make this assessment process problematic, making acquaintance with the rules that much more important for patients, families and practitioners.

Regulations state that NHS clinical commissioning groups (CCGs) must take reasonable steps to ensure that an assessment for CHC is carried out for a person if it appears to the CCG that such a person (a) may be in need of CHC, or (b) is already receiving CHC but may no longer be eligible for it.[1] The responsible CCG is normally where a person is registered with a medical general practitioner (GP).

The phrase 'may be in need' of CHC suggests a low legal threshold for triggering the assessment duty.[2] This means that even if there might just be a need for CHC, falling short, for example, of likelihood, the duty to assess would remain. The duty is not dependent on a request but is dependent on consent, assuming the person has the mental capacity to consent or dissent.

- **Taking 'reasonable steps' to assess.** To take reasonable steps to assess a person when there is an appearance of need is not the same as having an unqualified duty; for example, under section 9 of the Care Act 2014, local authorities have a duty to assess people who may be in need without such a qualification.

    What 'reasonable steps' means in practice and in detail will depend to an extent on individual context and circumstances, but in principle there would presumably be a difference between taking reasonable steps and, for example, taking every step no matter how onerous or leaving no stone unturned. By way of comparison, for instance, the taking of 'all practicable steps' under section 1 of the Mental Capacity Act 2005, to assist a person to take a decision for themselves, would be a stronger duty than merely to take reasonable steps.

- **Reasonable steps and delay in assessment.** One implication of taking 'reasonable steps' could in principle relate to how quickly, not just whether, the assessment is carried out. There is a general public law principle that if legislation stipulates a specific duty, then that

---

1   NHS Responsibilities Regulations 2012, r.21(2).
2   *R v Bristol City Council, ex p Penfold* [1998] 1 CCLR 315, High Court. In which a similar phrase was legally scrutinised, in relation to a local authority's duty of assessment.

duty should be carried out without undue delay.[1] If there are clear time limits in legislation or guidance, this will have a bearing on how the courts or ombudsman might view whether reasonable steps have been taken. Within CHC, the National Framework guidance does set out timescales. See **Delay**.

- **Assessing current or future need?** The duty in the regulations is to assess the present state of the person, not the future (in so many weeks, months or years), which means that declining to assess or to award CHC on the grounds that a person might at some point in the future improve would be legally suspect. Other than, as the guidance sets out, when people are discharged from hospital and assessment may be usefully delayed for a very few weeks, with the interim period normally being funded by the NHS. See **Hospital discharge**.

If and when a full assessment does take place, it must involve use either of the Decision Support Tool (DST) or, in end of life cases, the Fast Track Pathway Tool (to which the reasonable steps duty does not apply). In the case of the DST route, if a screening tool is used first of all, then it must be the Checklist.[2] For these three pieces of guidance, see **Checklist**, **Decision Support Tool** and **Fast Track Pathway Tool**.

A multi-disciplinary team must complete the DST (see **Multi-disciplinary team**) and an appropriate clinician the Fast Track Pathway Tool. Guidance states also that assessment should be carried out by appropriate professionals, in terms of both knowledge of the person and the condition. See **Expertise of assessors, and knowledge of the patient**.

---

1   *R(D) v London Borough of Brent* [2015] EWHC 3224 (Admin), para 19.
2   NHS Responsibilities Regulations 2012, r.21.

B

Breathing, see *Decision Support Tool*

C

Care Act 2014

The Care Act 2014 governs adult social care provided by local authorities. However, it is directly relevant to NHS Continuing Healthcare (CHC), provided under the National Health Service Act 2006, in a number of ways.

In summary, there is a legal boundary drawn between the two Acts, and local authorities are prohibited from providing under the Care Act both CHC and also registered nursing care.[1] These rules within section 22 of the Act are themselves based on principles set out by the Court of Appeal in the *Coughlan* legal case.[2]

This means that CHC eligibility, and decisions made about it, must be viewed and sometimes challenged not just in terms of what the NHS must provide, but what local authorities are not permitted to provide, which is why, for example, in one major legal case about CHC, the judge queried why the local authority had not, for whatever reason, participated in the case, given the considerable legal and resource implications for it.[3]

In addition, local authorities have a duty to refer to the NHS if they believe that a person may have CHC needs; a duty to cooperate with the NHS in relation to CHC assessments; and a duty to agree a dispute resolution procedure with the NHS clinical commissioning group (CCG). See **Cooperation**; **Dispute resolution between NHS and social services**; and **Referral for NHS Continuing Healthcare**.

Care Act 2014: prohibition on doing what the NHS is required to do

Section 22 of the Care Act states that:

> A local authority may not meet needs under sections 18 to 20 by providing or arranging for the provision of a service or facility that is required to be provided under the National Health Service Act 2006 unless – (a) doing so would be merely incidental or ancillary to doing something else to meet needs under those sections, and (b) the service

---

1 National Framework 2018, para 7.
2 National Framework 2018, para 44.
3 *R(Grogan) v Bexley NHS Care Trust* [2006] EWHC 44 (Admin), paras 32–35.

or facility in question would be of a nature that the local authority could be expected to provide.

The implications of this include the following.

First, the above wording is a rule about whether the quantity (incidental/ancillary) or quality (nature) of the care is beyond the remit of social services. Separate NHS regulations contain a very similar test and go on to say that if the health or nursing services *in their totality* exceed what would be within the remit of social services, then the person has a primary health need, in which case they are eligible for CHC and the NHS must arrange and be the sole funders of their care.[1]

So, this rule is stating that social services cannot lawfully meet a person's CHC needs. In addition, the rule is stating that there might be other provision, not amounting to CHC, but which would still be beyond the remit of social services (resulting in some cases in a joint package of care).

Second, the words 'incidental or ancillary' and 'nature' derive from legal case law.[2] See **Incidental or ancillary or of a nature beyond social services**.

Third, guidance attempts further to explain by stating that a local authority under the Care Act could, for example, commission 'elements of "general nursing" which can be provided by healthcare assistants or care assistants [but] this can only lawfully occur when this "nursing care" is both incidental or ancillary to the individual's accommodation and of a nature that a local authority can be expected to provide'.[3] But this could not, in any event, include any registered nursing care (see immediately below).

Nonetheless, the meaning of 'incidental or ancillary' may prove far from straightforward and raise its head, not only in CHC decisions but in decisions about joint funding when a person is not eligible for CHC. For instance, in the following case, the ombudsman simply declined to take a view about the meaning and application.

> **Speech and language therapy: incidental or ancillary?** In one ombudsman case, the question arose as to whether the local authority had the legal power, under the Care Act, to provide speech and language therapy for somebody it had placed in supported living accommodation, given the uncertainty that the NHS Trust would make adequate provision. The ombudsman, perhaps unsurprisingly,

---

1 NHS Responsibilities Regulations 2012, r.21.
2 *R(Coughlan) v North and East Devon Health Authority* [2001] Q.B. 213, para 30.
3 National Framework Practice Guidance 2018, para 2.4.

> declined to answer the question but instead criticised both the local authority and the NHS Trust for failing to work more cooperatively, to ensure that, one way or another, the person's health and social care needs were met.[1]

Care Act 2014: prohibition on arranging or providing registered nursing care

Section 22 of the Care Act states separately that a 'local authority may not meet needs under sections 18 to 20 by providing or arranging for the provision of nursing care by a registered nurse' (whether or not the registered nursing care required would otherwise be within the remit of social services in terms of quantity or quality of care. Formerly, local authorities could fund certain levels of registered nursing care, until the rules about this changed in 2001).[2]

Registered nursing care means provision 'by a registered nurse of a service involving: (a) the provision of care, or (b) the planning, supervision or delegation of the provision of care, other than a service which, having regard to its nature and the circumstances in which it is provided, does not need to be provided by a registered nurse'. A legal case further elaborated on what registered nursing care means, including the question of stand-by time.

> **Supreme Court definition of registered nursing care.** Registered nursing care is 'nursing care by a registered nurse [and] covers (a) time spent on nursing care, in the sense of care which can only be provided by a registered nurse, including both direct and indirect nursing time as defined by the Laing and Buisson study; (b) paid breaks; (c) time receiving supervision; (d) stand-by time; and (e) time spent on providing, planning, supervising or delegating the provision of other types of care which in all the circumstances ought to be provided by a registered nurse because they are ancillary to or closely connected with or part and parcel of the nursing care which she has to provide'.[3]

A local authority has the power to arrange a nursing home placement ('accommodation together with the provision of nursing care by a registered nurse') in two circumstances. The first is if the local authority has obtained

---

1 LGSCO, *Worcestershire County Council*, 2019 (17 009 661), paras 47–50.
2 *R(Grogan) v Bexley NHS Care Trust* [2006] EWHC 44 (Admin), para 26.
3 *R (on the application of Forge Care Homes Ltd and others) v Cardiff and Vale University Health Board and others (Secretary of State for Health intervening)* [2017] UKSC 56, para 44.

consent from the relevant CCG. The second is if the case is urgent and the arrangements are temporary, in which case the local authority must seek consent from the CCG as soon as feasible.[1]

The prohibitions above, about both registered nursing care and CHC, bar a local authority from doing those things under the Care Act. However, they do not necessarily affect a local authority's power to do them under the National Health Service Act 2006, on behalf of the NHS, by way of a formal joint working agreement under section 75 of the 2006 Act.[2]

Carers

Informal carers – for example, family members, friends and neighbours – have rights to assistance under the Care Act 2014 in relation to adult social care. This is to help them, essentially, remain willing and able to care for the adult in need for whom they are caring.[3]

In contrast, the National Health Service Act 2006 – which governs the provision of NHS Continuing Healthcare (CHC) – is silent about informal carers. Nonetheless, there are provisions in both legislation and guidance which may be of assistance to those carers of people in the community who have been assessed as eligible for CHC.

If an informal carer of a person with CHC status needs some form of break or respite, then the respite service itself – for instance, a sitting service in the person's own home, or a short break in a care home or hospice for the person being cared for – is clearly being provided to the person being cared for, i.e. the person with CHC status.

It follows that because, under legal regulations, the NHS clinical commissioning group (CCG) is responsible solely for arranging and funding CHC, then that respite falls to the NHS to provide.[4] Guidance confirms that this is the legal position:

> The CCG may need to provide additional support to care for the individual whilst the carer(s) has a break from his or her caring responsibilities and will need to assure carers of the availability of this support when required. This could take the form of the CCG providing the cared-for person with additional services in their own home or providing the necessary

---

1 Care Act 2014, s.22(3), (4), (5).
2 Care Act 2014, s.22(7).
3 Care Act 2014, ss.10, 19.
4 NHS Responsibilities Regulations 2012, r.20.

support to enable them to spend a period of time away from home (e.g. a care home).[1]

The CCG should, therefore, 'undertake an assessment of the carer's ability to continue to care, satisfying themselves that the responsibilities on the carer are appropriate and sustainable'.[2] The courts have explained it this way in a case about whether the respite care required for a child should be funded by social services or the NHS.

> **Respite for informal carer: social care or health care?**
>
> To my mind, it also shows how the purpose of the care should be regarded. It is spoken of as respite care for the mother. From one viewpoint, the purpose of its provision is so that the mother can have a few nights of unbroken sleep per week or some time by herself a week or to look after T. That could be seen as social care for the mother. But its nature and purpose is to provide medical care for D; the intention behind the provision of that medical care is her safety while her mother enjoys respite. There is nothing different in quality or care about the disputed provision.[3]

A similar conclusion was reached in a more recent case.

> **Health care by way of respite.** A CCG denied that it was providing health care in a respite facility for children with severe physical and learning disabilities despite the fact that, of 20 staff, half were nurses and the rest health care assistants. The court stated that in its view it was obvious that 'even if the primary motive or objective is to provide respite for the parents…the services being provided are health services nonetheless'.[4]

The ombudsman, too, has taken this view, and noted further that whilst it is for the CCG to decide on the carer's needs, it should take account of

---

1 National Framework 2018, para 327.
2 National Framework 2018, para 328.
3 *R(T) v London Borough of Haringey* [2005] EWHC 2235 (Admin), para 65.
4 *R(Juttla) v Hertfordshire Valleys Clinical Commissioning Group* [2018] EWHC 267 (Admin), paras 5, 11.

what the local authority's previous view of those needs was. If the CCG then decides not to continue to meet those needs – which the local authority would now be legally precluded from meeting because of the person's CHC status – it must at least explain why.[1] Other points include:

- **Informal carers and CHC eligibility**. The responsibility of the NHS both to provide respite care, where required, and other support to informal carers of a person with CHC needs, underlines the fact that CHC status does not depend on the identity of who is doing the main part of the caring. This is reinforced by guidance which notes that CHC eligibility 'is not determined or influenced either by the setting where the care is provided or by the characteristics of the person who delivers the care'.[2]

    This was underlined in the Health Service Ombudsman investigation, known as the *Pointon* case, in which the main carer of a man in his own home was his wife.[3] Likewise, in the *Haringey* case, in which a child's intensive tracheostomy care was being provided by her mother, but any additional care required in order to give the mother respite would be an NHS continuing care responsibility, beyond the legal limits of social services.[4]

- **Informal carers, CHC and training an informal carer (e.g. in manual handling)**. Guidance states further that the CCG should give consideration to meeting any training needs that the carer may have to carry out their role in caring for a person with CHC needs.[5] This could, for example, take the form of training in relation to manual handling, a common cause of difficulty and sometimes injury to informal carers.

- **Informal carers, CHC but continuing social services involvement**. Although respite provision would clearly be the responsibility of the NHS in a CHC case, when the carer needs a break, the carer may have other support needs which might still fall to social services to consider and to meet. Guidance states, for example, that this might be 'particularly relevant where the carer has needs in relation to

---

1 LGSCO, *Herefordshire Council*, 2018 (16 008 092), paras 45–46.
2 National Framework 2018, para 63.
3 *Cambridgeshire Health Authority* (E.22/02–03). In: Health Service Ombudsman. HC 704. *Selected investigations completed October 2003–March 2004*. London: TSO, 2004.
4 *R(T) v London Borough of Haringey* [2005] EWHC 2235 (Admin), para 65.
5 National Framework 2018, para 327.

education, leisure or work (unrelated to their caring role) as these fall outside the scope of NHS Continuing Healthcare but can be addressed through Care Act 2014 provisions'.[1]

Case management

When NHS clinical commissioning groups (CCGs) become responsible for meeting a person's NHS Continuing Healthcare (CHC) needs, they become responsible, too, for managing that person's case. This is implied by the legislation, since regulations state that CHC is a package of care arranged and funded solely by the NHS,[2] and is confirmed in guidance which states that the CCG is responsible for care planning, commissioning services and case management.[3]

In practice, CCGs sometimes ask local authorities to take on the case management of a person eligible for CHC. Local authorities are prohibited from doing this, since CHC is, in regulations, something the CCG is required to do 'solely' – and section 22 of the Care Act 2014 states that local authorities cannot do anything the NHS is required to do. At most, they could agree to do this under the National Health Service Act 2006, on behalf of a CCG, by way of an agreement made under section 75 of the National Health Service Act.[4] But, since CHC must be arranged and funded solely by the NHS, the local authority could, and arguably must, seek reimbursement.

Challenging behaviour

Behaviour is one of the domains of need which is assessed and recorded in the Decision Support Tool (DST) used in assessments for NHS Continuing Healthcare (CHC). See *Decision Support Tool*.

Behaviour is in practice a much-disputed domain, particularly in relation to people with learning disabilities, with local authorities and NHS clinical commissioning groups (CCGs) regularly taking opposing views about whether the person's needs are eligible for CHC. The disputes are seemingly driven as much by the high cost of caring for the person as by the legal position. They revolve regularly around the significance, in terms of CHC

---

1   National Framework 2018, para 329.
2   NHS Responsibilities Regulations 2012, r.20.
3   National Framework 2018, para 165.
4   A point referred to in the National Framework 2018, para 167.

eligibility, of the person's behavioural needs being 'well managed'. Guidance is clear that well-managed challenging behaviour is still challenging behaviour.

- **Challenging behaviour: well-managed need is still a need.**

    > Needs should not be marginalised just because they are successfully managed. Well managed needs are still needs. Only where the successful management of a healthcare need has permanently reduced or removed an on-going need, such that the active management of this need is reduced or no longer required will this have a bearing on CHC eligibility. This principle is incorporated into the domain descriptors of the DST. For example, in the behaviour domain the level of support and skill required to manage risks associated with challenging behaviour helps determine the domain weighting. In such cases the care plan (including psychological or similar interventions) should provide the evidence of the level of need, recognising that this care plan may be successfully avoiding or reducing incidents of challenging behaviour.[1]

Nonetheless, the view has, for example, been expressed that if challenging behaviour gives rise to hugely complex social care management, without the direct input on a regular basis of healthcare professionals, the person will not have a primary health need, even if the outcome of completion of the DST indicates eligibility for CHC.[2] This view seems questionable.

First, the National Framework statutory guidance is clear that eligibility should not be based on use (or not) of NHS-employed staff to provide care, need for/presence of 'specialist staff' in care delivery, or any other input-related (rather than needs-related) rationale.[3] And the *Pointon* case, which involved challenging behaviour and the bulk of the care being provided by the patient's wife, supports this approach in the guidance.

Second, sometimes CCGs appear to view learning disability as a social care need by definition and therefore not subject to the CHC rules (other than in relation to physical disabilities the person may also have); however, the regulations state that CHC applies in principle to people aged 18 or over 'to meet physical or mental health needs which have arisen as a result of disability, accident or illness'. Learning disability is clearly a disability; and

---

[1] Decision Support Tool 2018, para 27.
[2] Locke, D. *NHS law and practice*. London: Legal Action Group, 2018, para 16.30.
[3] National Framework 2018, para 65.

in any case, illness is defined in section 256 of the National Health Service Act 2006 so as to include any disorder or disability of mind, also therefore covering learning disability.

Third, such a view would in addition be vulnerable to an argument that it is not only contrary to the National Framework guidance but also potentially discriminatory under the Equality Act 2010, by singling out the characteristic of learning disability and treating it differently from other disabilities.[1]

Challenging decisions

For patients and their families, there are several options in terms of challenging a decision that has been made about NHS Continuing Healthcare (CHC).

These include seeking a local review by the NHS clinical commissioning group of its decision; beyond that, requesting NHS England to appoint an independent review panel; and, after that, asking the Health Service Ombudsman to investigate. An alternative is to attempt to bring a judicial review legal case. See *Disputes between a person and the NHS*; *Health Service Ombudsman*; *Independent review panels*; and *Judicial review*.

Sometimes, however, a challenge is also made against social services – for example, for not referring a person for CHC consideration or for providing (and financially charging for) services under the Care Act 2014, services which arguably should have been free of charge under the National Health Service Act 2006. If dissatisfied with the outcome of a complaint against social services, the person can request that the local ombudsman investigate.[2] See *Local Government and Social Care Ombudsman*.

Charging for services, see *Means-testing*

Checklist

The Checklist is a piece of statutory guidance published by the Department of Health and Social Care. It is used as a screening tool to judge whether a person should receive fuller assessment for NHS Continuing Healthcare (CHC) using the Decision Support Tool (DST). The Checklist is important for a number of reasons, flowing from both regulations and guidance. It is

---

1 National Framework Practice Guidance 2018, paras 35.1–36.1.
2 See e.g. LGO, *Hertfordshire County Council*, 2003 (00/B/16833).

the gateway, other than in end-of-life circumstances, to potential eligibility for CHC.

'Getting through' the Checklist stage is no guarantee that the person will then, on the full assessment using the DST, be eligible for CHC. But without negotiating the Checklist stage, there will normally be no possibility of eligibility – except in end of life cases and those rare cases when the Checklist is dispensed with and the DST is used straight away instead.

Once a completed Checklist is received by the NHS clinical commissioning group (CCG), it should make a decision about a person's CHC status and needs within 28 days; in other words, a completed Checklist has the effect of setting time running.[1]

In general, therefore, it is essential for patients, families and frontline practitioners to ensure that the Checklist is applied by CCGs according to the rules, and that it is completed accurately.

Importantly, therefore, guidance states that the individual should be given reasonable notice of the intention to undertake the Checklist and should normally be given the opportunity to be present at the completion of the Checklist, together with any representative they have. Furthermore, the outcome must be communicated clearly to them, including reasons, contained within a copy of the completed Checklist.[2]

There sometimes is a temptation for CCGs, in trying to save money, to stymie use of the Checklist and strangle potential eligibility at this first hurdle of the process, a temptation which can involve breaching the rules. These have already been summarised in Chapter 2 of this book.

In the following case, both social services and the CCG combined to delay a CHC decision for six months.

> **Six-month delay involving Checklist and final decision: both social services and CCG at fault.** Social services were informed that the condition of a care home resident had worsened. Consequently, a social worker completed a Checklist early in July but did not send it to the CCG until August; when she did so, it seemed she had not signed it. The CCG did not point out to social services the flaws in the Checklist. In any event, neither she nor the CCG did anything until November. Even then, a decision was not made until February, when eligibility was finally granted. The ombudsman found fault with both social services and the CCG.[3]

---

1 National Framework 2018, para 162.
2 National Framework 2018, paras 94, 100.
3 LGSCO, *Leicester City Council*, 2019 (18 001 026), paras 54–58.

Checklist: the only legally permitted screening tool for CHC

Regulations state that if a CCG uses an initial screening process to decide whether to undertake an assessment of a person's CHC eligibility, it must complete and use the Checklist, inform the person or somebody else lawfully acting on their behalf and make a record of the decision.[1] From this rule, a few key points follow.

First, the purpose of the Checklist, as stipulated in the regulations, must be adhered to: it is about deciding whether to conduct a CHC assessment. So, in the following case, the ombudsman found fault when a local authority completely misunderstood its purpose.

> **Checklist: not about whether a person has needs over and above funded nursing care.** A local authority stated that the CHC Checklist was 'used to determine if someone has nursing needs that are over and above what would normally be supported by community nursing services and is used for the determination of Funded Nursing Care (FNC)'. The ombudsman noted that this was 'incorrect'. The Checklist should be used 'to decide whether a person needs a full assessment for CHC'.[2]

Second, if no screening tool is used, then far more resource- and time-intensive assessments would need to be conducted by the CCG, using the Decision Support Tool. This is because the overarching duty is to take reasonable steps to assess a person for eligibility for CHC in all cases where it 'appears' to the CCG that 'there may be a need for such care'.

Such wording has been interpreted in legal case law as constituting a low threshold;[3] meaning in the context of CHC that, even were eligibility far from certain, there would still be a duty to assess. Use of the Checklist is therefore an essential way of avoiding unnecessary full assessments in cases where a person obviously falls far short of possible eligibility.

Third, if an alternative screening tool is used instead of the Checklist, the CCG will risk acting unlawfully. With this risk in mind, guidance sets out the obvious but limited circumstances in which it might not be necessary to apply the Checklist at all. They are as follows:

---

1   NHS Responsibilities Regulations 2012, r.21.
2   LGSCO, *Bedford Borough Council*, 2017 (16 015 651), para 45.
3   *R v Bristol City Council, ex p Penfold* [1998] 1 CCLR 315, High Court (in the context of social care legislation).

- **Clearly no need for CHC**. If practitioners are clear there is no need for CHC, the decision would require recorded reasons, and any doubt should lead to a Checklist being completed.

- **Short-term health needs**. The person is recovering from short-term health needs (but if there is doubt, a Checklist may need to be completed).

- **Direct referral for full assessment**. The CCG has agreed direct referral for full assessment of eligibility.

- **End of life**. The Fast Track Pathway Tool needs to be used instead, in case of a rapidly deteriorating condition that may be entering a terminal phase.

- **Mental health aftercare**. An individual is receiving services under section 117 of the Mental Health Act for their mental disorder, and this is meeting all of their assessed needs. [Unless there are separate physical needs which may need to be considered in relation to CHC.]

- **Previous decision**. A previous decision found the person not eligible for CHC and there has been no change in needs.[1]

Fourth, some CCGs, as part of an NHS England 'pioneer' programme, have been using what appears to be a pre-Checklist screening tool, in potential breach of the regulations. Referred to, for instance, in some areas as the '5Qs' approach, in others as '4Qs', they seem to be about filtering out patients from the CHC process,[2] not only going beyond the circumstances listed in the National Framework guidance above, but also asking questions inconsistent with the guidance and legal regulations.

Checklist: set at a low threshold, detailed evidence not required

One reason why some CCGs, and seemingly NHS England, dislike the Checklist is because it has been drafted to set a low threshold,[3] which means it should not be used stringently to bar people from fuller assessment under the Decision Support Tool.

---

1 National Framework 2018, para 91.
2 West Norfolk Clinical Commissioning Group. *West Norfolk Continuing Health Care innovation summary evaluation report*. King's Lynn: WNCCG, 2016, pp.18–19. And: Brennan, S. 'CCG accused of using flawed test to cut spending on elderly.' *Health Service Journal*, 3 January 2019.
3 National Audit Office. *Investigation into NHS Continuing Healthcare funding*. London: NAO, 2017, p.37.

Guidance states that the purpose of the Checklist is to encourage proportionate assessments of eligibility; that the threshold has intentionally been set low, in order to ensure that all those who require a full assessment of eligibility have this opportunity; that completing the Checklist is intended to be relatively quick and straightforward; and that it is not necessary to provide detailed evidence along with the completed Checklist, although a brief description of need (and source of evidence for this) should be included.[1] It notes also that the principle – that a well-managed need is still a need – applies equally to the Checklist stage at it does to the later, DST stage.[2] See **Well-managed needs**.

Whilst detailed evidence therefore is not needed, equally some is; otherwise, there is a risk of CCGs completing a negative Checklist and barring full assessment for CHC, without explanation.

Completing a funded nursing care assessment before a Checklist; then completing negative Checklist with no explanation: both unlawful. A court found fault when a Checklist was completed not only after an FNC assessment had taken place and not before (as it should legally have been) – but, in addition, the nurse had simply ringed the word 'No' against every need, without any comment whatsoever. More was needed.[3]

Likewise, the ombudsman found fault when a local authority officer completed a Checklist with a negative outcome; however, the reasoning and evidence was non-existent, stating only 'no indication for a full assessment' with no further explanation.[4]

Checklists need to be completed at the relevant time, in whatever setting, including care homes, the person is living. Furthermore, needs change: an earlier Checklist might not indicate the need for a fuller assessment; a second, later, Checklist might. The ombudsman has found fault when a CCG failed to appreciate this.[5]

---

1 National Framework 2018, paras 83–86, 97.
2 National Framework 2018, para 98.
3 *R(Dennison) v Bradford Districts Clinical Commissioning Group* [2014] EWHC 2552 (Admin), paras 12, 13, 17.
4 LGSCO, *Essex County Council*, 2018 (17 018 742), para 27.
5 HSO, Failure to assess for Continuing Healthcare. Summary 741, January 2015. In: HSO. *Report on selected summaries of investigations by the Parliamentary and Health Service Ombudsman December 2014 and January 2015*. London: HSO, 2015.

Checklist: consent
The Checklist should be completed only when a person has consented to this (and to the sharing of it) or, in case of lack of mental capacity, when a decision has been made in the person's best interests.[1]

Checklist: domains of need, scoring and eligibility for full assessment
The Checklist is set out in the form of 11 domains of need. Achieving a sufficiently high score overall against these domains is normally essential if the person is to be assessed more fully under the DST. It is therefore crucial that people, families and frontline practitioners ensure that the domains are completed appropriately.

The Checklist domains are the same as in the DST. They are breathing, nutrition, continence, skin integrity, mobility, communication, psychological and emotional needs, cognition, behaviour, drug therapies and medication, and altered states of consciousness. Each domain is broken down into three scoring levels, A, B and C. The outcome of the Checklist depends on the number of As, Bs and Cs identified.[2]

The Checklist states that a full assessment for CHC is required if there are: a) two or more domains selected in column A; b) five or more domains selected in column B, or one selected in A and four in B; or c) one domain selected in column A in one of the boxes marked with an asterisk (i.e. those domains that carry a priority level in the DST), with any number of selections in the other two columns.[3]

It also notes that occasionally a person should still proceed to a full assessment for CHC eligibility, even if they apparently do not meet the Checklist threshold, so long as there is a clear rationale for this decision.[4]

Checklist: who completes it?
Regulations state that it is the CCG that must 'complete and use' the Checklist. It is therefore clearly the responsibility of the CCG and, if staff from other bodies complete the Checklist, it must be with agreement and by arrangement with the CCG. But in reaching that decision the CCG must have regard to the National Framework, which is statutory guidance.

This guidance makes quite clear that the Checklist can be completed by a 'variety of health and social care practitioners, who have been trained in its

---
1   Checklist 2018, paras 11–12.
2   National Framework 2018, para 84.
3   Checklist 2018, para 15.
4   Checklist 2018, para 16.

use', including, for example, registered nurses employed by the NHS, GPs, other clinicians or local authority staff such as social workers, care managers or social care assistants. This should be by agreement between the CCG and local authority, but 'it is expected that it should, as far as possible, include staff involved in assessing or reviewing individuals' needs as part of their day-to-day work'.[1]

At the same time, guidance states that a person in need cannot complete the Checklist themselves.[2] Were a CCG to permit only a few nurse assessors (usually not known to the patient) to complete the Checklist, it would risk breaching the statutory guidance.

Children

For children, that is people aged under 18, the regulations and guidance about continuing care are not the same as for adults. The legal definition envisages more joint funding between education, health and social services authorities. And eligibility for children's continuing care does not presuppose eligibility for NHS Continuing Healthcare for adults.[3] Because of this difference, guidance sets out a transition process for when a person reaches the age of 18. See *Transition*. It is beyond the scope of this book to analyse the rules for children and their implications.

Clinical commissioning groups

NHS clinical commissioning groups (CCGs) are responsible locally for arranging and funding NHS Continuing Healthcare (CHC), except for a few categories of patient for whom NHS England is responsible (prisoners or serving military personnel and their families).[4] Formerly, their equivalents were called primary care trusts (PCTs) and, before that, health authorities. Some of the older legal or ombudsman cases referred to in this book involve PCTs or health authorities.

---

1 National Framework 2018, paras 92–93.
2 National Framework 2018, para 96.
3 NHS Responsibilities Regulations 2012, r.20. And: Department of Health. *National Framework for Children and Young People's Continuing Care*. London: DH, 2016.
4 NHS Responsibilities Regulations 2012, r.20.

Clinical commissioning groups: which one is responsible for funding CHC?

Sometimes disputes arise as to which CCG is responsible for meeting a person's CHC needs. Guidance states that care and treatment should not be refused because of the dispute, and that therefore interim responsibilities should be agreed. If the dispute cannot be resolved, it should be referred to NHS England.[1]

The guidance on establishing the responsible CCG is candidly called *Who pays?* It states that a placing CCG remains responsible for funding the CHC needs of the patient in care home or independent hospital accommodation. The original CCG would normally be identified by where the person was registered with a GP. However, CCG responsibility for commissioning health services *unrelated to the placement*, for example inpatient treatment in an NHS hospital, would be determined by where the person is registered with a GP.[2]

If a patient is provided with CHC in their own home and they decide to move home to another area (not into residential care), the responsible CCG would be determined by where the person is registered with a GP.

> **Identifying the correct CCG.** A CHC assessment was in process for a patient but, before it was completed, the person registered with a GP in a second area. At that time, the DST process had not been completed and no final decision had been made about eligibility or to provide services as a result of that decision.
>
> It was therefore the second CCG which was legally responsible for meeting the person's CHC needs – even though the first CCG, in error, had continued to make provision for years, something which it had in principle no legal power to do.[3]

If, when such uncertainties arise, a CCG refuses to get involved either with the family or with the other CCG, thus causing a delay of many months before responsibility is agreed, the ombudsman will find fault.[4]

---

1 National Framework 2018, para 213.
2 NHS England. *Who pays? Determining responsibility for payments to providers.* London: NHSE, 2013, paras 1, 60–64.
3 *R(Wolverhampton Council) v South Worcestershire Clinical Commissioning Group, Shropshire CCG* [2018] EWHC 1136 (Admin).
4 HSO, Woman in her eighties spent nearly ten months in hospital after she was ready to be discharged. Summary 1176, December 2015. In: HSO. *Report on selected summaries of investigations by the Parliamentary and Health Service Ombudsman October to December 2015.* London: HSO, 2016.

A decision by one CCG about eligibility may not be the same as that made by another, when a person moves area. Given the element of professional judgement contained within the CHC assessment process, this would not necessarily indicate fault or unlawfulness, as long as the process had been followed properly and reasons given.[1]

Clinical commissioning groups: overall responsibility

A CCG has power to 'delegate' CHC responsibilities to, for example, NHS trusts and local authorities. However, the CCG retains ultimate responsibility for ensuring that legal rules are complied with.[2]

In some areas, CCGs have delegated CHC assessments and decisions to what are called commissioning support units. If such a unit mishandles the CHC process, as in one particular case in which hundreds of referrals for CHC were ignored for many months, it would be the CCGs involved (there were three) that would be ultimately responsible.[3]

Delegation may get more complicated; for instance, in one case the CCG delegated aspects of CHC to a local authority which, in turn, further delegated these to an NHS Trust. The ombudsman pointed out that the ultimate responsibility remained with the CCG.[4]

Clinical commissioning groups: final decisions about CHC and pitfalls

CCGs are ultimately responsible for making decisions about CHC eligibility, but they do not have unfettered discretion to make arbitrary decisions. In other words, they must follow the rules set out in regulations and take account of statutory guidance.

For example, CCGs should not be interfering unduly with the recommendations of professionals involved in the multi-disciplinary team responsible for using and completing the Decision Support Tool (DST). Such interference should be exceptional and be supported by clear reasons:

- **Interference with multi-disciplinary team in exceptional circumstances only**. The guidance states that only 'in exceptional circumstances, and for clearly articulated reasons, should the multi-disciplinary team's recommendation not be followed'.[5] Exceptional circumstances include that the DST has not been fully completed,

---

1 See e.g. LGSCO, *Liverpool City Council*, 2017 (15 015 830), para 56.
2 National Framework 2018, para 10.
3 Heather, B. 'CSU blunder leads to hundreds of missed Continuing Healthcare alerts.' *Health Service Journal*, 20 September 2017.
4 LGSCO, *Northumberland Council*, 2018 (17 001 722), para 30.
5 National Framework 2018, para 153.

significant gaps in evidence, an obvious mismatch between evidence and recommendation, and that the recommendation would result in a CCG or local authority acting unlawfully (i.e. beyond their legally prescribed powers). Even then, there should be a referral back to the multi-disciplinary team (MDT), rather than the CCG simply proceeding to substitute its own judgement about need instead.[1]

The CCG itself (panel or otherwise) should therefore not be rescoring the DST, something which in practice is widely reported. More extreme in some areas, it appears that CCG panels sometimes supplant the role of the MDT altogether by scoring the DST from the outset.

Both practices would be legally challengeable not only because of what the National Framework guidance states, but also because the regulations themselves state that it is for the MDT to complete the DST,[2] not anybody else. Indeed, guidance states that CCGs should not be making decisions in the absence of recommendations from the MDT, other than in exceptional circumstances of urgency.[3]

The ombudsman has found fault, for example, when an MDT fails to complete the documentation and make a recommendation about CHC eligibility – and a local panel then makes the decision for itself, with missing evidence and no recorded rationale.[4] The following children's continuing care case involved similar issues.

Panel overriding professional recommendations with poorly recorded reasons. Following a meeting with a child's parents, the professionals discussed the disputed care domains. However, the panel's decision-making was documented in considerably less detail than the preceding discussion involving the parents. Furthermore, the panel noted the professional evidence that the unpredictability of the seizures could be an issue but agreed a score of 'moderate' only. Likewise, it identified an outstanding professional concern about whether or not the child was at risk of aspiration – but again agreed a 'moderate' score only. The ombudsman found a lack of clarity in the recording of both the decisions and their rationale.[5]

---

1   National Framework Practice Guidance 2018, paras 39.1–39.2.
2   NHS Responsibilities Regulations 2012, r.21(5).
3   National Framework 2018, paras 154–155.
4   PSOW, *Carmarthenshire Local Health Board*, 2010 (200801759), paras 70–76.
5   LGSCO, *Central Bedfordshire Council, Essex Partnership University NHS Foundation Trust, Bedfordshire Clinical Commissioning Group*, 2019 (16 002 323), para 72.

In other words, the role of the CCG is to check that the essentials of the decision-making process have been followed, not to supplant the professional judgements of the multi-disciplinary team:

> the CCG should not refer a case back, or decide not to accept a recommendation, simply because the multidisciplinary team has made a recommendation that differs from the one that those who are involved in making the final decision would have made, based on the same evidence.

In addition, the guidance states:

- **CCGs should not play a financial gatekeeping role**. In verifying MDT recommendations, the CCG could use an individual or a panel, although non-acceptance should never involve just one person acting unilaterally. The verification process should not 'be used as a gate-keeping function or for financial control... The final eligibility decision should be independent of budgetary constraints, and finance officers should not be part of a decision-making process.'[1]
- **CCGs should consider legal and ombudsman case law**. Guidance makes clear that legally CCGs should be aware of legal and ombudsman cases that 'have indicated circumstances in which eligibility for NHS Continuing Healthcare should have been determined, and where such an outcome would be expected if the same facts were considered in an assessment'.[2] The guidance refers to, as examples, the *Coughlan*[3] case and the cases contained in a 2003 Health Service Ombudsman report.[4] (Of course, other cases are relevant as well – e.g. the *Pointon* case.)

However, some of the above points contained in guidance were significantly undermined (arguably contentiously) by a court in late 2019. It stated that, whilst the regulations stipulate that the MDT must complete the DST, there is nothing to stop the CCG appointing an assessor to review the MDT's findings before they go for consideration by a panel – as long as the assessor is not directly varying the MDT's conclusions, and is simply part of a process of ensuring compliance and adherence to proper standards.

Furthermore, the court held that rejection by a CCG of MDT recommendations is not confined to exceptional circumstances only; and that, if further work on the DST is required, the CCG can remit the work

---

1 National Framework 2018, para 156.
2 National Framework 2018, para 157.
3 *R(Coughlan) v North and East Devon Health Authority* [2001] Q.B. 213.
4 Health Service Ombudsman. *NHS funding for long term care*. HC 399. London: The Stationery Office, 2003.

to an alternative MDT, not necessarily to the original one. It was held also that the effect of the regulations (overriding the guidance) is that the CCG is anyway not obliged to refer back (to an MDT) a DST with which it disagrees; it can simply proceed to take the final decision itself. As long as that decision is informed (but not dictated) by the DST.[1]

Clinical commissioning groups: eligibility not dependent on certain factors

The guidance states clearly that the reasons given for a decision on eligibility should not be based on the following:

- an individual's diagnosis
- the setting of care
- the ability of the care provider to manage care
- the use (or not) of NHS-employed staff to provide care
- the need for/presence of 'specialist staff' in care delivery
- the fact that a need is well managed
- the existence of other NHS-funded care, or
- any other input-related (rather than needs-related) rationale.[2]

In the following case, the ombudsman strongly criticised an NHS eligibility decision, the basis of which offended against at least two of the above points.

> **Faulty denial of eligibility on the basis of well-managed need and minimal input of NHS staff.** A 73-year-old care home resident had a history of Parkinson's disease and had experienced two strokes. The more recent of these had left her with right-sided weakness and dysphasia. She was an insulin-dependent diabetic, was partially sighted and had high blood pressure and abnormalities in thyroid function. Despite being assessed as having complex, unpredictable, unstable and risk-related needs, she was deemed to be ineligible for CHC. Her appeal to an independent review panel also failed.
>
> The denial of eligibility was based on the fact that the nursing home could generally manage her needs and that NHS staff were therefore not generally

---

1 *R(Gossip) v NHS Surrey Downs Clinical Commissioning Group* [2019] EWHC 3411 (Admin), paras 51, 71, 77, 93, 94.
2 National Framework 2018, para 65.

needed. The ombudsman found that the decision was not consistent with the primary need approach and with the *Coughlan* and *Grogan* cases. He stated that the NHS must take the decision again. Criticism was levelled at the health board, the multi-disciplinary team and the independent review panel.[1]

Clinical commissioning groups: legal accountability and giving reasons
It has been suggested that because the regulations themselves do not state that a CCG must accept MDT recommendations in all but exceptional circumstances (see above), the effect of the guidance is limited, not least because, in contrast, the regulations do state that a CCG, other than exceptionally, must accept the recommendation of an NHS England review panel.[2] A suggestion supported by the courts.[3]

However, CCGs (or their panels) which routinely reject MDT recommendations not only risk breach of the statutory guidance but also risk acting unlawfully if they do not supply relevant evidence and reasoning.

This was highlighted by the Court of Appeal in a case involving a joint health and social services continuing care panel. It had overruled, without plausible reasons or alternative evidence, the assessment and recommendations of the key practitioner involved with the person in need of care. This case reads almost like a roll call of the pitfalls into which CCG panels are at risk of falling.

Continuing care panel: ignoring expert evidence, relying on practitioners who had never seen the woman, financial gatekeeping, belittling of relatives, lack of recording of decision and reasons, closed minds. A local authority, via a continuing care panel, decided that a 95-year-old woman could not continue to live in the care home in which she had lived for many years. Instead she would have to move to a nursing home. Her daughter vigorously opposed the decision. The Court of Appeal ruled that the decision was manifestly flawed. A catalogue of serious criticism of the local authority underlay this judgment.

Reliance was placed by the local authority on the recommendations of the local continuing care panel, without ensuring that it had taken account of all relevant factors (which it had not). This meant the local authority was not reaching a lawful community care decision. The local authority had reached

---
1   PSOW, *Cardiff Health Board,* 2008 (200700482), paras 54–60.
2   Locke, D. *NHS law and practice.* London: Legal Action Group, 2018, para 16.115.
3   *R(Gossip) v NHS Surrey Downs Clinical Commissioning Group* [2019] EWHC 3411 (Admin), para 72.

> a decision without taking account of the most impressive and comprehensive assessment of the woman's needs, carried out by one of its own social work team managers who knew the woman best. Instead the authority had relied on the panel's recommendations, which in turn rested on the reports of health professionals who assessed the woman in hospital.
>
> Furthermore, a doctor who had endorsed these reports had not seen the woman. To make matters worse, one of the managers involved had misrepresented the dispute, portraying the woman's daughter as a lone voice without any professional support when in fact the team manager's assessment concurred with that of the daughter. The court concluded that the decision taken by the local authority was predetermined; those responsible had approached it with 'entirely' closed minds. The panel had portrayed itself as dealing with purely clinical issues yet had discussed the financial implications of a placement; this was therefore a legally irrelevant consideration for the panel. In addition, the panel had failed to keep a written record of its meetings; this was unacceptable and extraordinary. In turn, this meant that the decision was not reasoned, balanced or transparent.
>
> The court also found that article 8 of the European Convention on Human Rights had been breached. This was because the court could not accept that the decision-making process safeguarded the woman's physical and psychological integrity. Interference by the local authority had to be proportionate in terms of weighing up the doctor's and panel's recommendations in the wider context of the woman's needs and rights. The local authority had not done this. And it was not an academic matter since it was not in dispute that a change to a strange environment for such a frail person 'could have serious if not fatal consequences'.[1]

Unsurprisingly, therefore, the guidance states that the CCG:

> should give clear reasons for its decision on whether or not an individual has a primary health need. The CCG should set out the basis on which the decision of eligibility was made. The CCG should also explain the arrangements, and timescales, for dealing with a request to review an eligibility decision where the individual or their representative disagrees with it.[2]

The following case illustrates how the NHS appeared to breach the above rules in several ways, and therefore how it could and should have been challenged

---

1 *R(Goldsmith) v Wandsworth London Borough Council* [2004] EWCA Civ 1170, Court of Appeal, paras 68, 84, 87.
2 National Framework 2018, para 193.

– and probably would have been had time and circumstances allowed. (An appeal, or judicial review legal case, would have taken too long; and Court of Protection proceedings had intruded first.) The case is instructive, not least because of the unfortunate legal and practical complications that followed for the elderly couple concerned.

> **Woman with serious multiple health needs denied eligibility for CHC.** An elderly woman had multiple health problems, including vascular dementia, cerebrovascular disease, chronic pulmonary obstructive disease, ischaemic heart disease, hyperthyroidism and severe osteoarthritis in the neck, spine, legs and arms. She was often in pain. Her mobility was very limited and she was doubly incontinent. She had suffered a dense stroke, affecting her left side. She was awarded CHC at home.
>
> However, she then had a second stroke, after which CHC was withdrawn. The local authority took over the package of care but reduced it and failed to support her husband adequately with respite care; this partly contributed to her husband struggling to look after her, and to the local authority eventually trying to obtain (unsuccessfully) a Court of Protection order to remove his wife to a nursing home.[1]

The multi-disciplinary assessment in this case had identified a high level of needs in four domains (behaviour, cognition, mobility, drug therapies and medication: symptom control); moderate needs in six domains (psychological and emotional needs; communication; mobility; nutrition: food and drink; continence; skin, including tissue viability); and a low level of needs in two domains (breathing, altered states of consciousness).

The panel then proceeded to breach a number of rules in at least three ways: by rescoring the DST itself, by ignoring the views of a clinical specialist and by using consideration of funded nursing care as a reason for denying CHC eligibility. This led to the counter-intuitive decision to remove CHC eligibility from the woman even after she had suffered a second stroke.

> **Panel rescoring the DST, ignoring clinical specialist and using funded nursing care consideration wrongly.** *First*, the panel challenged the multi-disciplinary recommendations and lowered some of the scoring. (This is something which

---

1   *A London Local Authority v JH* [2011] EWHC 2420 (COP).

under the rules it is not meant to do; at most it should ask the multi-disciplinary team to reconsider.)

Second, the panel went on to consider the nature, intensity, complexity and unpredictability of the woman's needs and whether she had a primary health need. It considered she did not. (Yet her range of needs would suggest eligibility on the basis of the legal test set out in the key case of *Coughlan* and other relevant legal or ombudsman cases.)

The panel also disregarded the views of a specialist hospital doctor and two other professionals who described her needs as 'highly complex medical needs'. (According to the rules, mechanistic scoring of the DST is not meant to supplant the role of professional judgement.)

Third, the panel considered whether she had health care needs over and above what could be met by registered nursing care in the form of funding nursing care (FNC), were she in a nursing home. It concluded she did not. (This decision too would be in breach of the rules, because a CHC decision must be made before consideration of FNC; since even if a person's needs can be met through the registered nursing care in a nursing home, they could still be eligible for CHC, as was Pamela Coughlan in the key legal case already referred to.[1])

Cognition, see *Decision Support Tool*

Commissioning support units

Some NHS clinical commissioning groups (CCGs) appoint a commissioning support unit (CSU) to provide advice and back-office support, and to handle, amongst other things, procurement and commissioning of services. CSUs are independent companies and may be awarded multi-million-pound contracts by CCGs. In some areas, NHS Continuing Healthcare (CHC) is handled by CSUs, including assessment and eligibility decisions.

Like CCGs themselves, CSUs may be at risk of undermining rules about CHC in their determination to manage budgets and minimise expenditure.[2] Ultimately it will be the CCG held to be at fault by the ombudsman if the CSU gets things wrong.[3]

---

1   *A London Local Authority v JH* [2011] EWHC 2420 (COP).
2   Taylor, J. and Rigby, N. '"Medical opinions ignored" by NHS payment assessor, workers say.' *BBC News* (BBC East), 10 September 2017. Accessed on 17 July 2019 at: www.bbc.co.uk/news/uk-england-41187615. And: Heather, B. 'CSU blunder leads to hundreds of missed Continuing Healthcare alerts.' *Health Service Journal*, 20 September 2017.
3   e.g. LGSCO, *Leicester City Council*, 2017 (16 000 552), paras 11, 59–68.

Communication, see *Decision Support Tool*

Competence, see *Expertise of assessors, and knowledge of the patient*

Complexity

According to the National Framework guidance, complexity is one of the four characteristics of a person's needs that, alone or in combination, may demonstrate the existence of a primary health need, requiring NHS Continuing Healthcare (CHC) services. Complexity will relate to the quality or quantity of the care needed.[1]

Quality and quantity take on additional legal significance, besides being referred to in the guidance, since they are based on legal case law.[2] They represent the test in legislation about primary health need – the incidental/ancillary or nature test. See ***Incidental or ancillary or of a nature beyond social services***.

The decision about complexity will follow on from completion of the Decision Support Tool (DST). Thus, complexity represents 25 per cent of the possibilities referred to in the guidance and, according to the guidance, could alone – even without the presence of the other three characteristics (nature, intensity, unpredictability) – indicate eligibility for CHC. For patients, families and practitioners, therefore, reference to complexity – and the definition of it set out in guidance – can assume considerable importance.

Complexity can obviously apply, for example, in the case of many older people with multiple health conditions (sometimes referred to as co-morbidities or multiple pathology) which interact with each. In other words, the whole of the need becomes more than the sum of its parts. The term does not feature in legislation but is prominent in two pieces of statutory guidance, the DST and the National Framework.

If a primary health need is strongly indicated when the DST is completed, guidance states that detailed reference to the complexity of the needs will be less necessary. On the other hand, if there is less certainty from completion of the DST as to the existence of a primary health need, then 'careful consideration must be given to the four key characteristics of

---

1 National Framework 2018, para 60.
2 *R(Coughlan) v North and East Devon Health Authority* [2001] Q.B. 213, para 30.

nature, intensity, complexity or unpredictability of the individual's needs'.[1] The guidance states:

- **Complexity: interaction of needs and health conditions.**

    [Complexity] is concerned with how the needs present and interact to increase the skill required to monitor the symptoms, treat the condition(s) and/or manage the care. This may arise with a single condition, or it could include the presence of multiple conditions or the interaction between two or more conditions. It may also include situations where an individual's response to their own condition has an impact on their overall needs, such as where a physical health need results in the individual developing a mental health need.[2]

Consent

Guidance emphasises the importance of obtaining a person's consent for an assessment of eligibility for NHS Continuing Healthcare (CHC), or of recording a lack of capacity and a best interests decision (consistent with the Mental Capacity Act 2005) about whether to undertake the assessment. When relying on consent, it must be explicit, specific, informed and freely given.[3]

The guidance notes that although people with the requisite mental capacity are of course free to refuse CHC assessment and CHC itself, nonetheless this might have adverse consequences:

- **Lack of consent to CHC assessment.**

    If an individual with capacity does not consent to being assessed for NHS Continuing Healthcare or to sharing information which is essential for carrying out this assessment, the potential consequences of this should be carefully explained. This might affect the ability of the NHS and the local authority to provide appropriate services to them. The fact that an individual declines to be assessed for CHC does not, in itself, mean that a local authority has an additional responsibility to meet their needs, over

---

1 Decision Support Tool 2018, para 38.
2 National Framework 2018, para 59.
3 National Framework 2018, paras 72–73.

and above the responsibility it would have had if they had been assessed for NHS Continuing Healthcare.[1]

Consultation in decision-making

Decisions about NHS Continuing Healthcare (CHC) are primarily for an NHS clinical commissioning group (CCG) to take under the National Health Service Act 2006 and the relevant NHS regulations. However, local authorities play an important role since, amongst other things, the legal limits of what they are permitted to do must be established under the Care Act 2014; they have a duty to make referrals to the NHS; and they may anyway already have information about the person being assessed for CHC. See ***Care Act 2014***.

Consequently, there are rules relating to consultation and cooperation placed on both local authorities and CCGs. On the one hand, social services have duties towards the CCG:

- **Consultation: social services duty to provide advice and assistance to CCG, and to participate in multi-disciplinary assessment**. Social services must as far as is reasonably practicable provide advice and assistance to a CCG which consults in relation to a decision about a person's eligibility for CHC (including whether a person ceases to be eligible). In addition, if requested by the CCG, social services must cooperate by arranging for staff to participate in a multi-disciplinary team for the purpose of completing the Decision Support Tool.[2]

    The regulations also make clear that neither of these two duties affect the local authority's duty to assess a person under section 9 of the Care Act.[3] (This means that before CHC status has been established the section 9 duty will be in play, not just to ascertain the person's needs but also to establish the legal limits of what the local authority is permitted to do in order to meet those needs.) The regulations state also that if that assessment has already been completed, then the local authority must use the consequent information when providing advice and assistance to the CCG.[4] However, the local authority's duty to provide advice and assistance does not in itself trigger a duty to assess under section 9 of the Care Act 2014.[5]

---

1 National Framework 2018, para 73.
2 Care and Support (Provision of Health Services) Regulations 2014, r.3.
3 Care and Support (Provision of Health Services) Regulations 2014, r.3.
4 Care and Support (Provision of Health Services) Regulations 2014, r.3.
5 National Framework 2018, para 128.

Equally, the CCG in turn has duties towards social services:

- **Consultation: CCG duty to consult social services before a CHC decision about eligibility is made and before eligibility is withdrawn**. A CCG, as far as is reasonably practicable, must consult with social services before making a decision about a person's eligibility for CHC (including whether a person is no longer eligible for it). It must also cooperate with social services in arranging for staff to participate in a multi-disciplinary team for the purpose of a Decision Support Tool Assessment.[1]

More generally, there are also duties placed on local authorities and the NHS to cooperate about a range of matters within the Care Act 2014. See *Cooperation*.

The duty placed on the CCG to consult social services applies only so far as it is reasonably practicable. Thus, the courts have held that if social services is invited by the CCG to send representatives to panel meetings, but is unable to do so, the CCG nonetheless will have discharged its 'limited' duty to consult. And, the CCG, as the ultimate and sole decision-maker, can then proceed to a decision.[2]

Continence, see *Decision Support Tool*

Continuity of care

Social services have duties to provide advice and assistance to NHS clinical commissioning groups (CCGs), and to cooperate in terms of multi-disciplinary assessment for NHS Continuing Healthcare (CHC) eligibility. See *Cooperation*.

When complying with these duties social services must have due regard to the need to promote and secure the continuity of appropriate services for people in the following circumstances.

First, if their needs are currently being met under the Care Act 2014 or under section 117 of the Mental Health Act 1983 – on the day they are assessed to be eligible for CHC. *Second*, if they have been in receipt of

---

1 NHS Responsibilities Regulations 2012, r.22.
2 *R(Gossip) v NHS Surrey Downs Clinical Commissioning Group* [2019] EWHC 3411 (Admin), para 72.

CHC but are now assessed to be no longer eligible for it. *Third*, if they are otherwise assessed to be ineligible for CHC.[1]

This continuity duty in law seems to be aimed in practice at what guidance says should be avoided: unilateral withdrawal of care and funding. See **Withdrawal of care**.

The importance of continuity of care may arise in a number of guises. For instance, clear communication with a care home about when NHS funding is ceasing and when either the local authority or a resident, self-funding, will begin to pay.[2] And, in the following case, the CCG failed to consider the continuity issue when a person became eligible for CHC.

> **Assistance with finances for a person eligible for CHC.** A man in his 60s had a diagnosis of Huntington's disease. His cognitive impairment and behavioural problems stemming from this condition were so severe that he was unable to participate in assessments. He was also unable to express his needs verbally. He became eligible for CHC and moved to a new placement. He no longer had assistance, previously received from social services, with managing his finances.
>
> All this meant there was a gap in the provision of social security benefits. The consequence was lack of income, inability to buy toiletries or clothes and other necessities, wearing clothes belonging to deceased residents, inability to participate in activities to benefit fully from his care package, and suffering difficulty and distress.
>
> The ombudsman investigated; the CCG agreed to discuss with the Council any gap in service provision between what the social care needs assessment had identified was required and what would be provided by the CCG. The ombudsman stated that the two organisations should decide how any gaps in service provision would be covered and escalate the matter accordingly if they could not agree. The essential fault was that the CCG had failed to assess properly the man's needs. At a minimum, the Council should have been involved with the CCG's assessment.[3]

In another case, the importance of a CCG at least taking account of a previous assessment of need by a local authority was highlighted.

---

1 Care and Support (Provision of Health Services) Regulations 2014, r.3.
2 LGSCO, *Hertfordshire County Council*, 2017 (15 004 803).
3 LGSCO, *Sefton Metropolitan Borough Council*, 2018 (16 002 442).

> **CCG failing to consider information from local authority.** When a CCG took over responsibility from the local authority for a person when she became an adult, it stated that the assessment would be complex and time consuming. During this period, it reduced her care, before reinstating it when the assessment process was complete. The ombudsman found fault because the CCG had been aware of the local authority assessment of need and should have used that assessment as an indication of the person's health and social care needs, thus keeping in place the previous level of care, pending completion of its own assessment.[1]

When local authorities accept back into social care a person previously eligible for CHC, a pattern sometimes emerges of a rapid reduction in the amount or quality of care being provided for the person without proper consideration of a person's health and well-being. This can lead to needs not being met and to detriment to the person, the responsibility for which would lie at the door of the local authority,[2] especially if it had failed to challenge the withdrawal of CHC when the review took place and eligibility was withdrawn.

Cooperation

In practice, cooperation between health and social services is clearly desirable, given that people's health and social care needs are often interrelated. Specifically, in the context of NHS Continuing Healthcare (CHC), and if requested by an NHS clinical commissioning group (CCG), a local authority must cooperate by arranging for staff to participate in a multi-disciplinary team for the purpose of completing the Decision Support Tool.[3]

More widely, local social services authorities and NHS bodies, including CCGs, are required to cooperate with one another, both generally and in individual cases. This is under sections 6 and 7 of the Care Act 2014, where they are defined as statutory partners for the purpose of cooperation. And, under section 7, there is a duty on one partner to comply with a request from another. However, the duty to comply is not absolute; refusal must be in writing and on the grounds that the requested party considers that

---

1 LGSCO, *Staffordshire County Council (East Staffordshire Clinical Commissioning Group)*, 2019 (17 017 844), paras 67–68.
2 e.g. *A London Local Authority v JH* [2011] EWHC 2420 (COP). And: LGO, *Worcestershire County Council*, 2014 (12 004 137). And: LGSCO, *Knowsley Metropolitan Borough Council*, 2018 (17 005 594).
3 Care and Support (Provision of Health Services) Regulations 2014, r.3.

compliance with the request would be incompatible with its legal functions or have an adverse effect on them.

What this means, in the case of CHC for example, is that whilst social services could ask the NHS to meet a person's needs, or vice versa, neither could impose upon the other absolutely. So, for example, if the provision requested is beyond the legal remit of social services, it would be prohibited from making it. Or, if the local authority believed that the NHS should provide more services to meet a person's eligible needs, it could request this but could not impose upon the CCG how the latter should meet the person's needs.[1]

Coordinator

Guidance states that once an individual has been referred for a full assessment of eligibility for NHS Continuing Healthcare (involving the Decision Support Tool (DST)), the NHS clinical commissioning group is responsible for coordinating the process and should therefore appoint a coordinator.[2] Although a member of the multi-disciplinary team responsible for completing the DST could also fulfil the role of coordinator, the two functions then undertaken should be kept distinct.[3]

Cost-effectiveness

Patients and families sometimes feel strongly that provision of care should be delivered in a certain way or in a certain setting – for example, in their own home or in one care home rather than another. The obstacle may be that their preference involves greater expenditure than another, cheaper option, and this situation can give rise to conflict.

Guidance states that NHS Continuing Healthcare (CHC) can be delivered in a cost-effective way. Essentially, therefore, an NHS clinical commissioning group (CCG) can meet a person's needs by way of offering the cheapest option, *so long as that cheapest option is judged as capable of meeting the person's assessed needs*. This might not be in accordance with a person's wishes.

Human rights considerations may come into play, although they will not necessarily be decisive in excluding a cheaper or cheapest option. The

---

1 *R(T) v London Borough of Haringey* [2005] EWHC 2235 (Admin), para 101.
2 National Framework 2018, para 107.
3 National Framework Practice Guidance 2018, para 25.2.

discharge of duties in health and social care by offering a cost-effective (not necessarily the optimum) option is well established in both health and social care legal case law.[1] However, patients, families and practitioners should bear in mind that this does not mean that CCGs can simply take account of financial resources alone.

Cost-effectiveness: factors to weigh up
Guidance states that in meeting CHC needs, CCGs can take comparative costs into account but must consider a range of factors.

First, they should compare options in terms of real, not assumed, costs.

Second, if a person wishes to be supported at home, they should look at actual costs, at different ways of meeting needs (including, for example, assistive technology) and also what support family members can offer, without making assumptions about their ability to do so.

Third, related to the second, they must balance costs with the individual's wish to live in a family environment.[2]

Fourth, 'changes of provider or of care package should not take place purely because the responsible commissioner has changed from a CCG to a local authority (or vice versa)'.[3]

An example of what the guidance may have in mind on this last point is illustrated by the following local ombudsman case in which the outcome was disastrous for the service user.

> **Change of commissioner, cheaper placement, health needs not met, safeguarding.** A man had vascular dementia, diabetes, epilepsy and a history of stroke and cardiovascular accidents. He had limited mobility, needing help from two carers to mobilise, was doubly incontinent and needed support with all medication, food and fluid intake. His dementia limited his ability to communicate and he displayed challenging behaviour at times, including shouting and banging on the table. He became agitated in noisy environments.
>
> The NHS placed him in a care home which met his needs well, at £800 per week. But the NHS subsequently withdrew funding, handing over his care to the local authority which had an upper cost limit of £495 per week. It assessed that moving him would be detrimental but moved him all the same, relying on

---
1 *R(Davey) v Oxfordshire County Council* [2017] EWCA Civ 1308; *N v ACCG* [2017] UKSC 22.
2 National Framework 2018, para 177.
3 National Framework 2018, para 178.

> the new care home's assertion that it could meet his needs and not properly checking its suitability.
>
> His health declined, with apparent failings in care including difficulty in managing his behaviour, a pressure sore, inadequate documentation, being left in discomfort, being inappropriately clothed, and dehydration. In addition, the local authority failed to regard the son's comments as a complaint, failed to monitor the care provider's response to concerns raised, delayed in holding a strategy meeting, closed the safeguarding investigation without adequate explanation – and failed to review continuation of placements at the home.
>
> Furthermore, the decision to close the safeguarding investigation was not based on any report by the local authority, was not recorded and was contrary to its own policy. This was all fault.[1]

This was a case in which the local authority had refused to pay a higher rate for the required accommodation. However, the guidance warns CCGs as well that a higher rate may need to be paid if a person's needs require it. For example, a person with behavioural issues may require a larger room in a care home to help manage that behaviour, in which case the CCG should pay the extra cost.

Similarly, a person might need to remain in more expensive accommodation because of frailty, mental health or other needs.[2] Or, the more expensive accommodation may be needed because it is near family members who play an active role in the person's life – or because the person has lived there for many years and it would be significantly detrimental to the individual to move elsewhere.[3]

Balancing a person's needs and circumstances with limited resources was considered in the following legal case, in which the court held that whilst cost can be taken into account, a decision to meet a person's CHC needs in a care home – against her express wish to live in a family environment – would have to be clearly justified with reference to human rights.

> **Meeting CHC needs cost effectively in the light of human rights.** A severely disabled woman wished to continue living with her parents, whereas the primary care trust's preference was for her to move into a care home. Whilst not reaching

---

1 LGO, *Worcestershire County Council*, 2014 (12 004 137).
2 National Framework 2018, para 284.
3 National Framework 2018, para 285.

> a final decision on the course of action to be taken, the court found that article 8 of the European Convention of Human Rights had considerable weight in the decision to be made, that to remove her from her family home was an obvious interference with family life and so must be justified as proportionate. Cost could be taken into account, but the improvement in the young woman's condition, the quality of life in her family environment and her express view that she did not want to move were all important factors which suggested that removing her from her home would require clear justification.[1]

In a more recent case, nonetheless, the Supreme Court was clear that the ability to offer a more cost-effective option is not altered by the fact of a person's lack of capacity and the requirement to make a 'best' interests decision under the Mental Capacity Act 2005. This was because best interests decisions under that Act can only consider the 'available' options on offer under other legislation – which is, in the case of CHC, the National Health Service Act 2006.

Furthermore, the court went on to state that whilst human rights may come into play, cost-effectiveness decisions may nonetheless be justified in relation to the economic well-being of the country.

> **Best interests, human rights, cost-effectiveness and CHC.** A young man had severe physical and learning disabilities and lived in a care home with CHC funding. His parents wanted him to be able to visit them at home. This would require considerable, and skilled, carer input which the care home was unwilling to provide and which the CCG was not prepared to fund. In addition, the mother wanted to be able to assist, in the care home, the care home staff with his intimate care.
>
> On human rights issues, the court noted that:
>
> > decisions on health or social care services may also engage the right to respect for private (or family) life under article 8 of the European Convention on Human Rights, but decisions about the allocation of limited resources may well be justified as necessary in the interests of the economic well-being of the country.

---

1 *Gunter v South Western Staffordshire Primary Care Trust* [2005] EWHC 1894 (Admin). As summarised in: National Framework Practice Guidance 2018, para 46.1.

> As to best interests decisions under the Mental Capacity Act – since the man lacked capacity in relation to the decisions in question – the court stated that best interests could only relate to the 'available options' – in this case, the options being made available by both the care home and the CCG. Thus, the court, under the Mental Capacity Act, did not have power to order the CCG to fund what the parents wanted. Nor did it have power to order the actual care providers to do that which they were unwilling or unable to do.[1]

Coughlan case

The *Coughlan* legal case remains the most significant legal case relating to NHS Continuing Healthcare (CHC).[2] It is referred to throughout this book. Sometimes NHS clinical commissioning groups (CCGs) state wrongly that it is no longer relevant and decline to consider it when taking decisions – wrongly for a number of reasons.

First, the case represents high legal authority since it was decided by the Court of Appeal. *Second*, it has never been overruled or even doubted in any later legal case law. *Third*, a number of rules about CHC, enshrined in both section 22 of the Care Act 2014 and in the NHS Commissioning Board and Clinical Commissioning Groups (Responsibilities and Standing Rules) Regulations 2012, reflect directly the *Coughlan* case. *Fourth*, the Department of Health and Social Care has stated clearly in the National Framework guidance that the *Coughlan* case remains central to NHS Continuing Healthcare decision-making.[3] *Fifth*, the guidance states that when taking decisions about CHC, CCGs should consider indicative cases and the guidance mentions specifically the *Coughlan* case.[4] *Sixth*, the *Grogan* legal case is legal authority for the rule that a person in a nursing home with needs equivalent to Pamela Coughlan should be eligible for CHC.[5]

Nevertheless, despite these seemingly arguable and obvious points, the court in the 2019 *Gossip* case found that a CCG was not required to make reference to the *Coughlan* case when reaching a decision, even though the person concerned had ostensibly very similar needs to those of Pamela Coughlan.[6]

---

1 *N v ACCG* [2017] UKSC 22, paras 37, 44.
2 *R(Coughlan) v North and East Devon Health Authority* [2001] Q.B. 213.
3 e.g. National Framework Practice Guidance 2018, para 2.2.
4 National Framework 2018, para 157.
5 *R(Grogan) v Bexley NHS Care Trust* [2006] EWHC 44 (Admin), para 51.
6 *R(Gossip) v NHS Surrey Downs Clinical Commissioning Group* [2019] EWHC 3411 (Admin), para 97.

The National Framework guidance is arguably just reminding CCGs of the effect of the case as a matter of law; but the Framework is, in its own right, statutory guidance which should be followed in the absence of good reason. The key test which the *Coughlan* case outlined, and which is now reflected in legislation, is as follows.

> **Nature, incidental or ancillary, quality of care, quantity of care.**
>
> The distinction between those services which can and cannot be so provided is one of degree which in a borderline case will depend on a careful appraisal of the facts of the individual case. However, as a very general indication as to where the line is to be drawn, it can be said that if the nursing services are (i) merely incidental or ancillary to the provision of the accommodation which a local authority is under a duty to provide to the category of persons to whom section 21 refers and (ii) of a nature which it can be expected that an authority whose primary responsibility is to provide social services can be expected to provide, then they can be provided under section 21. It will be appreciated that the first part of the test is focusing on the overall quantity of the services and the second part on the quality of the services provided.[1]

---

1   *R(Coughlan) v North and East Devon Health Authority* [2001] Q.B. 213, para 30.

D

Decision-making process

The two main ways for people and their families to challenge decisions about NHS Continuing Healthcare (CHC), beyond local review or complaints processes, are judicial review legal cases and Health Service Ombudsman (and sometimes Local Government and Social Care Ombudsman) investigations.

The courts and ombudsmen look mainly at the decision-making process, not the final decision. That is, they do not generally want to step into the professional shoes of those making decisions and so will not directly question the 'merits' of decisions. Instead, they will look essentially to see that rules in the legislation were followed procedurally, with reasons given (and that professionally and clinically, there is plausible-looking evidence and reasoning underpinning the decision).

In addition, the courts will consider whether, legally, all relevant factors were considered and irrelevant factors excluded; whether the decision was rational (in the sense that it was not so outlandish as to be irrational); and whether there has been an unlawful fettering of discretion (by applying a rigid local policy in blanket fashion). See *Judicial review*.

If there is a problem with the decision-making process, the courts and ombudsmen will usually ask the NHS clinical commissioning group (or local authority) to retake the decision, this time properly. Usually, they will not themselves take the decision as to what a person's needs are and what they are eligible for.

Nonetheless, the Health Service Ombudsman (unlike the Local Government and Social Care Ombudsman) does have an express legal remit to look at the clinical judgement of health practitioners and has in the past sometimes done so and reached a decision directly about the level of a person's health needs and their associated CHC status. See **Health Service Ombudsman**.

Therefore, in challenges against the NHS made by patients and families – or even by local authorities (in a judicial review case) – it is generally the decision-making process that needs to be examined, rather than a head-on criticism of the final decision.

> **Legal fault in the process of CHC decision-making: *Grogan* case.** In the *Grogan* case, the judge found significant faults in the decision-making process but declined to take a view about the actual eligibility of the woman concerned. He ordered the NHS to take the decision again, by looking closely at her nursing needs and setting them against the right legal test. The faults were essentially that a physician had made a decision without referring to that legal test, and that more generally the NHS Trust's local criteria did not make clear reference to the primary health need legal test, meaning the NHS was at risk of being left adrift in a sea of confusing local factors which obscured the overall legal requirements.[1]

Likewise, the ombudsman has found fault when reference to primary health need is made but recording and rationale for the decision are absent.[2]

Decision Support Tool

The Decision Support Tool (DST) is a piece of statutory guidance published by the Department of Health and Social Care. Other than in end of life cases, it is through the DST that information about a person's assessed needs must be channelled in relation to NHS Continuing Healthcare (CHC). It is therefore crucial that patients, families (and practitioners) try to ensure that it is completed appropriately and accurately.

In other words, it is an administrative gateway to eligibility for CHC. It is meant to be used to bring together information relating to a person's assessed needs. Its obligatory use is intended to 'facilitate consistent evidence-based recommendations and decision-making regarding eligibility for NHS Continuing Healthcare'.

However, there are a few key points to make in summary because in practice it is easily misused and misunderstood. A number of the common pitfalls have already been listed (see Chapter 2).

- **Bringing together of assessment information**. The DST is 'not an assessment of needs in itself', merely pulling together assessment information.[3]

- **Outcome of DST scoring is not decisive: DST not to be used prescriptively**. The outcome of the 'scoring' on the DST is meant to

---
1   *R(Grogan) v Bexley NHS Care Trust* [2006] EWHC 44 (Admin), paras 91, 94, 95–105.
2   PSOW, *Carmarthenshire Local Health Board*, 2010 (200802583), para 75.
3   Decision Support Tool 2018, para 1.

be indicative, not decisive, a guideline only to CHC eligibility, not least because any such scored outcomes must be consistent with both legislation and with legal and ombudsman case law. The DST must not be used prescriptively.[1]

- **Multi-disciplinary team**. The DST must be completed by a multi-disciplinary team.

- **DST not discretionary**. Completion of the DST is not discretionary. It must be used, since regulations stipulate this. Once it is completed, the NHS clinical commissioning group (CCG) must decide whether a person has a primary health need; if so, the person is then eligible for CHC.[2]

Decision Support Tool: domains of need and scoring system

The DST consists of 12 care domains. Each domain breaks down into a number of scoring levels, with a description provided against each level. The scoring levels are named as: priority, severe, high, moderate or low, although not all domains necessarily contain the possibility of a priority or severe score. The domains are:

1. Breathing
2. Nutrition
3. Continence
4. Skin integrity
5. Mobility
6. Communication
7. Psychological and emotional needs
8. Cognition
9. Behaviour
10. Drug therapies and medication
11. Altered states of consciousness
12. Other significant care needs.

---

1 National Framework 2018, para 141.
2 NHS Responsibilities Regulations 2012, r.21(5) and (6).

The last domain, the 'empty' domain, is used to record any needs which do not fall into the other 11 domains. The severity of the need in question, in this twelfth domain, must be weighted using professional judgement.[1]

In terms of scoring the DST, and the implications, the following key points should be noted, as set out in the guidance. The scoring is meant to give an idea of the nature, intensity, complexity or unpredictability of a person's needs – and therefore of the quantity and quality of the care required. Generally, the DST indicates that the more domains of need there are, the greater the complexity may be; the higher the score on any one domain, the greater the intensity:

- **Variation in scoring possibilities**. Some domains can be scored higher than others, depending on how important the DST considers any particular domain to be in determining CHC eligibility.[2]

- **One or more 'priority' scores: usually indicates eligibility**. Guidance considers that if a person scores one 'priority' (available in the behaviour, cognition, breathing, drug therapies/medication domains), 'a clear recommendation (and decision) of eligibility for NHS Continuing Healthcare would usually be expected'.[3]

- **Two 'severe' scores: usually indicate eligibility**. If two severe scores are recorded, 'a clear recommendation (and decision) of eligibility for NHS Continuing Healthcare would usually be expected'.[4]

- **One 'severe' score with needs in other domains: careful consideration of eligibility required**. In case of one 'severe' score with needs in a number of other domains, 'careful consideration must be given to the four key characteristics of "nature", "intensity", "complexity" or "unpredictability" of the individual's needs. This consideration must be used to inform the decision as to whether or not the individual has a primary health need and therefore whether or not they are eligible for NHS Continuing Healthcare.'[5]

- **'High' or 'moderate' scores only: careful consideration of eligibility required**. If the scoring results in a number of 'high' and/or 'moderate' needs (but no 'priority' or 'severe' needs identified), 'careful

---

1   Decision Support Tool 2018, para 39.
2   Decision Support Tool 2018, para 25.
3   Decision Support Tool 2018, para 31.
4   Decision Support Tool 2018, para 31.
5   Decision Support Tool 2018, para 31.

consideration must be given to the four key characteristics of "nature", "intensity", "complexity" or "unpredictability" of the individual's needs. This consideration must be used to inform the decision as to whether or not the individual has a primary health need and therefore whether or not they are eligible for NHS Continuing Healthcare.'[1]

- **Professional judgement: importance of.** Whilst CHC decision-making is made within a legal and quasi-legal framework, guidance makes clear that the recommendation emerging from the DST should be on the basis of the multi-disciplinary team working 'collectively using professional judgement'.[2]

- **Recommendation of non-eligibility: clear reasons to be given.** 'Where an MDT [multi-disciplinary team] recommends an individual is not eligible for NHS Continuing Healthcare, a clear rationale that considers the four key characteristics must still be provided',[3] the characteristics being the 'nature', 'intensity', 'complexity' or 'unpredictability' of a person's needs.

- **Disagreement within the multi-disciplinary team: the higher level should be scored.**

    If, after considering all the relevant evidence, it proves difficult to decide or agree on the level, the MDT should choose the higher of the levels under consideration and record the evidence in relation to both the decision and any significant differences of opinion.[4]

The DST can be found online.[5]

Decision Support Tool: scoring and eligibility

Patients, families and practitioners should be aware that whilst great emphasis is placed on scoring within the guidance, it is not meant legally to be decisive. If treated as such, it could in some circumstances be challenged.

First, use of the DST is indeed mandatory but it creates a legal problem. It has been written by the Department of Health and Social Care in such a way as to set a high bar, or threshold, for potential eligibility, in particular

---

1 Decision Support Tool 2018, para 31.
2 National Framework 2018, para 147.
3 National Framework 2018, para 150.
4 Decision Support Tool 2018, para 21.
5 Decision Support Tool, accessed on 15 July 2019 at: www.gov.uk/government/publications/nhs-continuing-healthcare-decision-support-tool

the guidelines it lays down for scoring. The problem lies in the fact that in the *Coughlan* case, the Court of Appeal held that the patient came into a category of need wholly different from anything social services could legally meet. (At the time of the case, social services were legally permitted to provide what is now called funded nursing care in care homes.)

Her needs were essentially stable, her nursing needs relatively modest – but it is unlikely that she would qualify in practice for CHC if the DST's scoring system were now applied to her.[1]

This would be an unlawful outcome, not least because of the *Grogan* case which, seven years after *Coughlan*, confirmed that patients with levels of nursing need equivalent to Pamela Coughlan should not be assessed as eligible for (what would now be called) funded nursing care (FNC) but should be eligible for CHC.[2]

Second, the test in legislation deriving from the *Coughlan* case likewise sets a relatively low threshold for eligibility for CHC, arguably inconsistent with the high bar seemingly set by the DST. See **Incidental or ancillary or of a nature beyond social services**.

Third, the legal solution to this conundrum seems to be as follows. Guidance states that completion of the DST is to help answer the legal questions about the quality and quantity of care that a person requires,[3] these being the legal questions deriving directly from the legal case law. The DST is therefore not to be used prescriptively but simply as a guide to establishing legal eligibility. It does not directly determine eligibility but informs it.[4] The DST notes that:

> apart from more obvious cases, the domain descriptor levels will not determine eligibility but merely help inform consideration of the 'primary health need' test – using the four key characteristics of nature, intensity, complexity and unpredictability. These four key characteristics should be applied to the totality of needs.[5]

Although this in principle would seem to mean that a CCG would be free to deny eligibility even to those scoring highly on the DST, and to awarding eligibility in case of lower scores, it is the latter outcome which one would

---

1   Clements, L. 'NHS funding for continuing care in England: the revised (2009) guidance.' *Journal of Social Care and Neuro-disability*. Volume 1 (2010), Issue 1, pp.39–47.
2   *R(Grogan) v Bexley NHS Care Trust* [2006] EWHC 44 (Admin).
3   National Framework 2018, para 137. And: Decision Support Tool 2018, para 31.
4   National Framework 2018, para 141. And see: *R(Gossip) v NHS Surrey Downs Clinical Commissioning Group* [2019] EWHC 3411 (Admin), para 93.
5   Decision Support Tool 2018, para 19.

expect to be more common since the quantity/quality test deriving from the *Coughlan* legal case has set a relatively lower, rather than a higher, threshold for eligibility.

Decision Support Tool: individual domains and legal implications

The DST in itself is in principle a useful way of gathering relevant information about a person's needs. However, as already pointed out, there are concerns about the scoring system being out of line with the law and the understandable temptation to use the DST and scoring system prescriptively and narrowly.

There are various criticisms, falling into two main categories. Their implications are that the DST should precisely not be applied prescriptively and narrowly, even though this is what it invites by setting out a scoring system indicative of eligibility.

Perhaps most important is how the scoring system applies to patients with multiple health care needs, but without any one of these being scored as a 'priority' or without two of them being scored as 'severe'. Instead, patients may be scored as having a number of high and moderate needs; or perhaps just one severe need and a number of high or moderate needs.

The DST suggests that for such people careful consideration must be given to eligibility, suggesting in effect these may be borderline cases. Pamela Coughlan in the *Coughlan* case would almost certainly fall into this doubtful category outlined in the guidance; however, the court indicated that she was far from borderline and clearly eligible for CHC.[1] In other words, if CCGs apply the scoring system prescriptively to such types of patient, and find they are not eligible for CHC, they risk acting unlawfully.[2] See **Indicative cases**.

Second is a concern that a person with a particular and serious health condition and associated needs will sometimes wrongly be found not to be eligible for CHC if the scoring system is applied to them in respect of that particular need. Wrongly, simply because – under the primary health need test for CHC – the quantity of health- or nursing-related care needed would be likely to be more than just peripheral to meeting the person's needs or would be of a nature beyond the remit of social services.

The following examples would certainly suggest this, although it should be noted that anybody with a particular need as mentioned below would probably have other needs as well. This brings back the point dealt with

---

1 *R(Coughlan) v North and East Devon Health Authority* [2001] Q.B. 213, paras 30, 117.
2 *R(Grogan) v Bexley NHS Care Trust* [2006] EWHC 44 (Admin), para 51.

immediately above – the importance of considering the eligibility of a person with a combination of needs, even if none of those needs is scored very highly.

- **Breathing**. Tracheostomy care, requiring constant suctioning, was found in the *Haringey* legal case to point to a primary health need indicating CHC. This was because of the nature of such tracheostomy care, which the judge held was beyond that legally expected of social services.[1]

    However, under the DST scoring system, the person's needs in that case would have equated at most to a severe score, and that in itself would not, according to the DST, make a person eligible for CHC. This is an example suggestive of inconsistency between the DST (mere guidance, a tool) with a legal case (law, as opposed to guidance).

- **Nutrition**. In relation to the nutrition domain, one of the grounds for a 'severe' score is: 'unable to take food and drink by mouth, intervention inappropriate or impossible'. It has been pointed out that, taken literally, the patient would be already, or shortly, dead.[2] And yet even this, alone, would be insufficient to achieve CHC status since only one 'severe' score may fall short of CHC eligibility.

    For example, in 2003, the ombudsman found a person eligible for CHC who had suffered several strokes, had no speech or comprehension, was unable to swallow, required feeding by a percutaneous endoscopic gastrostomy (PEG) tube into the stomach, and was doubly incontinent.[3]

    Within the nutrition domain of the DST, a PEG tube would score only 'high' even if 'problematic'; likewise, total inability to communicate would score only 'high' in the communication domain. Even joined together, these two scores would fall far short of indicating eligibility on the DST, in apparent contradiction to the *Wigan* case.[4]

- **Incontinence, urinary or double**. Continence can be scored only up to 'high'. This is quite a strict limit when one considers what would be required in order to achieve even this, highest possible, score. Such a

---

1 *R(T) v London Borough of Haringey* [2005] EWHC 2235 (Admin), paras 61, 62, 70.
2 Clements, L. 'NHS funding for continuing care in England: the revised (2009) guidance.' *Journal of Social Care and Neuro-disability*. Volume 1 (2010), Issue 1, pp.39–47.
3 *Wigan and Bolton Health Authority* (E.420/00–01). In: Health Service Ombudsman. *NHS funding for long term care*. London: TSO, 2003.
4 See e.g. discussion in: Clements, L. 'NHS funding for continuing care in England: the revised (2009) guidance.' *Journal of Social Care and Neuro-disability*. Volume 1 (2010), Issue 1, pp.39–47.

level of need can lead to significant complications including infection. A 'high' score alone would get the person nowhere near to eligibility for CHC. But it is not easy to see how bladder washouts, manual evacuations and frequent re-catheterisation can fail to be continuing health care needs.

- **Skin**. In terms of skin, a severe score would require, for example, 'open wound(s), pressure ulcer(s) with full thickness skin loss with extensive destruction and tissue necrosis extending to underlying bone, tendon or joint capsule or above'. Even a score in the severe category would not *by itself* qualify a person for CHC eligibility, since the DST indicates that at least two domains need to be scored at severe. Yet to suggest that a person with necrosis to the bone, or multiple wounds not responding to treatment, does not qualify for CHC 'challenges reason'.[1]

    Furthermore, the domain scoring is to the effect that if pressure ulcers have so far been avoided by good care, no matter how great the risk and vulnerability, only a 'moderate' score can be achieved. The effect of this appears contrary to the National Framework guidance, which states that a well-managed need is still a need.[2]

- **Communication**. Communication can only be scored up to 'high'. Yet even this top score would in itself get the person, according to the DST, nowhere near eligibility for CHC. Even a total inability to communicate (a criterion for a high score) would be associated with, in many cases, significant safety issues for the patient. It is notable that some of the ombudsman cases in which eligibility was found included (amongst other needs) communication-related issues.[3]

- **Cognition**. To achieve a 'severe' score on cognition, a person would have extremely pronounced needs and exposure to risk: 'marked short or long-term memory issues, or severe disorientation to time, place or person. The individual is unable to assess basic risks even with supervision, prompting or assistance, and is dependent on others to anticipate their basic needs and to protect them from harm, neglect or health deterioration.'

---

1   Clements, L. 'NHS funding for continuing care in England: the revised (2009) guidance.' *Journal of Social Care and Neuro-disability*. Volume 1 (2010), Issue 1, pp.39–47.
2   National Framework 2018, para 142.
3   e.g. *Wigan and Bolton Health Authority* (E.420/00–01). In: Health Service Ombudsman. *NHS funding for long term care*. London: TSO, 2003.

Such a score, alone, would not point to eligibility, according to the DST's scoring system. Yet such a description of need would be comparable to the needs described in the *Pointon* ombudsman case, one of the indicative cases which needs to be considered, and which pointed clearly to eligibility for CHC. See **Indicative cases**.

- **Altered states of consciousness**. In relation to the domain of altered states of consciousness, a person described as being at high risk, at major risk of death and suffering several life-threatening fits a month would not come within the priority score. In fact, they would score only 'high'; which of itself would bring the person nowhere near CHC eligibility, according to the DST's scoring system. This would seem to be yet one more example of how the DST sets a scoring threshold inconsistent with the *Coughlan* case, and the incidental/ancillary or nature test.

    In a legal case involving just such needs, a local authority's decision to offer such obviously inadequate care to a man at serious risk of death from epilepsy was struck down as unlawful.[1] There was no mention of CHC in the case (presumably, it is not clear, because possibly prescriptive use of the DST had resulted, at some point in the past, in a decision of non-eligibility for CHC).

Delay

The Public Accounts Committee of the House of Commons found, in 2018, evidence of significant delays in assessment and decisions about people's NHS Continuing Healthcare (CHC) needs.[2] This followed a National Audit Office report to the same effect in 2017;[3] whilst Marie Curie continues to find delays involving end of life cases, delays which may mean people are dead by the time assessment and provision take place.[4] See **Fast Track Pathway Tool**.

It is true that the legislation about CHC contains no timescales. However, there is a general public law principle that if legislation stipulates a specific duty, then that duty must be performed without undue delay or within a

---

1 *R(Clarke) v London Borough of Sutton* [2015] EWHC 1081 (Admin), paras 26–30.
2 House of Commons Public Accounts Committee. *NHS Continuing Healthcare funding*. London: TSO, 2018.
3 National Audit Office. *Investigation into NHS Continuing Healthcare funding*. London: NAO, 2017.
4 Brennan, S. 'Report: "Patients dying in hospital waiting for community care."' *Health Service Journal*, 20 March 2019. And: Marie Curie. *Making every moment count: the state of Fast Track Continuing Healthcare in England*. London: Marie Curie, 2017, p.8.

reasonable period of time. And identifying a reasonable period of time will depend upon all the circumstances of the case.[1]

The relevant NHS regulations state only that the clinical commissioning group (CCG) must take 'reasonable steps' to assess a person where it appears 'there may be a need' for CHC.[2] This falls short of an unqualified duty. However, in relation to what would be reasonable in terms of time, statutory guidance states that in most cases, a decision about CHC should be made within 28 days of receipt of a completed Checklist,[3] a rule which, according to the evidence of the reports referred to immediately above, is by no means being followed. The various timescales (there are several) set out in the National Framework guidance are as follows:

- **Request for completion of Checklist: 14 calendar days.**

  Where the need for a Checklist is brought to the attention of the CCG through these routes it should respond in a timely manner, having regard to the nature of the needs identified. In most circumstances it would be appropriate to complete a Checklist within 14 calendar days of such a request.[4]

- **From completed Checklist or other notification to final decision about CHC: 28 days.**

  Decision-making on eligibility for NHS Continuing Healthcare should, in most cases, take no longer than 28 calendar days from the CCG (or organisation acting on behalf of the CCG) being notified of the need for assessment of eligibility for NHS Continuing Healthcare, e.g. an appropriately completed positive Checklist, or other notification that an assessment of eligibility is required.[5]

- **Decision about eligibility in hospital: far fewer than 28 days.**

  In the minority of cases where an assessment of eligibility is being carried out in an acute hospital setting, the process should take far fewer than 28 calendar days if an individual is otherwise ready for discharge.[6]

---

1 *R(D) v London Borough of Brent* [2015] EWHC 3224 (Admin), para 19.
2 NHS Responsibilities Regulations 2012, r.21(2).
3 National Framework 2018, Annex E, para 8.
4 National Framework Practice Guidance 2018, para 14.1.
5 National Framework 2018, Annex E, para 8.
6 National Framework 2018, para 163.

- **Multi-disciplinary team (MDT) recommendations: decision within 48 hours**.

    It is expected that CCGs will normally respond to MDT recommendations within 48 hours (two working days).[1]

- **End of life: Fast Track Pathway provision within 48 hours**.

    Action should be taken urgently to agree and commission the care package. CCGs should have processes in place to enable such care packages to be commissioned quickly. Given the nature of the needs, this time period should not usually exceed 48 hours from receipt of the completed Fast Track Pathway Tool.[2]

- **Unjustifiable delay**. If a CCG delays unjustifiably making a decision about CHC – in a case in which a person is subsequently assessed to have, and to have had, CHC needs – then the CCG must reimburse either the local authority or the person themselves. See *Reimbursement*.

If, without obvious reason, therefore, a CCG delays the CHC decision in excess of 28 days from receipt of the Checklist – for example, for four months – the ombudsman will find fault.[3]

The following example gives a flavour of what can all too often occur and cause significant distress. In this case, the 28-day period was exceeded by over 10 months.

> **21-month delay in decision-making and distress**. A former district surveyor cared for his wife who had colitis and suffered a stroke. Later, he himself then suffered from dementia, rectal cancer, stage 4 kidney disease, a poor heart and total incontinence. The process of applying for CHC for him was distressing. There were long delays – a written decision taking nearly two years overall. It took three months for a Checklist to be completed and a further 11 months for the Decision Support Tool. The nurse assessor recommended that he was not eligible for CHC. The family wanted to appeal but could not do so until the official decision was communicated in writing. This did not happen until ten months

---

1   National Framework 2018, para 162.
2   National Framework 2018, para 238.
3   LGSCO, *Essex County Council*, 2019 (17 015 113), para 58.

> after the assessment. His son rang the local CHC team every month, only to be told each time that they had a backlog.[1]

In another case, delay in completing the Checklist, delay of three months in completing the Decision Support Tool and delay in reimbursing the family for costs they had incurred in funding essential care meant that the man's sister had insufficient money to cover funeral costs when he died.[2]

Once eligibility has been established, approval of the actual care package may need to take place. The ombudsman, for example, has found fault when a panel persistently asks unnecessarily for further information, so as to delay approval of a care package for 15 weeks.[3]

Deprivation of liberty

Some people are subject to care arrangements which place them under continual supervision and control and not free to leave the place in which they are being cared for – but they lack the mental capacity to consent to these arrangements. In such circumstances, the arrangements must be legally authorised or sanctioned as a deprivation of liberty, either by a local authority or the Court of Protection.[4]

Detailed rules are contained in the Mental Capacity Act 2005 and in legal case law. In any event, if the best interests decision is made under the Mental Capacity Act 2005, the actual care arrangements would be made either by a local authority under the Care Act 2014, or by an NHS clinical commissioning group under the National Health Service Act 2006 in case of a person with NHS Continuing Healthcare (CHC) needs. Guidance points out that the CHC rules would apply as normal, irrespective of lack of capacity.[5]

---

1 Continuing Care Alliance. *Continuing to care: is NHS Continuing Healthcare supporting the people who need it in England?* London: CCA, 2016, p.14.
2 LGSCO, *Essex County Council (Mid-Essex Clinical Commissioning Group)*, 2019 (17 015 113).
3 PSOW, *Pembrokeshire County Council and Hywel Dda University Health Board*, 2015 (201404540 and 201409309), para 71.
4 Amendments to the Mental Capacity Act, due to come into force in 2020, will mean that hospitals and clinical commissioning groups will also be able to authorise a deprivation of liberty. See: Mental Capacity (Amendment) Bill 2019.
5 National Framework 2018, para 320.

Diagnosis

Guidance emphasises that the medical diagnosis of disease, illness, condition or impairment is not decisive as to whether a person has NHS Continuing Healthcare (CHC) needs since CHC eligibility concerns the level and type of the person's overall, actual day-to-day needs.[1]

Direct payments

A direct payment is a method of meeting a person's needs, by giving them money to use in order to purchase the assistance they need themselves. The overall purpose is to give a person more choice and control over how their needs are met and services provided.

Long since established in adult social care, it is only more recently that direct payments have been permitted legally in the NHS context[2] and direct payments for NHS Continuing Healthcare (CHC) are now possible. (Previously, people already receiving social care direct payments were sometimes concerned about being assessed as eligible for CHC. This was because they feared losing control and flexibility in their care arrangements.)

The law about direct payments for meeting CHC needs is now in place and clear. In short, for a person receiving CHC, the NHS clinical commissioning group must, on request, 'ensure that it is able to arrange for the provision of a relevant health service to an eligible person by means of a personal health budget'.

This means that, on request, anybody eligible must be allocated a personal health budget – unless it is not 'appropriate to secure provision of all or any part of the relevant health service by that means in the circumstances of the eligible person's case'.[3] If the request is refused, the CCG must communicate the decision in writing with reasons. The person can request a review and, again, the outcome of the review must be communicated in writing and with reasons.[4]

Once approved, the budget must be managed in one of three ways: a direct payment to the person, the CCG itself applying and using the budget to meet the person's needs, or the CCG transferring the money to somebody else to secure the care required.[5] The overall personal health budget is defined as an amount of money identified by the CCG as appropriate to secure the

---

1 National Framework 2018, para 55.
2 See e.g. *Gunter v South Western Staffordshire Primary Care Trust* [2005] EWHC 1894 (Admin).
3 NHS Responsibilities Regulations 2012, r.32B(4).
4 NHS Responsibilities Regulations 2012, r.32B(7)–32B(9).
5 NHS Responsibilities Regulations 2012, r.32B(2).

provision of CHC. How the budget is used is to be planned and agreed between the CCG and the person or their representative.[1]

Discrimination

The Equality Act 2010 governs discrimination law. Accordingly, guidance notes that access to NHS Continuing Healthcare (CHC) should be 'fair, consistent and free from discrimination' and that there should be no discrimination on the grounds of race, disability, gender, age, sexual orientation, religion or belief, or type of health need (whether the need is physical, mental or psychological).[2]

With this mind, an example of one local policy which appeared potentially to be discriminatory was to the following effect. It stated that if a person scored 'priority' on the behaviour domain of the Decision Support Tool (DST), the person would normally, as the DST clearly indicates, be eligible for CHC, unless they had a learning disability, in which case they would not.[3]

Dispute resolution between NHS and social services

Disputes about NHS Continuing Healthcare (CHC) are not necessarily confined to patients and their families challenging an NHS clinical commissioning group (CCG). They may also involve CCGs and local authorities disputing with each other the legal responsibility for meeting a person's needs. Regulations clearly envisage this, since they stipulate that a local authority and CCG must agree a dispute resolution procedure between them.

The procedure applies to a CHC eligibility decision or, where a person is not eligible for CHC, to the respective contribution that the local authority and CCG make to a joint funded package of care.[4] The CCG must, in operating the dispute procedure, have due regard to the need to promote and secure the continuity of appropriate services for the person involved.[5]

---

1 NHS Responsibilities Regulations 2012, r.32A.
2 National Framework 2018, paras 8, 69.
3 Personal communication, with evidence in writing, shared with the author.
4 NHS Responsibilities Regulations 2012, r.22(2). And: Care and Support (Provision of Health Services) Regulations 2014, r.4.
5 NHS Responsibilities Regulations 2012, r.22(3).

These are more than just vague words; a failure to achieve effective and timely dispute resolution can in some circumstances lead to needs being unmet.

> **Delay arguing about funding.** The ombudsman found fault when a five-month delay in funding a placement which would meet a person's needs meant that a person with learning disabilities and autism remained at home in a situation that was breaking down because of his compulsive and risky behaviours, a situation exacerbated by the health needs of his father (who, with his mother, looked after him). The ombudsman observed 'that the placement was not progressed solely because of the question of how it would be funded'.[1]

Apart from this rule in regulations, there are in any case good reasons for both CCGs and local authorities to challenge one another in some cases. This is particularly so in the case of local authorities, since a failure to do so could result in them acting unlawfully by providing services under the Care Act 2014 beyond their legal powers, and in them financially charging people whose needs should be met by the NHS free of charge.

Such an incentive notwithstanding, local authorities curiously have required, over the years, some encouragement to make challenges.[2] For example, the ombudsman has found fault when a local authority believed the NHS was acting unlawfully, failed to escalate the matter to dispute resolution and consequently continued to provide support to the person, support which it believed was beyond its legal remit.[3] Ease of challenge may also depend on the legally required dispute resolution procedure being in place; in one case, the ombudsman found fault with the NHS in this respect.[4]

The duty in regulations placed on both CCG and local authority to agree a dispute procedure demands also that they have regard to the National Framework guidance, which states that the CCG and local authority must ensure that the dispute resolution procedure encompasses the following:

---

1 LGSCO, *Staffordshire County Council*, 2018 (17 006 607), para 34.
2 Association of Directors of Adult Social Services. *Commentary and advice for local authorities on the National Framework for NHS Continuing Healthcare and NHS-funded Nursing Care.* London: ADASS, 2007, p.4.
3 LGO, *Northamptonshire County Council*, 2016 (14 007 296), paras 29, 31.
4 PSOW, *Aneurin Bevan Health Board and Caerphilly County Borough Council*, 2012 (2010001820 and 2010002050), para 28.

- **Informal stage**. This might, for example, involve consultation with relevant managers immediately following the multi-disciplinary team meeting to see whether agreement can be reached and to seek further information.
- **Formal stage**. This would involve managers and/or practitioners who have delegated authority to attempt resolution of the disagreement and can make eligibility decisions. It could involve an inter-agency CHC panel.
- **Escalation**. If the dispute remains unresolved, the dispute resolution agreement could involve further stages of escalation to more senior managers within respective organisations.
- **Arbitration**. A final stage, as a last resort, would involve independent arbitration to be triggered only by senior managers within the respective organisations. They must agree how the independent arbitration is to be sourced, organised and funded.
- **Timelines**. There must be clear timelines for each stage.
- **Interim funding of person's care**. There must be agreement as to how the person's care is to be funded during the dispute. People must 'never be left without appropriate support'.
- **Informing the person and their representative**. There must be arrangements to keep the person and/or representative informed.
- **Person requesting a review**. There must be 'arrangements in the event of an individual requesting a review of the eligibility decision made by the CCG'.[1]

The guidance on dispute resolution concludes that, since CHC decisions are ultimately for the CCG to take, it 'may choose to make [its] decision before an inter-agency disagreement has been resolved. In such cases it is possible that the formal dispute resolution process will have to be concluded after the individual has been given a decision by the CCG.'[2]

The implication of this guidance is that the dispute must still be carried to its conclusion, as opposed simply to abandoning it, following the CHC decision. Otherwise there would be little point having a statutory dispute procedure at all, if a CCG could simply curtail it.

---
1 National Framework 2018, para 210.
2 National Framework 2018, para 211.

Disputes between a person and the NHS

If people or their representatives (e.g. family members) wish to dispute an NHS Continuing Healthcare (CHC) decision, there are various possibilities. Which of these are most appropriate will depend on the circumstances of the particular case. The main possibilities are as follows.

- **Local review by the NHS clinical commissioning group (CCG)**. The person can ask the CCG to review the decision, using a local resolution procedure. 'A key principle of the local resolution process is that, as far as possible, if the CCG does not change the original decision, the individual or their representative has had a clear and comprehensive explanation of the rationale for the CCG decision.' Requests for review should be dealt with in a timely manner.[1]

- **Independent review panel: NHS England**. If the dispute has not been resolved through local resolution, the person can make a request to NHS England for an independent review of the decision, to challenge either the decision regarding eligibility for CHC or the procedure followed by the CCG in reaching its decision.[2] See *Independent review panels*. If the challenge is about anything else related to CHC, the normal NHS complaints process would have to be used instead.

- **Health Service Ombudsman**. Following the above reviews, the person could seek to take their challenge further to the Health Service Ombudsman. See *Health Service Ombudsman*.

- **Local Government and Social Care Ombudsman**. Sometimes CHC-related challenges involve the local authority, if it has arguably failed in its responsibilities – for instance, by not making a referral to the NHS as demanded by section 9 of the Care Act 2014. See *Local Government and Social Care Ombudsman*.

- **Judicial review legal case**. In some circumstances, a person might seek to take a judicial review legal case against the CCG or even the local authority. See *Judicial review*.

- **Members of Parliament, councillors and the press**. Sometimes, a less formal way of challenge is through a local MP or a local councillor.

---

1 National Framework 2018, paras 194–195.
2 National Framework 2018, para 196.

The House of Commons Library has from time to time produced briefing documents for MPs about CHC. Such briefing papers are aimed, amongst other things, at helping MPs support constituents. The most recent of these, published in 2018, notes the difficulties, lack of understanding and confusion inherent in the system of CHC.[1] A further option is to go the press, something that can bear fruit but can also be unpredictable and intrusive.

The guidance states that the local review processes of CCGs should function in a timely manner; when a woman appealed against a decision to take her off the Fast Track Pathway, on the grounds that she had become stable and needed an ongoing care package, it took the CCG three years from the original decision to conclude the review. The ombudsman found this to be clearly excessive.[2]

Disputes between a person and the NHS: reasons for challenge
Reasons for challenging decisions are not simply financial, substantial though such reasons are. If a person is wrongly deemed to have primarily social care rather than health care needs, there may be a greater chance of inadequate care being commissioned by social services. For example, in one case NHS withdrawal of CHC, on probably spurious grounds, led to the local authority commissioning a cheaper care home placement, resulting in physical and mental harm to the person.[3]

Similarly, following questionable withdrawal of CHC from a woman in her own home, the local authority reduced the support to her; this was a contributory factor to her main carer, her husband, struggling, and to the local authority then seeking to remove her to a care home by coercively depriving her of her liberty under the Mental Capacity Act 2005.[4]

Disputes between a person and the NHS: obstacles
Challenging decisions that have been made about CHC can be daunting for patients and their families.

---

1 See e.g. Powell, T. *Background to the National Framework for NHS Continuing Healthcare*. Standard note: SN/SP/4643. London: House of Commons Library, 2011. And: Powell, T. *NHS Continuing Healthcare in England*. Standard note: SN/SP/6128. London: House of Commons Library, 2014. And: Powell, T. and Mackley, A. *NHS Continuing Healthcare in England*. Standard note: SN/SP/6128. London: House of Commons Library, 2018.
2 LGSCO, *Halton Borough Council*, 2017 (16 007 858), paras 30–31.
3 LGO, *Worcestershire County Council*, 2014 (12 004 137).
4 *A London Local Authority v JH* [2011] EWHC 2420 (COP).

Reasons for this include the stress involved, not only in challenging 'authority' but in doing so at a time of chronic illness and need. Also stressful is knowing that what is at stake is not just a person's health and care, but their financial position and security. They may be at risk of losing the fruits of 40 years (their home and any savings) simply because a decision has been taken wrongly that their needs are social care rather than health care. To meet those needs they may therefore, again wrongly, have to pay.

This is made worse by the confusing rules and processes surrounding CHC decisions, leading in some cases to a loss of trust in the NHS and a feeling of betrayal when the decision seems to be more about finance than meeting a person's health care needs. During the process of the challenge itself, the patient and family may find themselves in a further unenviable position.

> **Financial burden on patient and family during challenge.** In one case, for instance, the challenge was ultimately successful and CHC eligibility was both awarded and backdated, but during this time the person's needs were deemed to be social care. The local authority arranged a care home placement and the person was expected to pay towards it. The family refused and were faced with a legal summons from the local authority for the unpaid care home costs.[1]
>
> In another such case, whilst the resident was pursuing a complaint to the Health Service Ombudsman about CHC, the local authority succeeded in placing a 'caveat' (restriction on the probate process, on death) on the person's will in relation to unpaid care home fees.[2]

Overall, it is unfortunate that the burden should fall to such an extent on patients and their families to make challenges in the first place.

First, if the rules were clear, and if CCGs applied them openly and consistently, this burden would arguably be reduced.

Second, if local authorities were to make more challenges of their own against CCGs, again the burden on patients and their families would be less. Local authorities should be doing this because they are legally prohibited from meeting the needs of people who have CHC needs (and who should

---

1 HSO, Mistakes in continuing care funding decision. Summary 490, October 2014. In: HSO. *Report on selected summaries of investigations by the Parliamentary and Health Service Ombudsman October to November 2014*. London: HSO, 2015.
2 LGSCO, *Essex County Council*, 2019 (17 017 282), para 22.

have been assessed as such) and are also obliged to have in place a dispute resolution procedure with the NHS.

Disputes between a person and the NHS: persistence, tenacity, patience

The existence of review or other dispute processes does not mean that people are able and willing to take advantage of them. As the Continuing Care Alliance has pointed out, many people 'decide not to appeal their decision on NHS CHC eligibility. This is not because they feel the decision was correct, but because they are too distressed and exhausted to go through the complex appeals process.'[1]

Thus, those CCGs that state that a lack of review requests or complaints (about CHC or indeed anything else) indicates that all is well are at risk of misplaced complacency. Even if a person and/or family is prepared to challenge, the CCG may still prove to be distinctly unhelpful and, essentially, obstructive.

> **Obstructiveness and then unwillingness to implement the review panel's recommendations.**
>
> I then said I wanted to take it to an IRP [independent review panel]. The CCG told me I had to apply for this through them, so I did. Nothing happened for three months. After chasing my CCG, they admitted they had got the information wrong and I actually had to go directly to NHS England. So, my appeal hadn't moved forward at all and I only found out because I kept calling and eventually someone told me. Once in touch with the IRP organisers, they thought I had a good case. They decided to uphold my appeal and requested my CCG grant NHS CHC. Even after this, the CCG didn't provide help straight away. If the CCG refuses to adhere to the IRP's ruling only the courts can enforce the decision. It doesn't seem like they are accountable to anyone.[2]

Equally, CCGs may unexpectedly concede a dispute, particularly if they realise that a patient, family or representative is alive to the rules and the

---

1   Continuing Care Alliance. *Continuing to care: is NHS Continuing Healthcare supporting the people who need it in England?* London: CCA, 2016, p.17.
2   Continuing Care Alliance. *Continuing to care: is NHS Continuing Healthcare supporting the people who need it in England?* London: CCA, 2016, p.18.

flaws in the decision-making that has taken place. In other words, sometimes sheer persistence may succeed, not least because CCG staff may not know the rules as well as they should, perhaps through lack of training and guidance, or they may be aware that the rules are being applied in a questionable way.

For example, in one reported instance, after withdrawal of CHC eligibility for a woman with cancer, the NHS refused to supply the previous documentation so that present and past assessments could be compared. However, as soon as they realised that the husband had been a chairman of a CHC independent review panel, his wife's eligibility was immediately restored.[1]

Equally, a CCG might doggedly resist and only extreme persistence in gathering, submitting and resubmitting clinical evidence over a long period of time – months or sometimes even years – bears any fruit, with potentially large sums of money having to be reimbursed by the CCG.

Ten-year battle with the NHS. The parents of a man with cerebral palsy and unable to use his arms and legs spent nearly all their life savings on his care, whilst battling for ten years with the CCG (and before that the primary care trust). Eventually, in 2019, the CCG agreed to repay them £300,000.[2]

Domains of need, see *Decision Support Tool*

Double scoring

Practitioners using and completing the Decision Support Tool are in practice sometimes warned by clinical commissioning groups to avoid 'double scoring' – recording needs arising from the same condition in more than one domain. However, the guidance itself is clear that there is no such rule, noting that 'a single condition might give rise to separate needs in a number of domains'.[3] Further guidance gives an example:

---

1 Care to be Different. *NHS Continuing Healthcare independent review – former chair speaks out.* 27 May 2014. Accessed on 14 June 2019 at: https://caretobedifferent.co.uk/nhs-continuing-healthcare-independent-review-former-chair-speaks-out
2 Phillips, N. (Victoria Derbyshire programme). 'Our life savings are spent on care that should be free.' *BBC News*, 11 June 2019. Accessed on 18 July 2019 at: www.bbc.co.uk/news/health-48555199
3 Decision Support Tool 2018, para 24.

- **Scoring cognitive impairment in more than one domain.**

    An individual with cognitive impairment will have a weighting in the cognition domain and as a result may have associated needs in other domains, all of which should be recorded and weighted in their own right. An individual with a severe cognitive impairment might or might not also exhibit associated challenging behaviour. Therefore, if challenging behaviour exists, recording this in the behaviour domain is necessary in order to give an accurate picture of needs, even though this behaviour might be linked to their cognitive impairment.[1]

In fact, a failure to double score could mean that a person's needs are not properly assessed and recognised and attract censure from the ombudsman. This happened in the following case, when the physical problem was addressed but not the cognitive difficulties underlying it.

> **Impact of cognition on nutrition and hydration.** A patient could physically swallow but had cognitive problems in recognising food. This led to a risk of choking. The assessment had focused too narrowly on the patient's ability to swallow. However, the cognitive issues meant she needed assistance and monitoring when eating; her weight and hydration were affected. The health board had failed to look at her needs holistically, in their totality.[2]

Dowry payments, see *Learning disability*

Drug therapies and medication, see *Decision Support Tool*

---

1 National Framework Practice Guidance 2018, para 30.1.
2 PSOW, *Aneurin Bevan Health Board and Caerphilly County Borough Council*, 2012 (2010001820 and 2010002050), para 30.

E

Education, health and care plans

Under the Children and Families Act 2014, some children or young people have an education, health and care (EHC) plan if the local authority decides that such a plan is necessary for special educational provision to be made for a child or young person.

The idea is to bring together the educational, health care and social care aspects of the child or young person's needs. The following paragraphs confine themselves to the *position of adults* with an EHC plan and the relevance to NHS Continuing Healthcare (CHC).

The plan itself is made by a local authority under the Children and Families Act 2014, and the educational provision is made directly under that Act. However, the health part of the plan legally contains what will be provided under the National Health Service Act 2006 in terms of 'any health care provision reasonably required by the learning difficulties or disabilities which result in the child or young person having special educational needs'. Provision for the meeting of such needs must be first approved by the relevant NHS clinical commissioning group.

The care part of a plan, referring to Care Act provision, must specify 'any social care provision reasonably required by the learning difficulties and disabilities which result in the child or young person having special educational needs'.[1]

Any health care or social care which educates or trains is to be regarded as educational and would therefore fall under the education part of the plan, with the responsibility for its provision resting ultimately with the local education authority.[2]

Education, health and care plans and Continuing Healthcare

The EHC plan of a younger person can continue up to and including the age of 24.[3] How then do these rules about EHC plans relate to CHC for

---

1 Children and Families Act 2014, s.37(2).
2 Children and Families Act 2014, s.21(5).
3 Children and Families Act 2014, s.46.

adults? In summary, the position would appear to be as follows, although it is not perhaps entirely clear.

First are the preparatory steps to assess a child for the transition from 'continuing care' for a child to CHC as an adult. These are set out in the National Framework guidance. See **Transition**.

Second, if a person aged 18 is eligible for CHC, the NHS is by default responsible for meeting both the health and social care needs of the adult.[1] And it is unlawful under section 22 of the Care Act 2014 for a local authority to meet CHC needs. This would seem to mean that the care part of the EHC plan would tend to be empty, with both health and social care needs being within the health part of the EHC plan, under the National Health Service Act 2006.

Third, however, NHS obligations to meet a person's health and social care needs in case of eligibility for CHC would not extend to meeting their educational needs. Any such provision should anyway be in the education part of an EHC plan and is for the local education authority ultimately to provide (see above).

However, *assistance to take advantage* of education or training (as opposed to providing the education or training itself) is part of the Care Act eligibility test.[2] Arguably, therefore, such assistance could perhaps, by extension, fall to the NHS for a person eligible for CHC. This is because the NHS would in effect be taking over social care responsibilities which would normally be the responsibility of social services under the Care Act. Equally, it is foreseeable that disputes about this could easily arise and this may prove to be a grey area.

All this may sound overly complicated; yet just such questions about how the CHC rules for adults interact with EHC plans have been arising in tribunals, including apparent attempts by local authorities to argue, contrary to the legislation, that the NHS should meet not just health and social care but also seemingly educational needs.[3]

---

1 NHS Responsibilities Regulations 2012, r.20.
2 Care and Support (Eligibility Criteria) Regulations 2015.
3 *NHS West Berkshire Clinical Commissioning Group v The First-tier Tribunal (Health, Education and Social Care Chamber) (interested parties: (1) AM; (2) MA; (3) Westminster City Council)* [2019] UKUT 44 (AAC), para 12. See also: LGSCO, *Cornwall Council*, 2019 (17 007 723), para 25.

Eligibility

Determining whether a person has a need for NHS Continuing Healthcare involves an eligibility test based on legal case law, regulations and statutory guidance. This is confirmed at the outset of the National Framework guidance.[1] This being so, patients and families are sometimes confused when they realise that such decisions made by the NHS are not about clinical needs but about who is going to pay to meet those needs.

End of life, see *Fast Track Pathway Tool*

Equipment

The rules governing eligibility for the provision of NHS Continuing Healthcare (CHC) apply not just to care but also to equipment, sometimes called aids to daily living. Guidance makes clear:

> Where an individual is eligible for NHS Continuing Healthcare and chooses to live in their own home, the CCG [clinical commissioning group] is financially responsible for meeting all assessed health and associated social care needs. This could include equipment provision.[2]

It states further that if there is a local equipment store, funded jointly by the local authority and the NHS, then standard equipment (in case of CHC) would be provided from that store but be chalked up, as it were, against NHS provision.

In case of special orders for equipment not kept in stock, this would be an NHS responsibility also. In the context of care homes, the care home would be expected to provide a basic level of equipment under the Health and Social Care Act (Regulated Activities) Regulations 2014 and the provisions of the contract that the CCG will have with the care home. If an individual resident with CHC needs has more specialised needs, it would fall to the CCG to meet those.[3]

In practice, CCGs sometimes ask social services, in particular occupational therapists, to carry out assessments for, and provision of, equipment for people whose CHC status is already established. However, CCGs are solely responsible for arranging and funding a CHC package of care, and section 22

---

1 National Framework 2018, p.3.
2 National Framework 2018, para 291.
3 National Framework 2018, para 301.

of the Care Act places prohibitions on social services in relation to CHC. So, such formal assessment and provision could not be carried out under the Care Act. Nonetheless social services, by agreement under section 75 of the National Health Service Act 2006, could carry these out on behalf of the CCG (with reimbursement), but under the National Health Service Act 2006 and not the Care Act 2014.

Evidence of need

Guidance states that the purpose of evidence of a person's needs, gathered in assessment for NHS Continuing Healthcare eligibility, is to ensure an accurate picture of the individual's needs and 'not to convince a court of law that those providing the evidence are telling the truth'.

Evidence required should be proportionate and reasonable, and a detailed diary may be needed to demonstrate the nature and frequency of the needs and interventions, and their effectiveness. It also notes that oral evidence is relevant, and that the person and family should be fully involved in the assessment.[1]

> **Proportionate evidence.** A continuing demand by a local panel for ever more evidence was fault when investigated by the ombudsman if, in the circumstances, this insistence was designed to avoid taking a decision and the refusal to award eligibility on the existing evidence appeared perverse.[2]

Equally, there have been persistent concerns expressed that sufficient evidence about a person's needs is sometimes not sought and obtained by NHS clinical commissioning groups (CCGs) or is downplayed or marginalised. Clearly one way in which inadequate evidence will become apparent is if assessors are not sufficiently expert and competent in relation to the particular health conditions and their implications. See ***Expertise of assessors, and knowledge of the patient***.

Alternatively, if, particularly in the case of informal carers, evidence from the family is ignored, dismissed or simply suppressed, the ombudsman will object.[3] Likewise, if evidence is generally marginalised.[4]

---

1 National Framework Practice Guidance 2018, paras 21.2, 21.5, 31.1–31.3.
2 PSOW, *Carmarthenshire Local Health Board*, 2009 (200800779), para 56.
3 LGSCO, *Lancashire County Council*, 2017 (16 000 404), paras 24, 43.
4 e.g. PSOW, *Cardiff and Vale University Health Board*, 2017 (201701350). And: PSOW, *Cwm Taf University Health Board*, 2017 (201700989).

> **Downplaying of evidence by a nurse assessor.** A nurse assessor might state that a person with dementia who has suffered a stroke 'needs assistance with dressing and washing'. A more accurate description would be that:
>
>> [she] needs constant care, day and night, for even the most basic things such as getting clothes on, maintaining vital oral health and protecting her skin from the impact of poor hygiene. She is unable to carry out even the most basic tasks for herself – in any way. Without such care and intervention, she would suffer painful injury, distress and potentially fatal skin breakdown.[1]

The All Party Parliamentary Group on Parkinson's found that assumptions are sometimes wrongly made about people's needs.

> **Cognition and emotional needs.**
>
> Examples were provided with dementia and other conditions such as motor neurone disease where assessments had found that if someone had little cognition, it was felt that this meant that they had no emotional or psychological needs. The Alzheimer's Society said this contradicted current research around cognition, as it is believed that people with low levels of cognition still experience emotions and psychological needs and that these needs still require support.[2]

In the following example, the CCG would have been applying a legally dubious interpretation of mobility by equating it with 'shuffling about in bed'.

> **Unable to walk, stand or turn over but assessed as mobile.**
>
> During the assessment they used the DST [Decision Support Tool] to assess the severity of Tom's needs. The criteria can be interpreted differently by the people conducting the assessment. I believe the team assessing Tom

---

1 Care to Be Different. *Check carefully what Continuing Healthcare assessors write down about your relative's care needs.* Accessed on 8 August 2019 at: https://caretobedifferent.co.uk/nhs-continuing-healthcare-assessors-describe-care-needs
2 All Party Parliamentary Group on Parkinson's. *Failing to care: NHS continuing care in England.* London: Parkinson's UK, 2013, p.18.

> manipulated some of the information. For example, when assessing his mobility, they decided that because he could shuffle about in bed, he was mobile and therefore did not qualify. What's their definition of mobility? He couldn't walk, stand or even turn over in bed, which I think means he was immobile. It was very clear to me that the assessment was a sham. It was awful to watch. Tom was completely reliant on others to provide his care. I felt the assessors seriously downplayed most of his problems.[1]

The CCG may simply not seek the evidence, placing the burden on the patient's representatives or family to produce it.

> **The NHS wrongly placing the burden on the family to gather evidence.** The ombudsman has held, however, that it is an NHS responsibility 'to gather the evidence and records needed'.[2]
> Likewise, the ombudsman has found fault when, instead of gathering relevant information from a care home itself, the NHS told him he would have to pay the care home for the relevant records relating to his wife. The NHS needs:
>
>> to consider all relevant evidence, including care records. Inevitably there will be times when they will have to pay an administrative overhead to get the information they need. The NHS should not depend on patients or their relatives paying these costs.[3]

Expertise of assessors, and knowledge of the patient

The Public Accounts Committee, in 2018, referred to evidence of a lack of knowledge amongst assessors of NHS Continuing Healthcare (CHC) of the condition they were assessing.[4]

---

1 Continuing Care Alliance. *Continuing to care: is NHS Continuing Healthcare supporting the people who need it in England?* London: CCA, 2016, p.13.
2 HSO, Trust wrongly asked for clinical evidence to support claim for NHS Continuing Healthcare funding. Summary 880, March 2015. In: HSO. *Report on selected summaries of investigations by the Parliamentary and Health Service Ombudsman February and March 2015.* London: HSO, 2015.
3 HSO, Older man left frustrated and out of pocket in Continuing Healthcare assessment (CHC) claim. Summary 24, February 2014. In: HSO. *Selected summaries of investigations by the Parliamentary and Health Service Ombudsman. Volume 1, report 1 (February and March 2014).* London: HSO, 2014.
4 Continuing Care Alliance. *Continuing to care: is NHS Continuing Healthcare supporting the people who need it in England?* London: CCA, 2016, pp.4, 6.

NHS CONTINUING HEALTHCARE

To the extent that this is so, it is not what either regulations or guidance stipulate, and could form a ground of challenge to a decision as a procedural failing.

The regulations state that when a full assessment is carried out using the Decision Support Tool, it must be multi-disciplinary in nature.[1] The National Framework guidance then states that the multi-disciplinary team should usually involve professionals who are knowledgeable about the needs of the person and, if possible, have recently been involved in the person's assessment, treatment or care.[2]

The guidance indicates that it is best practice that 'where the individual concerned has, for example, a learning disability, or a brain injury, someone with specialist knowledge of this client group is involved in the assessment process'.[3]

In end of life cases, involving use of the Fast Track Pathway Tool, the regulations themselves stipulate that the Tool must be completed by an appropriate clinician responsible for the diagnosis, treatment or care of the person.[4] Thus, the clinician should be 'knowledgeable about the individual's health needs, diagnosis, treatment or care'.[5]

> **Absence of an appropriate medical clinician undermined the decision about end of life care.** A woman was diagnosed with anaplastic ganglioglioma, a very rare type of brain tumour of the central nervous system. She was denied fast track end of life provision by the NHS clinical commissioning group (CCG). This was on the basis of a prognosis given by a doctor in general medicine, who gave no reasons for it and whom the ombudsman (advised by their clinical adviser) found to lack the knowledge and expertise required. The appropriate clinician would have been the consultant oncologist. The CCG was therefore at fault.[6]
>
> **Faulty denial of eligibility; absence of diabetes nurse.** A 73-year-old care home resident had a history of Parkinson's disease and had experienced two strokes. The more recent of these had left her with right-sided weakness and dysphasia. She was an insulin-dependent diabetic, was partially sighted and had high blood pressure and abnormalities in thyroid function. The ombudsman found fault

---
1 NHS Responsibilities Regulations 2012, r.21.
2 National Framework 2018, para 121.
3 National Framework 2018, para 126.
4 NHS Responsibilities Regulations 2012, r.21(8), (13).
5 National Framework 2018, para 221.
6 LGSCO, *Essex County Council*, 2017 (16 007 609), paras 26–29.

with the decision to deny eligibility and noted that it would have been helpful to have had a specific review with a diabetes nurse contributing to the assessment process.[1]

Nurse assessor and social worker unknown to the patient and Parkinson's nurse excluded. CHC eligibility was denied to a man with Parkinson's disease, which confined him to bed, judged to have three months to live. A nurse assessor, together with a social worker the family had never met, visited, asked a few cursory questions and focused on the fact that he didn't fall over any more (even though the reason for this was his deteriorating condition), concluding that he was therefore better.

The man's daughter began gathering her own evidence, getting hold of her father's notes from the GP, district nurses and social workers; she then presented the case before a CCG panel and won. But this was only after very considerable distress caused to her and particularly to her father.[2]

---

1 PSOW, *Cardiff Health Board,* 2008 (200700482), para 50.
2 Deith, J. 'Continuing healthcare: the secret fund.' BBC Radio 4 *File on 4,* 23 November 2014. Accessed on 18 July 2019 at: www.bbc.co.uk/programmes/b04p86c4

F

Family involvement, see *Person and family involvement*

Fast Track Pathway Tool (end of life)
Alternative to use of the Checklist and Decision Support Tool (DST) to determine NHS Continuing Healthcare (CHC) is the Fast Track Pathway Tool (FTPT).[1] This is applied in end of life circumstances; regulations stipulate that if the fast track applies, then the Checklist and DST must not be used. It can be accessed online.[2]

The FTPT represents in principle a much faster process, which is necessary for obvious reasons. For patients, families and practitioners, who may struggle to obtain a timely decision and provision of services, awareness that the process is meant to be relatively simple and speedy is important.

In summary, the regulations state that the fast track applies when a registered medical doctor or registered nurse responsible for the diagnosis, treatment or care of the patient under the National Health Service Act 2006 decides (a) that the person has a primary health need arising from a rapidly deteriorating condition and (b) that the condition may be entering a terminal phase and completes the FTPT, giving reasons for their decision. The normal test in the regulations to determine a primary health need in circumstances other than end of life is expressly omitted: namely whether the care required is more than incidental or ancillary to what social services is providing, or of a nature beyond that expected of social services. See ***Incidental or ancillary or of a nature beyond social services***.

Once this has been done, the NHS clinical commissioning group (CCG) must decide that the person is eligible for CHC. If a person nearing the

---

1 NHS Responsibilities Directions, r.21(8)–(9).
2 Fast Track Pathway Tool 2018, accessed on 19 July 2019 at: www.gov.uk/government/publications/nhs-continuing-healthcare-fast-track-pathway-tool

end of their life does not qualify via the FTPT, they may still do so via the Checklist and DST.[1] A number of key points arise from these legal rules, points amplified in guidance and which could be used by patients, families and practitioners to query or challenge decisions:

- **Minimum of delay without quibble: 48 hours.** Guidance states that the intention is to identify individuals who need to access CHC quickly, with minimum delay. The completed FTPT, with clear reasons, is sufficient to establish eligibility.[2] This follows from the regulations: 'In order to comply with Standing Rules a CCG must accept and immediately action a Fast Track Pathway Tool where the Tool has been properly completed.'[3] Therefore, the decision about eligibility should usually be made within 48 hours of receipt of the completed Tool.[4]

- **Appropriate clinician's knowledge.** 'The appropriate clinician should be knowledgeable about the individual's health needs, diagnosis, treatment or care and be able to provide an assessment of why the individual meets the Fast Track criteria.' The clinician can be employed in the voluntary or independent sector with a specialist end of life role, but only if they are providing services pursuant to the National Health Service Act 2006 (i.e. on behalf of the NHS).[5]

- **Strict time limits should not be applied, and a non-restrictive approach to eligibility should be taken.** Eligibility is established by applying the words of the regulations, including 'rapidly deteriorating' and 'may be entering a terminal phase'. Thus, guidance states that the FTPT should be supported by a prognosis where available, but that 'strict time limits should not be imposed'.

    The guidance goes further by deprecating a restrictive approach to the meaning of the criteria: 'rapidly deteriorating' should not be interpreted narrowly as only meaning an anticipated specific or short time frame of life remaining; and 'may be entering a terminal phase'

---

1 NHS Responsibilities Regulations 2012, r.21(8), (9).
2 National Framework 2018, para 218.
3 National Framework 2018, para 236.
4 National Framework 2018, para 238.
5 National Framework 2018, paras 221–222.

is not intended to be restrictive to only those situations where death is imminent.'[1]

- **End of life: non-eligibility**. If a person is assessed as not being eligible under the FTPT, but is still nearing the end of their life, eligibility under the DST might still be possible since deterioration of a condition is relevant to completion of the DST.[2]

- **Decision-maker: the CCG must accept the decision of the doctor or nurse other than exceptionally**. The decision-maker in substance is the appropriate clinician, the doctor or the nurse; if they complete the FTPT as indicated in the regulations, the CCG must decide that the person is eligible for CHC. This would suggest that, other than when there are clear indications that the requirements in the regulations have not been substantially followed, the CCG has no legal room to refuse to accept the recommendations.

    Accordingly, guidance states that, 'exceptionally, there may be circumstances where CCGs receive a completed Tool which appears to show that the individual's condition is not related to the above criteria at all'.[3] In one example where the ombudsman found the CCG's refusal to accept a fast track recommendation justified, despite reference to weight loss experienced by the person, the care home, the district nursing service and the GP all agreed that the woman was generally well when the FTPT was submitted, and there was anyway no reference to a rapidly deteriorating condition.[4]

- **Restricting the occurrence and frequency of reviews**. Guidance states that once eligibility is established, reviews will be necessary to ensure that the care arrangements are adequate. Although review of eligibility might sometimes be required, this will be only in 'certain situations' as opposed to it being standard, and any such review should be carried out sensitively.

    If the eligibility decision reached through the FTPT is appropriate, guidance notes a review of eligibility is unlikely to be needed. However, were eligibility to be reviewed and consideration given to

---

1   National Framework 2018, para 227.
2   National Framework 2018, para 230.
3   National Framework 2018, para 237.
4   LGSCO, *Tameside Metropolitan Borough Council*, 2018 (17 012 483), para 21.

withdrawing funding, this should not happen without a full DST being completed by the multi-disciplinary team.[1]

Fast Track Pathway Tool: delay and other problems
Guidance makes clear that since the effect of the regulations is that the appropriate clinician is the decision-maker, it is only exceptionally and with good reason that a CCG should query a completed Tool. Otherwise it should accept it and make provision without delay. In the following case this did not happen, and the ombudsman found fault.

> **Wrongful refusal to action Fast Track Pathway Tool, followed by delay.** The patient's consultant submitted a fast-track application for continuing care funding, expecting the primary care trust (PCT) to admit her to a nursing home within 48 hours. The GP wrote a letter in support of the application. The PCT did not accept it and instead insisted in carrying out a full continuing care assessment. This took three months. During this period, she deteriorated to such an extent that social services intervened and arranged admission to a nursing home.
>
> The ombudsman found fault: the PCT had possessed enough information to accept the fast-track application, and this should have led to a nursing home admission within 48 hours. The PCT then failed to carry out the full continuing care assessment quickly.[2]

In practice, delay is of concern. In 2019, the organisation Marie Curie reported that, for 2017–2018, around 10 per cent of approved fast track applications did not result in the patient receiving a care package. Given that 67,729 people were found eligible annually for fast track CHC in England, these findings suggest more than 6700 people could have died in hospital while waiting for community care. More than a third of approved packages were never provided in 25 CCG areas, while more than 40 per cent were never provided in six areas.[3]

---

1 National Framework 2018, paras 243–244.
2 HSO, NHS failed to arrange fast-track care package. Summary 309, July 2014. In: HSO. *Selected summaries of investigations by the Parliamentary and Health Service Ombudsman July to September 2014*. London: HSO, 2015.
3 Brennan, S. 'Report: "Patients dying in hospital waiting for community care."' *Health Service Journal*, 20 March 2019.

In 2017, Marie Curie had reported that many CCGs did not keep data on fast track cases. Where Marie Curie could obtain information, this suggested wide variations in the time taken to put care in place. Just 28 per cent of CCGs were, on average, putting care in place within 48 hours of receipt of the completed Tool. Thirty-two per cent had an average wait of more than a week, with some reporting average waiting times exceeding two weeks.[1] For instance, delay and obfuscation might be experienced as follows.

> **Motor neurone disease, delay in fast track, ignoring expert opinion and death without award of CHC.**
>
> Dad had MND [motor neurone disease] and it was progressing fast. He couldn't talk at all or convey expression through his face. He couldn't move, so had to be hoisted. He was fed through a tube into his stomach, couldn't go to the toilet and his breathing was compromised. I moved Dad in with me and was caring for him while trying to work full time. It was a lot of pressure.
>
> Our district nurse was really supportive and requested a fast track NHS CHC assessment for us. She made the request just before New Year. At this time our palliative care consultant said she didn't think Dad had long to live. Despite this, the assessment didn't happen quickly, and took place in mid-February. I experienced so much worry and anxiety during this time, as I waited to find out whether he would be eligible. Though logically, I didn't know how much more could have been wrong with him in order to make him qualify.
>
> When the assessor finally came, it was clear to me she didn't know anything specific about MND. She said they should only be doing fast track assessments for someone who is end of stage and then followed that by saying, 'which he clearly is not'. Dad died two days later.[2]

In the following case, the ombudsman's criticism was pointed, as the CCG breached various rules in the regulations and the guidance, including the application of a policy about eligibility, stipulating a rigid time period in terms of how long a person was expected to live – and also restricting the setting in which eligibility was possible.

---

1 Marie Curie. *Making every moment count: the state of Fast Track Continuing Healthcare in England.* London: Marie Curie, 2017, p.8.
2 Continuing Care Alliance. *Continuing to care: is NHS Continuing Healthcare supporting the people who need it in England?* London: CCA, 2016, p.16.

> **Applying blanket timescales and blanket restrictions of setting for end of life care.** A man with dementia, advanced kidney disease and other medical conditions was admitted to hospital, where terminal kidney cancer was diagnosed. NHS staff stated that the fast track tool could only be used if the person had less than four weeks to live. The social worker said this was based on 'local guidelines on the ward regarding life expectancy'. Two consultants and two members of the discharge team at the Trust said it was the CCG's policy not to allow fast track funding unless the person's prognosis was less than four weeks.
>
> The ombudsman stated that, regardless of where the rule originated, it appeared that the professionals were applying it contrary to the National Framework guidance. This was fault. In addition, the CCG had a policy that it would not fund placements in residential (as opposed to nursing) care homes: a restriction of setting which was also contrary to the National Framework guidance.
>
> The ombudsman was not convinced by the CCG's argument that it had refused the residential care on grounds of safety, especially since the man's hospital consultant supported the placement as appropriate. The ombudsman noted that:
>
>> CCGs have responsibility for commissioning safe care, and if they believe a proposed placement will not meet a person's needs safely then they are entitled to say so. However, they should give a specific justification for this based on the individual, rather than a general restriction on a particular type of accommodation. In this case, I consider that the CCG is at fault for failing to either accommodate the family's preferred place of care or provide a proper justification for not doing so.[1]

Although a duty is placed on the CCG to act once in receipt of the completed Tool, there is no explicit duty placed on the appropriate clinician to complete it in the first place. If, for example, general practitioners, district nurses and others are not given information, or even training, by CCGs about the fast track, they may never know to use it.

Oddly, the duty in regulations on a CCG to take reasonable steps to assess people's eligibility for CHC applies only to the Checklist/DST, not to the FTPT.[2] However, the National Framework is clear that CCGs should ensure

---

1 LGSCO, *Lancashire County Council*, 2017 (16 000 404), paras 52–61.
2 NHS Responsibilities Directions, r.21(8)–(9).

that training is available to practitioners[1] – and so this could be challenged if nurses and doctors in its area are unaware of the FTPT and how to use it.

The ombudsman has found fault directly with a GP practice, because of its lack of knowledge about the fast track process.

> **Failings in GP practice; lack of understanding of CHC and the fast track.** A woman had type 2 diabetes, an auto-immune condition affecting the liver, had suffered a stroke and had kidney disease. She was admitted to hospital with low sodium levels and increased drowsiness. Following discharge home, her GP visited her on 20 January. In hindsight, he said that she met the criteria for fast track funding, but he did not consider this at the time. This resulted in the award of CHC funding being delayed. She died on 1 March.
>
> The GP practice acknowledged the GP should have discussed this with the family and made checks with social care or nursing staff about CHC funding. The GP committed to improving his understanding of CHC and the fast track process with other GPs at the practice; the ombudsman stated that this would address the systemic fault involved.[2]

Lastly, some CCGs state that three eligibility criteria must be met under the regulations: a primary health need (using the usual CHC test involving the incidental/ancillary and nature test), a rapidly deteriorating condition – and a possible terminal phase (see above).[3] However, the first of these is almost certainly wrong, since the regulations expressly exclude, from the fast track decision-making process, the incidental/ancillary and nature test for determining a primary health need.

This is because the regulations in effect state that if a person has a rapidly deteriorating condition that may be entering a terminal phase, then a primary health need will in any event be present. Otherwise, there would be no point having special rules for end of life, in the form of the fast track, if the usual test anyway had to be satisfied. Indeed, the National Framework

---

1 National Framework 2018, para 21.
2 LGSCO, *Wolverhampton City Council, The Royal Wolverhampton NHS Trust, Wolverhampton CCG, Grove Medical Centre*, 2019 (17 013 455), paras 21–33.
3 See e.g. Nottingham North and East CCG Governing Body and Others. *NHS continuing healthcare and joint packages of health and social care services commissioning policy*. Nottingham: NNECCG, 2017.

guidance refers only to the two criteria set out in the regulations, not the third criterion that is apparently being applied by some CCGs.[1]

Final decisions about CHC eligibility, see *Clinical commissioning groups*

Funded nursing care

Funded nursing care (FNC) is a type of NHS funding for people in nursing homes only and is distinct from NHS Continuing Healthcare (CHC). It replaced the Registered Nursing Care Contribution (RNCC) which was previously paid at three different rates. For patients, families and practitioners it is important to have an idea of the rules because, misapplied by NHS clinical commissioning groups (CCGs), they can result in CHC being wrongly denied. Key points about FNC include the following.

First, and in summary, it applies to people who are not eligible for CHC and are in a nursing home (either funded by the local authority or by themselves as a self-funder).

Second, the CCG must have assessed that the person requires registered nursing care and that the need can be most appropriately met in a nursing home.

Third, section 22 of the Care Act 2014 prohibits social services from providing or arranging registered nursing care, which is why the CCG is obliged to pay this amount.

Fourth, the weekly amount of FNC payable to care homes in 2019–2020 is £165.56 (except for some people who were originally on a 'higher rate' of RNCC, prior to 2007, in which case the amount is £227.77).[2] Other key points include the following:

- **Eligibility for CHC must be considered before a funded nursing care decision.** Regulations state that if it appears to a CCG that a person might have CHC needs, then it must carry out an assessment for CHC (using the Decision Support Tool (DST)), before an assessment for funded nursing care.[3] Given that most people in nursing homes will have significant needs, it is arguable that this legal

---

1 National Framework 2018, paras 224–235.
2 NHS Responsibilities Regulations 2012, r.20.
3 NHS Responsibilities Regulations 2012, r.21(2), (3).

rule is tantamount to saying that a significant number of people in nursing homes will require assessment using the Checklist if not the DST – before funded nursing care is considered.

Guidance reinforces this order of assessment, stating that 'eligibility for NHS Continuing Healthcare must be considered, and a decision made and recorded (either at the Checklist or DST stage), prior to any decision on eligibility for NHS-funded Nursing Care'.[1] Despite this clear rule, it is by no means clear how far, in practice, CCGs follow it. Not to do so is clearly unlawful, on the face of regulations, but the rule was in any case identified as such by the courts even before the regulations were in place.[2]

- **Duty to assess for funded nursing care**. The CCG must carry out an assessment where it appears to it that a person (for whom it has responsibility) (a) is resident in relevant premises (a nursing home) or may need to become resident in such premises; and (b) may be in need of nursing care. The duty does not arise if the person has been assessed as eligible for CHC.[3]

- **Duration of eligibility for funded nursing care**. Guidance states that people are entitled to continue to receive FNC until they are reviewed as no longer needing it, they no longer live in a nursing home, they become eligible for CHC or they die.[4] (The last is a somewhat redundant point to make.)

- **Requirement of fair and transparent contracts to prevent care homes pocketing, wrongly, the FNC payment**. Guidance states that contracts between individuals and care homes, or local authorities and care homes, should be fair and transparent.[5] Amongst other things, this is to avoid care homes benefiting from the FNC, rather than the person themselves (see below).

- **Registered nursing care: what it is**. Section 22 of the Care Act 2014 prohibits local authorities from providing or arranging registered nursing care. It is defined in the Act as 'provision by a registered nurse of a service involving (a) the provision of care, or (b) the planning,

---

1 National Framework 2018, para 250.
2 *R(Grogan) v Bexley NHS Care Trust* [2006] EWHC 44 (Admin).
3 NHS Responsibilities Regulations 2012, r.28.
4 National Framework 2018, para 253.
5 National Framework 2018, para 257.

supervision or delegation of the provision of care, other than a service which, having regard to its nature and the circumstances in which it is provided, does not need to be provided by a registered nurse'.

- **Review of funded nursing care and whether a new Checklist is required.** Guidance states that a Checklist will normally be required on review of FNC, but not always, if there has been no material change.[1]

One not uncommon practice by care homes, particularly though not only in the case of self-funding residents, is to increase the weekly fee once FNC is awarded, rather than to reduce it by the amount of the FNC payment. This means that the resident does not benefit from the weekly payment by the NHS; the ombudsman has repeatedly stated that care home contracts must be clear from the outset about how the fee relates to any FNC payments.

For example, the ombudsman may find fault if the contract is silent altogether about FNC,[2] or if the contract is clear about the care home fee reducing by the amount of FNC, but then the care home in practice does the opposite, effectively breaching the contract.[3]

Funded nursing care: relationship to NHS Continuing Healthcare

The legal requirement that CHC consideration take place before the decision about FNC is not a mere technicality, as the courts have pointed out,[4] not least because a need for registered nursing alone, depending on that level of need, could in some cases still mean that the person is eligible for CHC, as the courts put it about the RNCC (predecessor of FNC).

> **Registered nursing care need equating to CHC eligibility, not FNC.**
>
> A proper application of *Coughlan* and the Primary Health Need Approach would mean that if any of the RNCC bands describe a degree and nature of nursing care equivalent to that needed by Miss Coughlan a person who

---

1 National Framework 2018, paras 258–260.
2 LGSCO, *Acer Healthcare Operations Limited*, 2018 (18 003 826), para 30. Also: LGSCO, *Hayes Cottage Nursing Home Ltd*, 2017 (16 017 793), para 25. Also: LGSCO, *Morris & Co*, 2018 (17 011 162), para 23.
3 LGSCO, *Springfield Healthcare (Seacroft Green) Limited*, 2018 (17 009 182), para 16.
4 *R(Grogan) v Bexley NHS Care Trust* [2006] EWHC 44 (Admin).

> had those needs should...be found to be eligible for Continuing NHS Health Care.[1]

Therefore, on registered nursing needs alone, any such needs which approximated to those in the *Coughlan* case would, by definition, be more than incidental or ancillary and of a nature beyond that social services remit, meaning that the person would have a primary health need. See ***Incidental or ancillary or of a nature beyond social services***.

Funded nursing care: consideration of only after CHC consideration

The risk is that if assessments for CHC and FNC are done in the wrong order, then significant numbers of people in nursing homes could be denied CHC eligibility, since if the FNC decision is made first, then a CHC decision, to consider the level of the nursing (and health care needs), may never be taken.

Even if done in the right order, it may be that the CHC consideration is wrongly influenced by assessors who are aware of the FNC test and are perhaps steered towards denial of CHC by that awareness – even when the degree of the person's needs (even if being met through registered nursing care in a nursing home) in law should be regarded as a primary health need.[2]

Alternatively, as the ombudsman has pointed out, NHS bodies might wrongly view continuing care as merely at the upper end of what is covered by funded nursing care, and thus fail to consider the totality of the person's needs by focusing wrongly on their nursing needs only.[3]

In the following legal case, the NHS failed to follow the rules by completing the RNCC (now FNC) assessment first, and only then completing a Checklist entirely negatively with no evidence or reasoning supplied, even though the negative scoring on the Checklist contradicted some of the points made in the nursing assessment.

> **Unlawfully completing the FNC assessment first, before the NHS Continuing Healthcare decision.** The completed RNCC assessment document simply identified that the woman required a medium level of nursing care, with a one-sentence explanation of why that was. There was also a Checklist document

---

1   *R(Grogan) v Bexley NHS Care Trust* [2006] EWHC 44 (Admin), para 51.
2   For this issue, albeit in relation to previous rules about registered nursing care, see: *R(Grogan) v Bexley NHS Care Trust* [2006] EWHC 44 (Admin), paras 61, 91.
3   Health Service Ombudsman. *Annual report 2003–4*. London: TSO, 2004, para 22.

headed 'West Yorkshire Continuing Care', described as a screening tool. There was a statement printed on the front stating that it 'must always be used before undertaking an RNCC determination'.

However, first, the Checklist was completed by a nurse ringing the word 'No' in relation to every aspect of care but without any comment under any of the headings despite the fact that the document had a section for comments under each heading. Second, some of the responses on this document appeared to conflict with observations on the 'Nursing Needs Assessment Tool'. Third, the Checklist was signed on a date later than the RNCC determination had been signed. The judge held that this approach was irrational and unreasonable.[1]

---

[1] *R(Dennison) v Bradford Districts Clinical Commissioning Group* [2014] EWHC 2552 (Admin), paras 12, 13, 17.

G

Gap between health and social care

The divide between health and social care – that is, between the National Health Service Act 2006 and the Care Act 2014 – means that in respect of NHS Continuing Healthcare (CHC) needs, a legal gap is (or at least was previously) possible. This meant that a person could in principle have needs which would not be eligible for CHC under the National Health Service Act 2006 but would be beyond the legal remit and powers of local authorities under the Care Act. This possibility was recognised in the *Grogan* case.[1]

Notwithstanding this risk, the court in that case noted that the Department of Health's policy was that there should in practice be no gap, which meant that the determination of CHC should not just depend on the 'primary health need' test, but also on the limits of what social services lawfully could provide.[2] This approach was enshrined in 2012 regulations, the effect of which would appear to have either removed, or all but removed, the gap.

The NHS regulations now state clearly that if a person's health or nursing needs in their totality are more than incidental or ancillary to the provision of social services – or of a nature that is beyond what social services is expected to provide – then the CCG must decide the person has a primary health need.[3] Similarly, section 22 of the Care Act prohibits social services from providing services that fall into either of these categories.

This approach, of delineating limits to social services provision, and basing a CHC decision on what is above those limits, is in any case supported by earlier legal case law: 'the elements of degree [of need] should be considered against the limit of the lawful provision of social services together with incidental or ancillary nursing by the local authority rather than simply by reference to "primary health need"'.[4]

---

1   *R(Grogan) v Bexley NHS Care Trust* [2006] EWHC 44 (Admin), paras 38, 47.
2   *R(Grogan) v Bexley NHS Care Trust* [2006] EWHC 44 (Admin), para 47.
3   NHS Responsibilities Regulations 2012, r.21(7).
4   *R(Grogan) v Bexley NHS Care Trust* [2006] EWHC 44 (Admin), para 47.

In other words, the effect of the NHS regulations is to place a greater burden on the NHS to lower the primary health need test for CHC eligibility in order to descend to social services limits, thus avoiding the gap. Were there any doubt, the National Framework confirms the effect of the regulations, stating that *non-eligibility* for CHC is possible where what is required could lawfully be provided by social services. It also notes, in this respect, that whilst there is an upper legal limit to what social services can provide, there is no lower limit on what the NHS can provide – meaning that the NHS eligibility boundary can come down in a way in which the social services boundary cannot rise.[1]

Grogan case

The *Grogan* legal case remains significant and is referenced throughout this book. Albeit dating from 2006, it analysed carefully and painstakingly the implications of the legal rules on which NHS Continuing Healthcare (CHC) rests.

Amongst other things, it confirmed that CHC decisions must evidence how key legal questions have been decided, including the primary health need decision, and not be obscured by local criteria and policies. Consideration of CHC must take place before consideration of funded nursing care (FNC; then referred to as the Registered Nursing Care Component). And nursing needs on a par with or above those in the *Coughlan* case would mean that a primary health need would exist and FNC would not only be unlawful but would not, in effect, even be considered (since the CHC decision must come first).[2]

Guidance

The body of NHS Continuing Healthcare (CHC) rules is made up of primary legislation in the form of Acts of Parliament, of regulations and of guidance. By definition, guidance is not law, but if it is designated as 'statutory guidance' – basically guidance which is referred to in some way in legislation – then it carries significant legal clout. To the extent that if it is not followed without sound reason when it states what 'must' be done, the NHS or social services, for example, may be held to be in breach of their

---

1 National Framework 2018, paras 57–59.
2 *R(Grogan) v Bexley NHS Care Trust* [2006] EWHC 44 (Admin).

legal duty.[1] Even non-statutory guidance, which is not so strong, must still be had regard to.[2]

CCGs and social services would normally be well served in respecting this approach, notwithstanding the *Gossip* case about CHC. In this seemingly contentious case, the judge, though stating that the National Framework must not be ignored, nonetheless found that the CCG had considerable discretion to depart from it – without giving detailed reasons or even, to an extent, referring at all to the elements of the guidance from which it had chosen to diverge.[3] (Reflecting on this case, it is hard to see how a CCG can evidence that it has not ignored guidance, if it has not referred to it at all when coming to its decision.)

All the main guidance can be characterised as a form of statutory guidance. As far as NHS clinical commissioning groups are concerned, regulations mandate the use – in CHC assessment and decision-making, in dispute resolution and in responding to independent review panel recommendations – of, variously, the National Framework, the Checklist, the Decision Support Tool and the Fast Track Pathway Tool.

As far as local authorities are concerned, regulations state that they must have regard to the National Framework when referring people to the NHS who might have CHC needs,[4] as well as when resolving disputes and – by implication – when cooperating in terms of multi-disciplinary assessment to determine CHC eligibility.[5]

---

1 *R(Rixon) v Islington London Borough Council* [1997] E.L.R. 66, pp.2–3.
2 *R(Rixon) v Islington London Borough Council* [1997] E.L.R. 66, pp.6, 11.
3 *R(Gossip) v NHS Surrey Downs Clinical Commissioning Group* [2019] EWHC 3411 (Admin), see e.g. 94, 97.
4 Care and Support (Assessment) Regulations 2014, r.7.
5 Care and Support (Provision of Health Services) Regulations 2014, rr.3, 4.

H

Health care needs

Eligibility for NHS Continuing Healthcare is premised legally on a person being assessed as having a primary health need. One obvious question therefore is just what the definition of a health care need is. There is none in legislation; so, guidance attempts, well, to guide:

- **No definition of health care need**.

    Whilst there is not a legal definition of a healthcare need (in the context of NHS Continuing Healthcare), in general terms it can be said that such a need is one related to the treatment, control or prevention of a disease, illness, injury or disability, and the care or aftercare of a person with these needs (whether or not the tasks involved have to be carried out by a health professional).[1]

This attempt at some sort of a definition is informative to a degree, since it includes care and aftercare, meaning that health care is not confined just to treatment. To try to make things clearer, the guidance then attempts to say what health care is not, by outlining social care in contrast. Yet this, too, is legally undefined. The best the guidance can do is to point to legal 'eligibility criteria' in the Care Act 2014 and to say that social care needs relate to those criteria. It states:

- **Social care under the Care Act 2014, distinct from health care**.

    These criteria set out that an individual has eligible needs under the Care Act 2014 where these needs arise from (or relate to) a physical or mental impairment or illness which results in them being unable to achieve two or more of the following outcomes which is, or is likely to have, a significant impact on their wellbeing:

    - managing and maintaining nutrition;
    - maintaining personal hygiene;

---

1   National Framework 2018, para 50.

- managing toilet needs;
- being appropriately clothed;
- being able to make use of the home safely;
- maintaining a habitable home environment;
- developing and maintaining family or other personal relationships;
- accessing and engaging in work, training, education or volunteering;
- making use of necessary facilities or services in the local community, including public transport and recreational facilities or services; and
- carrying out any caring responsibilities the adult has for a child.[1]

At the least the following can be extrapolated in order to try to distinguish health care from social care.

First, none of the above is suggestive of 'treatment' for a health condition; treatment therefore remains an NHS responsibility.

Second, in terms of care required in relation to any of those outcomes, it cannot include registered nursing care because of the separate rule in section 22 of the Care Act that local authorities are not permitted to provide or arrange registered nursing care.

Third, a range of care interventions would in any case seem not to fall under those outcomes, and so would or could not be part of a duty on social services to meet a person's needs. For example, tracheostomy care, pressure care (tissue viability), pain management, catheter care, bowel evacuation, management of epilepsy, management of percutaneous endoscopic gastrostomy for nutrition and medication, assistance with medication. However, these examples are typically what social services increasingly – in cases which are not eligible for NHS Continuing Healthcare – are being asked to commission by way of social care, and which there may be a legal objection to.

---

1   National Framework 2018, paras 51–52.

Fourth, social services, in any case, only have a duty to meet needs by providing care and support if a person has eligible needs; and part of the eligibility test is that the person is unable to achieve *two* or more of the above outcomes.

Fifth, social services are permitted under the Care Act to meet need, even if there is no eligibility, but this is a power only, not a duty. In other words, were a health-related task not to fall within the eligibility outcomes, there would in any case be a discretion only, but not a duty, to provide.

Health Service Ombudsman

Under the Health Service Commissioners Act 1993, the Health Service Ombudsman (HSO) investigates complaints against the NHS, including those relating to NHS Continuing Healthcare (CHC). Normally the complainant must have gone through the NHS body's own complaints procedure first – or, in the case of many CHC disputes, through the local clinical commissioning group's (CCG) CHC dispute process. See ***Disputes between a person and the NHS***.

The HSO has played a key role in highlighting CHC issues. For example, the *Leeds* report in 1994, a trenchant overview report in 2003 criticising the Department of Health, and the *Pointon* case in 2005 concerning CHC in people's own homes.[1]

The HSO is not a court of law and recommendations are not binding, but NHS bodies normally comply with recommendations. In respect of CHC, the HSO is important because he or she represents usually an easier route of challenge than the law courts.

In addition, the National Framework guidance states that CCGs must take account of ombudsman cases when they make decisions about CHC. See ***Indicative cases***.

The ombudsman's remit extends to complaints about NHS-funded health care services provided in a private hospital and to complaints about any NHS-funded health care services for privately funded patients in an NHS hospital. Key points include:

- **Maladministration, hardship, injustice, failure in service**. The ombudsman looks to see whether hardship or injustice has resulted

---

1 *Leeds Health Authority* (E.62/93–94). In: Health Service Commissioner. *Failure to provide long term NHS care for brain damaged patient*. London: HMSO, 1994. And: Health Service Ombudsman. *NHS funding for long term care*. London: TSO, 2003. And: *Cambridgeshire Health Authority* (E.22/02–03). In: Health Service Ombudsman. HC 704. *Selected investigations completed October 2003–March 2004*. London: TSO, 2004 (*Pointon* case).

from maladministration, from failure in a service that has been provided or from failure to provide a service which it was a function of the NHS body concerned to provide.[1]

- **Clinical judgements and merits of decisions.** The HSO can also question, directly, clinical judgements in a way in which the local government ombudsman cannot question professional judgements in the social care context. This is because whilst both ombudsmen are precluded legally from questioning the 'merits' of a decision, nonetheless in the case of the HSO, this prohibition is disapplied in the case of clinical judgement.[2] This allows the HSO to investigate not just the decision-making process underpinning a CHC decision, but also the clinical judgements relied on, as occurred, for example, in the *Pointon* and *Wigan* cases.[3]

- **Joint investigations by the HSO and local government ombudsman.** With increased joint working and integration within health and social care, the HSO can investigate jointly with the local ombudsman.[4] In the case of CHC disputes, where fault can lie not just with the NHS but also social services, people may be well advised in some circumstances to make a complaint against both the CCG and the local social services authority. Otherwise, one or other of the ombudsmen may not be able to look at all of the issues disputed.[5] For example, complaining to the local government ombudsman only in respect of the failure of NHS hospital staff to complete a Checklist would be a misdirected complaint.[6]

Health services generally

Guidance makes the point that if a person is receiving NHS Continuing Healthcare (CHC), they continue to be entitled to 'access to the full range of primary, community, secondary and other health services',[7] as indeed would a person not eligible for CHC, but with various health needs.

---

1 Health Service Commissioners Act 1993, s.3(1).
2 Health Service Commissioners Act 1993, s.3(4), (6).
3 Health Service Ombudsman. HC 704. *Selected investigations completed October 2003–March 2004.* London: TSO, 2004 (*Pointon* case). And: *Wigan and Bolton Health Authority* (E.420/00–01). In: Health Service Ombudsman. *NHS funding for long term care.* London: TSO, 2003.
4 Health Service Commissioners Act 1993, s.18ZA.
5 LGSCO, *Kent County Council*, 2018 (18 000 211), para 17.
6 LGSCO, *Solihull Metropolitan Borough Council*, 2018 (17 007 577), para 34.
7 National Framework 2018, para 304.

Home adaptations

Home adaptations are most often provided for disabled or ill people through the Care Act 2014 (usually, but not only, minor adaptations) and the Housing Grants, Construction and Regeneration Act 1996 (usually more major adaptations in terms of 'works' to the dwelling).

The latter Act sets out criteria for disabled facilities grants (DFGs), payable by local housing authorities for works of adaptation to meet the disabled occupant's needs. However, the NHS, too, has legal powers to adapt people's homes and always has had; as evidenced, for instance, by long-standing guidance on the provision by the NHS of adaptations for people requiring renal dialysis in their own homes.[1]

In the case of NHS Continuing Healthcare (CHC), however, NHS clinical commissioning groups (CCGs) are legally obliged to meet not just people's health care but also their social care needs, and thus may incur added responsibility for adaptations. Minor adaptations, normally provided under the Care Act, would become instead the responsibility of the CCG, as guidance makes clear.[2]

In the case of a need for major adaptations, the guidance clarifies that an application should, as normal, be considered for a DFG. Were this, however, not available or fail to cover the full cost of the adaptation assessed as needed, CCGs should consider helping, were this the most cost-effective option for meeting a person's CHC needs.

- **CCG responsibility for assisting with major home adaptations.**

    The CCG retains responsibility for deciding with the individual how their needs will be met, including in situations where property adaptation is assessed as an appropriate option. DFGs are means tested and the individual might not be entitled to a grant or the grant might not cover the full cost of the adaptation. CCGs are reminded that in such circumstances they must give consideration to the option of funding the adaptation if this is a cost-effective solution.[3]

---

1 HSG(93)48. Department of Health. *Home dialysis patients: costs of metered water for home dialysis.* London: DH, 1993. And: HSC(IS)11. Department of Health and Social Security. *Services for chronic renal failure.* London: DHSS, 1974.
2 National Framework Practice Guidance 2018, para 56.1.
3 National Framework Practice Guidance 2018, para 56.4.

Hospices

A hospice is one of the settings in which a person might be eligible for NHS Continuing Healthcare status and funding.[1]

Hospital discharge

Hospital discharge rules, in relation to NHS Continuing Healthcare (CHC), are contained in both legislation and guidance. For patients, families and practitioners, knowledge of these rules can be important since at stake are compliance with legal duties, patient welfare and finance, and local authority and NHS clinical commissioning group (CCG) budgets.

One key legal rule about hospital discharge, deriving from the Care Act 2014, is that if a person is occupying an acute NHS hospital bed, the NHS cannot request that social services assess (under the Care Act) and arrange discharge, unless the NHS has first considered CHC eligibility.

This is because the assessment notice to be served by the hospital on social services must contain a statement that the NHS body has considered whether or not to provide the patient with CHC, and the result of that consideration. (Acute care is defined, so as to exclude mental health acute care.)[2] This duty is referred to in other, CHC-focused regulations, as well as a set of legally binding directions on hospital discharge.[3]

For hospital patients being discharged, the CCG remains the overall decision-maker. However, it is the NHS Trust that is responsible for applying the Checklist and the Decision Support Tool (DST) before making a recommendation to the CCG. Likewise, it must make a recommendation to the CCG if an appropriate clinician has completed the Fast Track Pathway Tool (end of life).[4]

In the following two cases, the ombudsman found fault over a failure to consider CHC eligibility.

---

1 National Framework 2018, para 63.
2 Care Act 2014, schedule 3. And: Care and Support (Discharge of Hospital Patients) Regulations 2014, r.3(1).
3 NHS Responsibilities Regulations 2012, r.21(3). And: Delayed Discharges (Continuing Care) Directions 2013, para 2 (as amended).
4 Delayed Discharges (Continuing Care) Directions 2013, para 2 (as amended).

HOSPITAL DISCHARGE

> **No Checklist before discharge and handing over to social services.** An NHS hospital told social services to discharge a person without having done a Checklist; when asked by the local authority about this, the NHS member of staff stated, without semblance of evidence and reasoning, that as far as he was concerned, he would not meet the criteria for health care funding. The ombudsman found fault.[1]
>
> **Assumptions made, needs not considered, Checklist not completed by NHS.** An NHS hospital referred a person to social services for discharge but had not considered first his eligibility for CHC. It said it assumed this had been considered previously in the community. But this did not correspond with the evidence, which was that a nurse had advised the family to seek a CHC assessment.
>
> In any case, even had eligibility been considered previously, the hospital should have considered whether his overall needs had changed since admission, and whether that might lead to a different decision about eligibility. There was evidence that he had spoken to a doctor about CHC after entering hospital and the doctor planned to speak to colleagues about it. The failure to consider CHC properly was fault on the part of the NHS.[2]

Hospital discharge: consideration of CHC after discharge

Guidance now states that, 'in the majority of cases, it is preferable for eligibility for NHS Continuing Healthcare to be considered after discharge from hospital when the person's ongoing needs should be clearer'.[3]

This means, in such cases, that the NHS cannot serve the assessment notice on social services and that the legal transfer, as it were, from the National Health Service Act 2006 to the Care Act 2014 cannot take place. The consequence, as guidance explains, is that interim services, following hospital discharge, should be arranged and funded by the NHS until the CHC consideration and decision takes place.

The guidance spells out the implications of this legal situation and the various options. Because of the complications, uncertainties and haste that tend to accompany hospital discharge, it is worth quoting in full the relevant paragraphs from the guidance, for the avoidance of doubt about the implications.[4]

---

1 LGSCO, *Devon County Council*, 2018 (16 010 515), paras 53–54.
2 LGSCO, *Kent County Council*, 2018 (17 013 200), paras 52–55.
3 National Framework 2018, para 109.
4 National Framework 2018, para 114.

- **Importance of NHS-provided interim care following discharge**.

    In order to ensure that unnecessary stays on acute wards are avoided, there should be consideration of whether the provision of further NHS-funded services is appropriate. This might include therapy and/or rehabilitation, if that could make a difference to the potential of the individual in the following few weeks or months. It might also include intermediate care or an interim package of support, preferably in an individual's own home.

    In such situations, assessment of eligibility for NHS Continuing Healthcare, if still required, should be undertaken when an accurate assessment of ongoing needs can be made. The interim services should continue until it has been decided whether or not the individual has a need for NHS Continuing Healthcare. There must be no gap in the provision of appropriate support to meet the individual's needs.

- **Checklist deferred until after discharge: provision of interim NHS services on discharge**.

    Rather than completing a Checklist in hospital a decision is made to provide interim NHS-funded services to support the individual after discharge. In such a case, before the interim NHS-funded services come to an end, screening, if required, for NHS Continuing Healthcare should take place through use of the Checklist and, where appropriate, the full MDT [multi-disciplinary team] process using the DST (i.e. an assessment of eligibility).

- **Negative Checklist completed in hospital: local authority takes responsibility for services after discharge**.

    A 'negative' Checklist is completed in an acute hospital (i.e. the person does not have a need for NHS Continuing Healthcare) in which case, where appropriate, an Assessment Notice may be issued to the local authority.

- **Positive Checklist completed in hospital, provision of interim NHS services on discharge**.

    A 'positive' Checklist is completed in an acute hospital and interim NHS-funded services are put in place to support the individual after discharge until it is either determined that they no longer require a full assessment (because a further Checklist has been completed which is now negative) or a full assessment of eligibility for NHS Continuing Healthcare is completed.

- **Checklist and DST completed in hospital: dependent on outcome, either CHC or local authority responsible on discharge.**

    A 'positive' Checklist is completed in acute hospital and (exceptionally and for clear reasons) a full assessment of eligibility for NHS Continuing Healthcare takes place before discharge. In a small number of circumstances, it may be decided to go directly to a full assessment within the acute hospital, without the need for a Checklist. If the full assessment does not result in eligibility for NHS Continuing Healthcare then, where appropriate, an Assessment Notice may be issued to the local authority.

- **Pre-existing care package reinstated following discharge but pending CHC consideration: rules and backdating of funding where necessary.**

    Where the individual has an existing package or placement which all relevant parties agree can still safely and appropriately meet their needs without any changes, then they should be discharged back to this placement and/or package under existing funding arrangements.

    In such circumstances any screening for NHS Continuing Healthcare, if required, should take place within six weeks of the individual returning to the place from which they were admitted to hospital. If this screening results in a full assessment of eligibility and the individual is found eligible for NHS Continuing Healthcare through this particular assessment, then re-imbursement will apply back to the date of discharge.[1]

The guidance adds that there will be some circumstances in which, in or out of hospital, even a Checklist might not be necessary before serving the assessment notice since it might be 'clear to the professionals involved that there is no need for NHS Continuing Healthcare'. There is evidence of some hospitals using an alternative form of screening tool within the hospital to evade consideration of CHC using the Checklist and DST and going

---

1   National Framework 2018, para 112.

beyond the above circumstances set out in the guidance. Since regulations state that the only screening tool that can be used is the Checklist, this risks unlawfulness. See ***Checklist***.

More generally, it is unclear to what extent local NHS 'discharge to assess' policies are compliant with the law and guidance, as described immediately above. For instance, in some areas, use of alternative screening tools (rather than the Checklist), the provision of 'interim funded nursing care', the provision of 'urgent nursing funded payments' (UNFPs) and the restriction of fully funded interim NHS services to nursing home placements may all be questionable.

I

Incidental or ancillary or of a nature beyond social services

The terms 'incidental or ancillary', and 'nature', derive originally from legal case law, the *Coughlan* case. They are the key legal questions, which ultimately an NHS clinical commissioning group (CCG) must answer before it decides about NHS Continuing Healthcare (CHC).

For patients, families and practitioners, therefore, how these two questions are referred to and answered is particularly important, especially because the *Coughlan* case, from which they stem, sets a relatively *low* threshold for CHC eligibility.

The terms are now embedded in NHS regulations and in the Care Act 2014 as well. They form a dual test. 'Incidental or ancillary' refers to the *quantity* of care a person needs and is directly relevant to deciding whether a person has CHC needs or not. The word 'nature' refers to the *quality* of care required.[1] Another way of putting this is to consider the scale and type of care required.[2]

The NHS regulations (in relation to nursing home placements) state that in deciding whether a person has a primary health need and so has CHC needs, the CCG must consider whether nursing or other health services required are, as a whole, more than incidental or ancillary to that placement – or, in any case and in any setting, whether the care required is of a nature beyond which social services is expected to provide. If so, the CCG must decide the person has a primary health need and is eligible for CHC:

- **Health or nursing services more than incidental or ancillary or of a nature beyond that which social services can provide**.

    In deciding whether a person has a primary health need in accordance with paragraph (5)(b), a relevant body must consider whether the nursing or other health services required by that person are:

---

1 *R(Coughlan) v North and East Devon Health Authority* [2001] Q.B. 213, para 118.
2 *R(T) v London Borough of Haringey* [2005] EWHC 2235 (Admin), para 62.

a. where that person is, or is to be, accommodated in relevant premises, more than incidental or ancillary to the provision of accommodation which a social services authority is, or would be but for a person's means, under a duty to provide; or

b. of a nature beyond which a social services authority whose primary responsibility is to provide social services could be expected to provide, and, if it decides that the nursing or other health services required do, when considered in their totality, fall within sub-paragraph (a) or (b), it must decide that that person has a primary health need.[1]

Guidance states that the incidental/ancillary test should be applied not just in the context of care homes, but also people's own homes, since the related Care Act rule does so.[2] It presumably makes this point because although the nature test in these regulations is not restricted to placements in accommodation, the incidental or ancillary test is.

Mirroring these NHS regulations which apply to CCGs is the Care Act 2014, which applies to local social services authorities. It prohibits social services from meeting needs in any setting by arranging services which the NHS is required to provide – unless those services are merely incidental or ancillary to what is being provided under the Care Act *and* are of a nature which social services could be expected to provide.

- **Merely incidental or ancillary and of a nature that social services can provide.**

    A local authority may not meet needs under sections 18 to 20 by providing or arranging for the provision of a service or facility that is required to be provided under the National Health Service Act 2006 unless (a) doing so would be merely incidental or ancillary to doing something else to meet needs under those sections, and (b) the service or facility in question would be of a nature that the local authority could be expected to provide.[3]

The discrepancy just referred to between the NHS regulations and the Care Act, relating to the question of setting and the application of the incidental/ancillary test, is not the only discrepancy. The Care Act refers to 'merely' incidental or ancillary, echoing the *Coughlan* case, which also included the

---

1 NHS Responsibilities Regulations 2012, r.21(7).
2 National Framework 2018, para 59.
3 Care Act 2014, s.22.

word 'merely'.[1] The word 'merely' would therefore simply seem to add to the meaning of 'incidental or ancillary', in the sense of the health or nursing care required being clearly no more than peripheral, minor, marginal.

Incidental or ancillary or of a nature beyond social services: application of these terms

From the above rule, local authorities are able to provide other nursing care outside of the definition of registered nursing care. See **Care Act 2014**.

And, other than that, they are able to provide any other health or nursing service not significant in quantity and not of a nature which is beyond that expected of social services.

First, in terms of 'incidental or ancillary'. Synonyms for 'incidental' could include 'minor', 'peripheral', 'in the background', 'by-the-way', 'inessential' or 'marginal'; for 'ancillary', they could include 'subordinate' or 'supplementary'. Even so, deciding this may not prove easy. The ombudsman avoided answering whether helping a person receiving CHC to manage his money and property was incidental or ancillary, and so could have been carried out by the local authority. Instead, the ombudsman criticised both the local authority and the CCG for not working together better to ensure his needs were met.[2]

On the other hand, for example, the nursing that an elderly lady with dementia required in a care home was held to be merely incidental or ancillary because it was distinguishable from the nursing required in the *Coughlan* case, and therefore did not amount to CHC eligibility. It was a case before the rules changed which barred a local authority from providing registered nursing care; so today the finding that the nursing services were merely incidental or ancillary would have meant either the NHS paying for the funded nursing care if it was registered nursing care, or the local authority paying if it was not.

> **Nursing services incidental only to the provision of care home accommodation: no eligibility for NHS Continuing Healthcare.** A woman aged 89 had been an independent lady, living alone in her own home. She was admitted to hospital with a broken hip, and in consequence of that admission was diagnosed as suffering from dementia and frontal lobe syndrome. Having made a medical

---

1   *R(Coughlan) v North and East Devon Health Authority* [2001] Q.B. 213, para 118.
2   LGSCO, *Derby City Council*, 2018 (17 015 873), paras 38–40.

> recovery from her physical injury, she was transferred to a mental health residential home caring for patients with mental health needs.
>
> It was argued on her behalf that she should be entitled to CHC. This was on the basis that what she needed was not accommodation to which nursing services were incidental, but nursing services themselves, in the same way as, or by analogy with, psychiatric nursing services which a patient would receive if being treated under the Mental Health Act 1983.
>
> The primary care trust concluded that her needs were for general nursing and that she did not require the therapeutic intervention of registered nursing staff or psychiatric care. The court would not interfere with this decision based on the evidence, held that it was distinguishable from the *Coughlan* case and that 'the care required would appear to fit the criterion of being merely incidental or ancillary to the provision of accommodation'. Therefore, the woman did not fall within the CHC category and would be liable to pay the local authority for her care.[1]

Second, in terms of nature, tracheostomy care has, for example, been held by the courts to be beyond the scope of social services, by its very nature. It was:

> care designed to deal with the continuing medical consequences of an operation, which if not met will give rise to urgent or immediate medical needs: tube replacement and unblocking, to avoid very significant risks of a life-threatening nature. The advice on management is provided by a hospital. The training is provided by the medically qualified. (The mother could provide the care but needed respite by way of somebody else managing the tracheostomy.)[2]

The word 'expected' (of social services under the Care Act) in relation to the nature test is not explained or elaborated upon and, considered in isolation, gives rise to some uncertainty. It runs the risk of circularity. And it does not seem objective; for instance, who is doing the expecting and when? For instance, NHS district nurses once upon a time were largely responsible for bathing services in people's own homes; this task has largely migrated to social care in the last 40 years.[3]

---

1 *Brewins v Canterbury and Coastal Primary Care Trust* [2003] EWHC 3354 (Admin).
2 *R(T) v London Borough of Haringey* [2005] EWHC 2235 (Admin), paras 61, 62, 70.
3 See e.g. Twigg, J. 'Deconstructing the "social bath": help with bathing at home for older and disabled people.' *Journal of Social Policy* 26, 2, 1997, 211–223.

The *Coughlan* case in which the word originates provides no further explanation; nor does the National Framework guidance. That said, this legal case is as good a source as any for giving meaning to the words 'incidental', 'ancillary' and 'nature', simply by considering the description of Pamela Coughlan's needs in the law report. The Court of Appeal concluded that her needs were of a 'wholly different category' to anything within the remit of social services.[1] And the courts subsequently held that other people with equivalent needs would be eligible for CHC since they too would be beyond the legal remit of social services.[2]

Independent review panels

Guidance states that disagreements between a person and an NHS clinical commissioning group (CCG) should be resolved, if possible, informally. See ***Disputes between a person and the NHS.***

However, if resolution is not achieved, both regulations and guidance set out a procedure for review of the decision by means of an independent review panel (IRP) appointed by NHS England. The key rules in the regulations are as follows:

- **Request by individual**. It is for the individual subject to their decision, or somebody acting on their behalf, to make a request to NHS England for an IRP to be convened.

- **Procedure followed using the Decision Support Tool (DST) or decision made about primary health need**. The review must be about the procedure followed by the CCG in assessing (using the DST) or about the primary health need decision made by the CCG.

- **Local resolution procedure**. The local resolution procedure must have been used first, unless NHS England is satisfied that this would cause undue delay.

- **Panel**. NHS England may appoint a review panel consisting of a chair, a CCG representative (not from the CCG involved), and a local authority representative (not from the local authority involved).

---

1 *R(Coughlan) v North and East Devon Health Authority* [2001] Q.B. 213, Court of Appeal, paras 31, 118.
2 *R(Grogan) v Bexley NHS Care Trust* [2006] EWHC 44 (Admin), para 51.

- **Procedure and operation of the panel.** These are to be determined by the Chair, having regard to the National Framework guidance.

- **Notice of decision.** NHS England must, as soon as reasonably practicable, give notice in writing of the review decision and the reasons for it to the person and to the CCG.

- **CCG implementation of review decision.** The CCG must implement the review panel's decision as soon as reasonably practicable, unless there are exceptional reasons not to do so. In deciding the latter, it must have regard to the National Framework guidance.[1]

A number of points can be made.

First, the regulations state that the CCG must accept the IRP's recommendations other than exceptionally.

Second, the convening of an IRP by NHS England is a power, a discretion, not a duty. However, guidance states that it expects refusal to 'be confined to those cases where the individual falls well outside the eligibility criteria, as set out in the standing rules (the relevant NHS regulations), or where the case is very clearly not appropriate for the independent review panel to consider'.[2] On this basis in the following case, the ombudsman found fault.

> **Improperly not convening a review panel.** In respect of the discretion to convene a panel not being exercised, the Health Service Ombudsman referred to the guidance at the time (which read the same as the current guidance) which stated that the decision not to convene should be confined to those cases where the patient falls outside the criteria or is otherwise clearly not appropriate for the panel to consider. In the particular circumstances, the ombudsman criticised the failure to convene a panel, although the woman involved could not be seen 'as anything other than borderline', given the 'scoring' she had received when assessed.[3]

Third, guidance notes that, following a panel decision, the person still has the right to complain to the Health Service Ombudsman.[4]

---

1 NHS Responsibilities Regulations 2012, r.22.
2 National Framework 2018, para 206.
3 *Herefordshire Health Authority* (E.1321/98–99). In: Health Service Ombudsman. HC 19. *Investigations completed April–September 1999*. London: TSO, 1999.
4 National Framework 2018, paras 196–206.

Fourth, the role of the IRP is limited to considering only how the NHS Continuing Healthcare (CHC) procedure was used by the CCG in assessing (using the DST) or the primary health decision. Its role does not cover issues concerning use of the Checklist at the screening stage.

Fifth, the IRP's remit does not extend, for instance, to considering a dispute about the level or type of services provided by way of meeting CHC needs. (This issue arose in one case about the type of care home accommodation the person needed once CHC eligibility had been established. The IRP exceeded its legally prescribed remit and made a recommendation about such essentially extraneous matters; there was no obligation on the CCG to follow it.)[1]

Sixth, the ombudsman will expect the IRP to give adequate reasons for its decision. It will be a fault if an IRP fails to provide sufficient evidence for its decision of non-eligibility, raising considerable doubts about whether the decision was 'robust and properly made' because of significant omissions in the decision-making process.[2] In another case, the IRP found in a retrospective funding case that the patient was eligible for one period but not another. However, the son was unaware of any change in his father's condition between the two periods. The IRP's reasoning in its decision letter was insufficiently detailed by way of explanation, and there were flaws in the evidence on which the IRP based its decision. This was fault.[3]

Seventh, self-evidently, the IRP should follow the rules relevant to CHC in the regulations and the guidance and consider relevant evidence; otherwise the ombudsman may find fault. For example, it would be troubling if such a decision-making body, at a higher level, was either unacquainted with, or untroubled by, the rules.

> **IRP ignoring the rules about primary health need and funded nursing care (FNC).** An IRP's decision was challenged as unreasonable, clinically unsound and based on inappropriate considerations. Contrary to the National Framework, it had considered whether Mrs A's needs were being met by the staff at the care home through the provision of registered nursing care in the form of FNC instead of considering first of all, as demanded by the Framework, that a decision about primary health need be made first.

---

1 *R(S) v Dudley Primary Care Trust* [2009] EWHC 1780 (Admin), para 23.
2 PSOW, *Hywel Dda University Health Board*, 2018 (201700015).
3 PSOW, *Cardiff and Vale University Health Board*, 2016 (201501974).

> The Health Board agreed to reissue the decision letter providing a full and robust explanation of the reasons why it was felt that a primary health need did not exist, while ensuring that any references to FNC were excluded from the decision.[1]

It would be equally troubling if an IRP were to take a decision but fail to consider all the relevant information, as happened, for example, when the obviously relevant notes of a negotiation meeting were ignored.[2] And it would also be a concern if an IRP went ahead with a decision without the relevant clinical advisor being present, and was therefore unable to discuss with her significant questions and to consider the rationale behind her earlier decision-making.[3]

Eighth, the IRP should inform, in writing, the person who is appealing about the details of the process, so that they know what to expect and whether to proceed.[4]

Lastly, a legal challenge, following an IRP decision, should be made against the IRP rather than the CCG, even if it is being argued that the very same, core errors made by the CCG had infected the IRP decision as well.[5]

Independent review panels: efficacy

For patients and families, appeal to an IRP may be an effective way of getting a decision re-examined and possibly overturned. The quality of the IRP's process and decision may, however, vary. Equally, the process may not be straightforward and not necessarily satisfactory, as a former Chairman of an IRP related.

> **Independent review panels in practice.** Appeals were handled differently from area to area. Some allowed family members to attend and speak. For others, it was a paper exercise behind closed doors. Sometimes a number of appeals were crammed together on a single day and it was questionable whether panel members read the case notes adequately. There may be evidential gaps and

---

1 PSOW, *Cardiff and Vale University Health Board*, 2018 (201705777).
2 PSOW, *Powys Teaching Health Board*, 2016 (201408376).
3 PSOW, *Powys Teaching Health Board*, 2016 (201506835). Also: PSOW, *Betsi Cadwaladr University Health Board*, 2017 (201504580).
4 PSOW, *Powys Teaching Health Board*, 2016 (201408376).
5 *R(Gossip) v NHS Surrey Downs Clinical Commissioning Group* [2019] EWHC 3411 (Admin), para 41.

> medical jargon panel members may not understand. Flawed information may be relied on. It could be a complicated and bureaucratic process. It may be vital for the family to attend to have any chance of success. There may be long waits for an appeal to be heard, months, maybe even years.[1]

The ombudsman has also found fault in relation to the Chairman of an IRP, in the way in which a decision was taken not to convene an IRP, a decision based precisely on the flawed information in dispute.

> **Flawed decision of Chairman of IRP.** The ombudsman was concerned about the Chairman's decision that a woman was so far outside the eligibility criteria for continuing care that an IRP was not warranted. The document provided to the Chairman from the coordinator included inaccurate statements about the views of the multi-disciplinary team professionals. In addition, the decision-making process provided no explanation of how the primary health need approach had been applied in the finding of non-eligibility. Even though these flaws were evident, the Chairman still ruled out a hearing.
>
> Logically, the ombudsman pointed out that '[if] the process for determining Mrs H's eligibility for NHSFCC [NHS Funded Continuing Care] was flawed, the Chair should not have relied on information collected during this flawed process to formulate her own view on eligibility'. The Chairman also noted that she had received insufficient training or updates and felt isolated in her role.[2]

Indicative cases

The National Framework statutory guidance indicates specifically that when NHS Continuing Healthcare (CHC) decisions are made, indicative legal and ombudsman cases should be considered. For patients, families and practitioners, this may be important if, for example, the eligibility decision, following use of the Decision Support Tool (DST), is unfavourable. This is because the scoring system contained within the DST is, if applied rigidly to determine eligibility, arguably not consistent with the case law.

---

1 Care to be Different. *NHS Continuing Healthcare independent review – former chair speaks out.* 27 May 2014. Accessed on 14 June 2019 at: https://caretobedifferent.co.uk/nhs-continuing-healthcare-independent-review-former-chair-speaks-out
2 PSOW, *Carmarthenshire Local Health Board*, 2010 (200801759), paras 63, 75.

The word 'indicative' refers to how a patient with an equivalent level of need to a patient in previously decided legal or ombudsman cases might be eligible now. The guidance is referring to cases in which the courts or the ombudsman went beyond purely reviewing the decision-making process and took the further step of stating that the person concerned was eligible for CHC. The guidance points out, of course, that generalisations should not be made, in the sense that every case is different.[1]

Relying on this last point, a court in 2019 held, arguably questionably, that even in the case of a patient with apparently very similar needs to Pamela Coughlan, it was open to the CCG to make a finding of non-eligibility, without referring at all to the *Coughlan* case, or any of the ombudsman cases.[2] And thus without being able to demonstrate that it had even considered these indicative cases.

Nonetheless, the courts have stated, for example, that a person with needs 'equivalent' to Pamela Coughlan in the *Coughlan* case should be found, in law, to be eligible for CHC.[3] The word 'equivalent' means that one is looking not for needs that are the same but for what could be a range of needs at a comparable level.

Therefore, a broad-brush approach needs to be taken in extrapolating from the cases below and applying them to individual eligibility decisions. A general representation of the patients in these cases would be people with multiple health care conditions requiring ongoing care. No one condition need necessarily be intense or unpredictable (although it might be); the cases suggest that even without these characteristics of intensity or unpredictability, a person might still be eligible.

In other words, the cumulative effect of several health care conditions must be taken into account in determining the overall nature and complexity of a person's needs. For instance, in one ombudsman case, fragmented and poorly recorded decision-making suggested that the cumulative impact – of the patient's seizures, reflux and hip dysplasia on his night care needs – had not been considered. This was fault.[4]

Importantly, some of these patients may not score so highly on the DST (see above) but could still be eligible – which is why the DST guidance states that the scoring is not decisive. And even if their needs might be

---

1   National Framework 2018, para 157.
2   *R(Gossip) v NHS Surrey Downs Clinical Commissioning Group* [2019] EWHC 3411 (Admin), para 97.
3   *R(Grogan) v Bexley NHS Care Trust* [2006] EWHC 44 (Admin), para 51.
4   LGSCO, *Central Bedfordshire Council, Essex Partnership University NHS Foundation Trust, Bedfordshire Clinical Commissioning Group*, 2019 (16 002 323), para 73.

capable of being met by registered nursing care alone in a nursing home, some patients might still be eligible for CHC and so should not be awarded funded nursing care.

More generally, the guidance anyway states that it 'is based on statutory responsibilities, case law [and] input from the Parliamentary and Health Service Ombudsman'.[1] This means, of course, that a range of other legal and ombudsman cases are generally relevant, not just the indicative cases. Throughout this book these other cases are referred to, a notable example being the *Grogan* case.[2]

Indicative cases: substantive cases

The cases immediately below are just such indicative cases, in terms of there being a 'substantive' decision about eligibility, not just about a flaw in the decision-making process – or, failing that, a strong indication that the person's needs were likely to be eligible. Some are particularly important, such as the *Coughlan* case, from which rules in NHS regulations and in the Care Act 2014 are derived.

> ***Coughlan* case: tetraplegia, incontinence, breathing difficulties, regular nursing required, in a wholly different category to anything that social services could lawfully fund.** A woman who had been badly injured in a road traffic accident in 1971 had resided in an NHS unit since then. The NHS was now attempting to move her to a nursing home, where responsibility for her care would fall to the local authority (social care) and be means-tested. She was described as tetraplegic, doubly incontinent, requiring intermittent catheterisation (every two to three hours), partially paralysed in respiratory function, requiring a corset to keep abdominal organs in place, subject to problems attendant on immobility and also to recurrent, pounding headaches caused by an associated neurological condition (which was potentially fatal).
>
> The Court of Appeal held that:
>
> the needs of Miss Coughlan and her fellow occupants were primarily health needs for which the Health Authority is as a matter of law responsible... Whether it was unlawful [for social services to meet the needs] depends, generally, on whether the nursing services are merely (i) incidental or ancillary to the provision of the accommodation which a local authority is

---

1 National Framework 2018, para 11.
2 *R(Grogan) v Bexley NHS Care Trust* [2006] EWHC 44 (Admin).

NHS CONTINUING HEALTHCARE

> under a duty to provide and (ii) of a nature which it can be expected that an authority whose primary responsibility is to provide social services can be expected to provide. Miss Coughlan needed services of a wholly different category.
>
> Thus, the duty fell upon the NHS to meet her needs by way of continuing care, not social services.[1]

The following legal case involved a child, but the judge considered that the rules established in the *Coughlan* case, applying to adults, applied to children as well.

> *Haringey* case: constant tracheostomy care, beyond the legal remit of social services, therefore eligibility for NHS Continuing Healthcare. A woman was caring for her child at home. Shortly after birth the child was admitted to Great Ormond Street Hospital where she was diagnosed as having a haemangioma of the lip (a tangle of abnormal vessels that form an abnormal communication between the arterial and venous systems – a disfiguring, but non-life threatening condition), a subglottic haemangioma (which obstructs her airways) and a subglottic stenosis, a narrowing of the passages in her larynx. Because of the last two conditions she had a tracheostomy (tube in the throat) fitted and it was anticipated that this would have to remain in place for several years.
>
> During the day, the tube might need suctioning as regularly as every 15 minutes, although the period between suctioning was often longer. At the time of the case, suctioning was needed about three times a night. Suctioning required disposable catheters attached to a battery-operated suction machine.
>
> In addition, the tube itself required replacing regularly, about once a week, or when there was an emergency such as if the child pulled the tube out altogether. If the child was not suctioned or if the tube came unstuck, the child would suffocate and die within minutes or suffer serious brain damage in a shorter time. The tapes which kept the tube in place also needed changing if they became loosened, wet, dirty or chafed.
>
> The woman had another, older disabled daughter who visited home fortnightly. The woman was struggling to cope. She was receiving a certain

---

1 *R(Coughlan) v North and East Devon Health Authority* [2001] Q.B. 213, Court of Appeal, paras 31, 118.

amount of assistance from the NHS primary care trust but felt she needed more, especially in light of her exhaustion resulting from sleep deprivation.

The case centred mainly on the provision of ten extra hours of help a night. The primary care trust (PCT) did not accept that this was required. But, in any case, the section 3 (of the NHS Act) target duty could not be enforced, even had she needed more. Although human rights considerations could 'crystallise' this target duty into a specific, enforceable duty, nonetheless this case did not raise the question of human rights breaches under articles 2, 3 or 8 of the European Convention on Human Rights.

Beyond social services legal limits. The mother had turned to social services for the extra assistance. But the court found that the particular nursing care required, including tube replacement and unblocking, was nursing care of a type beyond that which social services legally could provide. In deciding this it accepted that the limits of social services provision outlined in the *Coughlan* case, under adult social care legislation, applied to children's social care legislation as well.

Scale and type of nursing care. The scale and type of nursing care was particularly important, as was the question of whether its provision was incidental or ancillary to the provision of some other service which the social services authority was lawfully providing, and whether it was of a nature which such authority could be expected to provide.

This was care designed to deal with the continuing medical consequences of an operation, which if not met would give rise to urgent or immediate medical needs: tube replacement and unblocking, to avoid very significant risks of a life-threatening nature. The advice on management was provided by a hospital. The training was provided by the medically qualified.

To hold that social services might be obliged to provide such care under section 17 of the Children Act 1989 or section 2 of the Chronically Sick and Disabled Persons Act 1970 would have meant turning a social services authority into a substitute or additional NHS for children. The local authority was not the 'default provider' in having to meet needs which fell primarily in the province of other bodies (in this case, the NHS). Thus, the PCT was not obliged to provide the extra care, and the local authority was not empowered to.[1]

The following are Health Service Ombudsman cases, not establishing law in the way in which a legal case does, but to the point, especially given that the

---

1   *R(T) v London Borough of Haringey* [2005] EWHC 2235 (Admin), paras 61, 62, 70.

National Framework guidance, as already noted above, states that they are highly relevant to decisions about eligibility for CHC.

> *Pointon* case: CHC eligibility in a person's own home, even though informal care was providing most of the care. A man with Alzheimer's disease was now living at home, being cared for by his wife and other personal assistants paid for by social services. He was totally reliant on them for his needs to be met. He was subject to epileptic seizures, muscular spasms, panic attacks and episodes of choking, visual spatial difficulties and hallucinatory experiences. He required constant supervision.
>
> The ombudsman found that he should have been assessed as eligible for CHC, since the NHS had not considered psychological needs nor the fact that a person could have CHC needs in their own home, not just in a nursing home or hospital. The NHS should have been funding the respite care which his wife required in order to be able to continue to manage caring.
>
> The report of an independent medical consultant commissioned by Mrs Pointon took the view that Mr Pointon's symptoms 'stemmed solely from a health condition that was severe, complex and unpredictable, needing 24-hour care and frequent interventions to prevent him harming himself'. A consultant psychiatrist and consultant geriatrician confirmed this opinion – but the PCT's nurse assessors had disagreed with these doctors.[1]

> *Wigan* case: several strokes, comprehension, communication, swallowing, PEG (percutaneous endoscopic gastrostomy) feed, double incontinence: eligibility for NHS Continuing Healthcare. A woman had suffered several strokes, had no speech or comprehension, was unable to swallow and required feeding by a PEG tube into the stomach, and was doubly incontinent.
>
> The ombudsman stated:
>
>> It is clear from the information I have seen about Mrs N's condition that she was extremely dependent and required a high level of physical care: like Miss Coughlan, she was almost completely immobile; and she was doubly incontinent. I have seen no evidence that she had breathing difficulties as Miss Coughlan had; but she required PEG feeding, which Miss Coughlan did not. She was unable to communicate verbally. I cannot see that any authority could reasonably conclude that her need for nursing care was

---

1 *Cambridgeshire Health Authority* (E.22/02–03). In: Health Service Ombudsman. HC 704. *Selected investigations completed October 2003–March 2004*. London: TSO, 2004 (*Pointon* case).

merely incidental or ancillary to the provision of accommodation or of a nature one could expect Social Services to provide... It seems clear to me that she, like Miss Coughlan, needed services of a wholly different kind.[1]

Berkshire case: dementia, behaviour, intensive and complex care package, eligible for NHS Continuing Healthcare. A woman had vascular dementia, confusion and challenging behaviour; she had been assessed as having multiple and complex nursing and medical problems and needed help with all daily living except eating. These conditions required an 'intensive and complex' personal care package, well beyond the customary level of care offered by a nursing home.

The ombudsman stated that she could not 'see how the total amount of nursing care such a patient would need would be likely to be merely incidental or ancillary to the provision of accommodation, or of a nature which a local authority could be expected to provide'.[2]

Shropshire case: full assistance with personal care (washing, dressing, feeding, toileting), double incontinence, safety, mobilisation. A woman in a nursing home was assessed as requiring full assistance with all personal care tasks including washing, dressing, feeding and toileting. She was doubly incontinent, dependent on others for her safety and could mobilise only with assistance. The health authority refused a request for an independent review.

The ombudsman was advised by her independent clinical assessor that it was debatable whether the significant nursing care required could properly be regarded as incidental or ancillary. The ombudsman recommended that a reassessment take place to determine the status of the woman.[3]

Shropshire (2nd) case: all personal care, urinary catheter, faecal incontinence, puréed diet, PEG feed, partial paralysis, contractures, re-positioning, communication, safety. A woman was discharged to a nursing home without continuing care funding. The assessment included the fact that she was unable to manage any aspect of personal care independently, had an in-dwelling urinary catheter, suffered from occasional faecal incontinence, required a soft puréed diet, had a PEG feed, needed a hoist for all transfers because of hemiparesis and contracture, required re-positioning every two hours in order to

---

1 *Wigan and Bolton Health Authority* (E.420/00–01). In: Health Service Ombudsman. *NHS funding for long term care.* London: TSO, 2003.
2 *Berkshire Health Authority* (E.814/00–01). In: Health Service Ombudsman. *NHS funding for long term care.* London: TSO, 2003.
3 *Shropshire Health Authority* (E.5/02–03). In: Health Service Ombudsman. HC 787. *Selected investigations completed December 2002–March 2003.* London: TSO, 2003.

> manage pressure risks, communicated by eye contact and head movement, could not speak, and was totally reliant on others for safety.
>
> The ombudsman's assessor concluded that the health authority's decision to deny continuing care status was debatable. The ombudsman recommended that the health authority re-determine whether the woman should have Continuing Healthcare status.[1]

There are older ombudsman decisions, preceding even the *Coughlan* case. In terms of the relevance of these, the *Coughlan* case did not change the law but merely interpreted the implications of the existing National Health Service Act 1977. The ombudsman cases preceding 1999 were decided against that same Act. Thus, if the *Coughlan* case remains relevant – which it does – so too do some of these older ombudsman cases. In the following case, the ombudsman referred to section 3 of the 1977 Act, just as the Court of Appeal did in the *Coughlan* case itself.[2]

> *Leeds* case: incontinence, no communication, visual impairment, occasional epilepsy, kidney tumour, no active medical treatment but substantial nursing required: NHS Continuing Healthcare eligibility. A health authority had decided not to provide directly or pay for elsewhere (e.g. a nursing home) continuing care for people with neurological conditions: the health authority's neurosurgical contract did not refer to institutional care at all. The person discharged was doubly incontinent, could not eat or drink without assistance, could not communicate, had a kidney tumour, cataracts in both eyes and occasional epileptic fits.
>
> There was no dispute that when he was discharged he would not need active medical treatment but he would need 'substantial nursing care'. The health authority defended its position with reference to resources, priorities and national policy (which was being followed by other health authorities).
>
> The Health Service Ombudsman found a failure in service. He cited section 3 of the National Heath Service Act 1977, including section 3(1)(e) which refers to aftercare, and stated:

---

1   *Shropshire Health Authority* (E.2119/01–02). In: Health Service Ombudsman. HC 787. *Selected investigations completed December 2002–March 2003.* London: TSO, 2003.
2   *R(Coughlan) v North and East Devon Health Authority* [2001] Q.B. 213, Court of Appeal, para 22.

INDICATIVE CASES

> This patient was a highly dependent patient in hospital under a contract made with the Infirmary by Leeds Health Authority; and yet, when he no longer needed care in an acute ward but manifestly still needed what the National Health Service is there to provide, they regarded themselves as having no scope for continuing to discharge their responsibilities to him because their policy was to make no provision for continuing care. The policy also had the effect of excluding an option whereby he might have the cost of his continuing care met by the NHS. In my opinion the failure to make available long-term care within the NHS for this patient was unreasonable and constitutes a failure in the service provided by the Health Authority. I uphold the complaint.
>
> The ombudsman recommended that the health authority reimburse nursing home costs already incurred by the man's wife and meet future costs and also that it should review its 'provision of services for the likes of this man in view of the apparent gap in service available for this particular group of patients'.[1]

The following two cases, also older but still under the same primary legislation as the *Coughlan* legal case, are similar.

> **Head-injured woman requiring sustained nursing care, mental stimulation, physiotherapy: eligibility for NHS Continuing Healthcare.** A woman sustained severe head injuries in a road traffic accident. She was admitted to the neuro-surgical unit of a hospital. After she was over the acute stage some six months later, she was discharged to a private nursing home charging £200 per week. The district health authority (DHA) denied it was responsible for funding her placement. Basically, the health authority considered that it lacked the resources to fund non-acute health needs for such a patient.
>
> The relevant hospital consultant told the ombudsman that although she no longer needed to be in the unit, she still required nursing care, mental stimulation and physiotherapy. She would remain severely incapacitated and would require 'sustained nursing care for the rest of her life'.
>
> The ombudsman found it 'incontrovertible, therefore, in the light of the level of continuing care [she] will require...that the DHA had a duty to continue to provide the care...at no cost to her or her family'. This meant the DHA should

---

1   *Leeds Health Authority* (E.62/93–94). In: Health Service Commissioner. *Failure to provide long term NHS care for a brain damaged patient.* London: HMSO, 1994.

meet the cost of provision and should reimburse the complainant (the woman's son) who had receivership from the Court of Protection.[1]

North Worcestershire case: stroke, depression, incontinence, feeding, diabetes, Crohn's disease, hypertension, blood disorder, eligibility for NHS Continuing Healthcare. A 55-year-old man had a stroke and was admitted to hospital. Six months later, his wife was told that nothing more could be done for him and a nursing home would be required. He was discharged; the health authority refused to pay for the nursing home placement or even the transport to the home.

His general practitioner wrote to the family's MP to the effect that the man was in the nursing home because:

> he continues to have several serious medical problems for which he is under consultant medical care. Because of his stroke he cannot walk and because he is a relatively young man his severe stroke condition causes him to be chronically depressed. He is incontinent of urine and has difficulty feeding himself although he does so. His diabetes is controlled by insulin. His care is coordinated by a consultant physician at the Alexandra Hospital, Redditch, but the specialist nature of his blood condition requires that he is also under the care of a consultant haematologist at the same hospital. He is likely to remain under the consultant for the rest of his life because of the serious state of his Crohn's disease [inflammatory disease of the bowel], his diabetes and his idiopathic thrombocytopenia [a blood disorder]. In addition, he has hypertension and is on treatment for that as well.

The chairman of the regional health authority had stated to the district health authority that the man appeared to have very complex needs and 'that begs the question, if people like [the patient] do not qualify for continuing care by reason of ill-health, then who does?'

The Health Service Ombudsman found that 'the continuing care of a highly dependent patient like the complainant's husband is a service which the NHS should provide'. The policy adopted by the district health authority represented a 'failure to provide a service which it is the authority's function to provide'. The ombudsman recommended that the authority pick up the cost of the nursing home placement and make an *ex gratia* payment to the man's wife to cover the cost of the care already incurred.[2]

---

1 HSO, W.478/89–90. In: Health Service Commissioner. HC 482. *2nd report 1990–1991*. London: HMSO, 1991.
2 *North Worcestershire Health Authority* (E.264/94–95). In: Health Service Commissioner. HC 11. *Selected investigations completed April to September 1995*. London: HMSO, 1995.

Indicative cases: examples in which CHC responsibility was accepted and not contested

In the following legal cases, the contested matters were not about eligibility for CHC itself but about other matters – for example, how the needs were going to be met. In other words, they are examples in which the NHS had already accepted that the patients concerned were eligible.

> ***Whapples* case: uncontested acceptance of hysterical paraplegia, underlying eligibility for NHS Continuing Healthcare.** A 57-year-old woman had been partially sighted since birth. As a child she lived in various residential homes during which time she was traumatised. Physical disability developed gradually. By the time she was 27 the woman was bed-ridden. She was diagnosed with 'hysterical paraplegia', an unfortunate label applied to her severe disability which had no discernible physiological cause. The paralysis continued to develop to the extent that the appellant became quadriplegic.
>
> As long ago as 1986 the woman first wrote to say that she wanted to disassociate from community services. Her condition was described as chronic, progressive and untreatable. In 2009, it was noted following hospital tests that she had severe wasting of her lower limbs. She was in need of physiotherapy. At this time there was no structured care being provided to the appellant. A close friend provided day-to-day care with help on a voluntary basis from two retired nurses. The assessment described as the 'ideal situation' that she should be provided with a care package involving two carers, including to turn her in bed at night.[1]
>
> ***Kemp* case: Alzheimer's, diabetes, polymyalgia rheumatica, respiratory disease, arthritis, challenging behaviour, underpinning eligibility for NHS Continuing Healthcare.** The patient suffered from senile dementia of an Alzheimer's type. This was complicated by the fact that he also had diabetes, which had on occasion rendered him hypoglycaemic, as well as polymyalgia rheumatica (inflammatory disease), respiratory disease and rheumatoid arthritis. On occasion he behaved aggressively and with disinhibition. His son challenged the decision to deny CHC but a special review panel confirmed the decision. The son persisted and a second review panel met but declined to decide. Finally, a third panel awarded CHC.

---

1 *R(Whapples) v Birmingham Crosscity Clinical Commissioning Group* [2015] EWCA Civ 435, paras 4–6.

The final decision followed a report by a professor of psychiatric nursing. Amongst other matters, he indicated that the level of dementia from which he assessed the claimant to be suffering was such that:

> there is no reasonable body of nurses or doctors who would not say that Mr Kemp's dementia falls at the severe end of the spectrum of severity...that the claimant's sexual disinhibition, double incontinence, propensity to pull at doors, attempts to abscond, unpredictable sleep pattern and array of physical health problems were such that, in aggregate, he required overall the skills of a registered nurse...and that his need to be in the Nursing Home was driven primarily by his healthcare needs.

The case found its way to court, but the NHS did not deny CHC eligibility; the dispute was about the extent of reimbursement for care home charges to be made to the patient.[1]

***N v ACCG* case: severe physical and learning disabilities, autism, epilepsy, no speech, choking, intensive level of care required, underpinning eligibility for NHS Continuing Healthcare.** A young man in a care home was funded under CHC by the clinical commissioning group. He had severe learning and physical disabilities together with autism and an uncommon epileptic condition resulting in frequent seizures and risk of sudden death. A nurse had to be available at all times to administer emergency drugs to him if the need arose. He had poor muscle tone and used a wheelchair. He was doubly incontinent.

He had the cognitive ability of a child aged less than one year. He had no speech but could express his feelings by facial expression, sounds and gestures. He needed help with feeding as he was vulnerable to choking; he required 2:1 care with his personal care and accessing the community. Overall, he had to have his carers nearby at all times, and during the night he had one sleeping member of staff and one member of staff who stayed awake to look after him.

The case was not about whether he was eligible for CHC, but how his needs should be met, including questions of cost-effectiveness.[2]

---

1   *Kemp v Denbighshire Local Health Board* [2006] EWHC 181 (Admin), paras 3, 21, 33.
2   *N v ACCG* [2017] UKSC 22.

Informal carers, see *Carers*

Input (of care)

Sometimes NHS clinical commissioning groups appear to argue that it is irrelevant what level or quantity of input of care is required to provide care for a person – for example, the number of carers required to manage a person with challenging behaviour. However, such a position would seem not to be in accordance with either law or guidance.

First, one of the legal questions that must be asked relates to the *quantity* of care being provided. This is about whether the health or nursing needs are incidental or ancillary to what is being provided; the requirement to decide this is referred to in the NHS regulations, the Care Act 2014 and legal case law. See ***Incidental or ancillary or of a nature beyond social services***.

Second, guidance states that in deciding about a primary health need, consideration should be given to various characteristics, including the intensity of a person's needs – and that the number of carers required at any one time could be one of the relevant questions.[1]

Intensity

According to the National Framework guidance, intensity is one of the four characteristics of a person's needs that, alone or in combination, may demonstrate the existence of a primary health need and therefore eligibility for NHS Continuing Healthcare (CHC).

The decision about this will follow on from completion of the Decision Support Tool (DST), but with a view to establishing whether what is required is merely incidental or ancillary (quantity of care) to what social services would otherwise provide, or is of a nature (quality of care) beyond the legal remit of social services. See ***Incidental or ancillary or of a nature beyond social services***.

Thus, intensity represents 25 per cent of the possibilities contained within the guidance and can alone form the basis of a primary health need, even without the presence of the other three characteristics (nature, complexity and unpredictability). For patients, families and practitioners, therefore, reference to intensity – and the definition of it set out in guidance – can assume considerable importance. Key points about it include the following:

---

1   National Framework Practice Guidance 2018, para 3.4.

- **Intensity: legal significance of the term**. The term does not occur in legislation but in statutory guidance: both the National Framework and the DST.[1] Since the regulations state that the DST must be used to assess CHC and regard be given to the National Framework, so intensity becomes a quasi-legal consideration. Further, guidance states that intensity relates to the quantity of care required, a legal consideration referred to in both case law and legislation in relation to the term 'incidental or ancillary'.

- **Intensity: careful consideration of**. If a primary health need is strongly indicated when the DST is completed, guidance implies that detailed reference to the intensity of the needs will be less necessary. On the other hand, if there is less certainty from completion of the DST as to the existence of a primary health need, then 'careful consideration must be given to the four key characteristics of nature, intensity, complexity or unpredictability of the individual's needs'.[2] See *Decision Support Tool*.

- **Intensity: quantity, severity, continuity**. Guidance states intensity 'relates both to the extent (quantity) and severity (degree) of the needs and to the support required to meet them, including the need for sustained/ongoing care (continuity)'.[3]

- **Intensity: questions to ask**. Guidance goes on to set out questions that may help the consideration of intensity, involving the quantity, severity and continuity of needs: severity of need, how often intervention is required and for how long, how many carers/care workers are required at any one time, and whether the care relates to needs over several domains.[4]

Interim provision of care during assessment and decision

Guidance states that a person only becomes eligible for NHS Continuing Healthcare once a decision on eligibility has been made. Therefore, during the decision-making process, existing arrangements for provision and funding of care should continue, unless urgent adjustment is required related

---

1 National Framework 2018, para 59; Decision Support Tool 2018, para 18.
2 Decision Support Tool 2018, para 38.
3 National Framework 2018, para 59; Decision Support Tool 2018, p.43.
4 National Framework Practice Guidance 2018, para 3.4.

to the person's needs changing and/or to the legal limits of provision by the local authority or NHS clinical commissioning group.[1]

This general rule should be read, however, in relation to hospital discharge, which take on an added legal dimension because of specific rules about this in schedule 3 of the Care Act 2014. See *Hospital discharge*.

---

1   National Framework 2018, para 105.

J

Joint funding

Regulations define NHS Continuing Healthcare (CHC) as a 'package of care arranged and funded solely by the health service in England for a person aged 18 or over to meet physical or mental health needs which have arisen as a result of disability, accident or illness'.[1] The word 'solely' has a clear meaning in language and law.

The implications of this rule, therefore, are that in the case of a person with CHC eligibility, their assessed health and social care needs cannot be met by means of joint funding. As the courts have pointed out, this is akin to an 'all or nothing' approach,[2] a position confirmed by the National Framework guidance which notes that only if a person does not have CHC needs is a variety of joint funding arrangements possible.

- **Joint funding if a person is not eligible for CHC.**

    If a person is not eligible for NHS Continuing Healthcare, they may potentially receive a joint package of health and social care. This is where an individual's care or support package is funded by both the NHS and the local authority. This may apply where specific needs have been identified through the [Decision Support Tool] that are beyond the powers of the local authority to meet on its own.

    This could be because the specific needs are not of a nature that a local authority could be expected to meet, or because they are not incidental or ancillary to something which the Local Authority would be doing to meet needs under sections 18–20 of the Care Act 2014. It should be noted that joint packages can be provided in any setting.[3]

---

1 NHS Responsibilities Regulations 2012, r.20(1).
2 *Grogan v Bexley NHS Care Trust* [2006] EWHC 44 (Admin), para 15.
3 National Framework 2018, para 263.

- **Joint funding and range of health services.**

    Apart from NHS-funded Nursing Care, additional health services may also be delivered by existing NHS services or funded by the NHS, if these are identified and agreed as part of an assessment and care plan. The range of services that the NHS is expected to arrange and fund includes, but is not limited to, primary healthcare; assessment involving doctors and registered nurses; rehabilitation/reablement and recovery (where this forms part of an overall package of NHS care, as distinct from intermediate care); respite healthcare; community health services; specialist support for healthcare needs; and palliative care and end of life healthcare.[1]

The first of the above two points could cause confusion. This is because it refers to needs that go beyond the remit of social services, in relation to the incidental/ancillary or nature test. Yet NHS regulations clearly state that if a person's health or nursing needs are beyond the legal reach of social services on the basis of this very test, the NHS clinical commissioning group (CCG) must find a primary health need and therefore eligibility for CHC, which of course precludes joint funding.[2]

However, the test in regulations is whether, *in their totality*, the health or nursing services a person requires are more than incidental or ancillary to what social services would otherwise be providing, or are of a nature beyond that expected of social services. If so, the person has a primary health need and is eligible for CHC.[3]

The guidance therefore seems to suggest that, if as a whole the health or nursing services do not exceed the social services remit but do so only fractionally or piecemeal so to speak, then joint funding is called for. Certainly, the judge in the *Grogan* legal case seemed to envisage joint funding on this sort of basis in some cases.[4]

Nonetheless, such distinctions relying on a vague term such as 'totality' may be fine ones, and it is not surprising that joint funding is much disputed in practice. For patients and families, the decision one way or another – CHC or joint funding – can have considerable financial implications in

---

1 National Framework 2018, para 265.
2 NHS Responsibilities Regulations 2012, r.21(7).
3 NHS Responsibilities Regulations 2012, r.21(7).
4 *R(Grogan) v Bexley NHS Care Trust* [2006] EWHC 44 (Admin), para 105. See also: *R(Gossip) v NHS Surrey Downs Clinical Commissioning Group* [2019] EWHC 3411 (Admin), para 109.

that the social care part of a joint package would have to be paid for by the patient (or, if the latter has insufficient resources, by the local authority). For example, if local authorities and CCGs delay in agreeing joint funding, the ombudsman may find fault if there is a delay in care being provided, and if a CCG unreasonably delays both agreeing the health care component of the joint package and backdating a payment due to the family.[1]

Thus in one case, a person at home needed manual evacuation of her bowel, to be performed by district nurses, so many times a week. However, immediately afterward, she would need cleaning up and then hoisting. Uncertainty, over whether the latter two tasks were a health or social care responsibility, contributed in part to an overall delay of 21 months in completion of the assessment. The ombudsman found fault with the local authority.[2]

Joint working

Cooperative and joint working is legally encouraged in legislation. For example, section 3 of the Care Act 2014 states that local authorities must consider integration with the NHS, and sections 6 and 7 of the same Act state that local authorities must cooperate with NHS bodies and vice versa. Section 75 of the National Health Service Act 2006 gives the NHS and local authorities powers to enter joint working agreements, including pooled budgets and carrying out legal functions on behalf of each other.

However, working jointly does not mean disregarding legal rules in trying to please or placate a joint working partner. One of the reasons why local authorities have hesitated sometimes to challenge decision-making by the NHS about NHS Continuing Healthcare has been because of a form of what might loosely be called political pressure to work cooperatively and not to rock the local boat. But joint working (and cooperation) should be about adhering to, not undermining, legal functions and rules. See **Cooperation**.

Judicial review

Judicial review is a type of legal case in which the courts scrutinise the decision-making process underlying a decision made by a public body. It has been used in NHS Continuing Healthcare (CHC) cases, in which a person challenges the decision made by the NHS in respect of CHC eligibility. And, occasionally, it has been used by local authorities to challenge a clinical

---

1 LGSCO, *Sheffield City Council*, 2019 (17 002 402), paras 62–65.
2 LGSCO, *Somerset County Council*, 2019 (16 016 755), paras 14, 23, 36.

commissioning group in the CHC context. A few key points include the following:

- **Judicial review: permission**. Permission is required from a judge to bring a judicial review case.

- **Decision-making process**. The courts in the main consider the decision-making process, not the substance or merits of a final decision. Thus, if the challenge succeeds and the decision is overturned, then typically the public body must reconsider the decision, this time adhering to the rules.

  An example of this was the *Grogan* case, in which it was clear that the NHS decision about CHC was unlawful because it had failed to apply the right legal questions relating to the establishment of a primary health need. But the judge did not go on to find that the woman in question was eligible for CHC; instead he struck down the original decision but stated the NHS would have to do the assessment again.[1]

- **Avoiding undue interference**. The courts are wary of interfering unduly and will not do so unless the decision has breached legislation or strayed too far from certain legal principles of fair and rational decision-making. They might avoid 'over-zealous textual analysis' of a decision and give practitioners some leeway in how they have made and recorded a decision.[2] For instance, two differing assessment decisions relating to the same person could both be lawful if the correct process was followed in each.[3]

- **Alternative remedy**. Sometimes the local authority (or NHS) complaints process might be deemed to be anyway a more appropriate, alternative remedy, in which case the courts might decline to consider a case.[4] The NHS may argue this to defeat legal claims and prevent even a hearing taking place. However, the courts have held, for example, that if a particular CHC dispute is about a matter of law, or about the application of guidance in the legal context, it is appropriately dealt with by the courts.[5]

---

1   *R(Grogan) v Bexley NHS Care Trust* [2006] EWHC 44 (Admin), para 106.
2   *R(Ireneschild) v Lambeth LBC* [2007] EWCA Civ 234, paras 57, 71.
3   *R(GS) v London Borough of Camden* [2016] EWHC 1762, paras 32–33, 47.
4   *R(Cowl) v Plymouth CC* [2001] EWCA Civ 1935, para 27. And: *R(Ireneschild) v Lambeth LBC* [2007] EWCA Civ 234, para 72.
5   *R(Dennison) v Bradford Districts Clinical Commissioning Group* [2014] EWHC 2552 (Admin), para 19. And see: *R(Gossip) v NHS Surrey Downs Clinical Commissioning Group* [2019] EWHC 3411 (Admin), para 44.

- **More anxious scrutiny.** Human rights issues can sometimes lead to closer or more 'anxious' scrutiny, when a court checks not just that relevant factors have been considered but also what weight has been given them in terms of proportion and balance.[1] In one continuing care panel case, the Court of Appeal found a breach of human rights concerning the manifestly flawed decision about a 95-year-old woman's continuing care needs.[2]

In judicial review cases, including CHC cases, unlawful decision-making might come in various forms – for instance, breaching legislation explicitly by making a funded nursing care decision before considering CHC by means of a Checklist.[3] Or it might involve taking account of irrelevant factors, such as a person's financial resources, which, given that NHS health care is not a means-tested service, cannot be considered.[4]

Other examples of unlawful decision-making include: failing to follow binding legal case law, such as the *Coughlan* case, by not asking the legally required questions relating to whether there was a primary health need;[5] an absence of a legally required decision-making process by completing a negative Checklist with no comment, explanation or evidence whatsoever, amounting to unreasonableness;[6] and applying a blanket policy (sometimes referred to as a fettering of discretion) such as appearing to rule out CHC in all settings save hospitals.[7]

Equally, in the following case, an argument that the denial of eligibility for a woman with significant mental health needs was irrational was defeated since there was evidence of reasoned views by the multi-disciplinary team with which the court would not interfere.

> **No irrationality in denying eligibility in a case of a mentally disordered woman.** A woman in her mid-30s suffered from dissociative identity disorder. The annual cost of her care was around £675,000. She had needed three carers during the day and two during the night. The carers provided support with daily living,

---

1 *R(Daly) v Secretary of State for the Home Department* [2001] UKHL 26, para 26. And: *R(A and B) v East Sussex County Council* [2003] EWHC 167 (Admin), para 166.
2 *R(Goldsmith) v Wandsworth London Borough Council* [2004] EWCA Civ 1170.
3 *R(Dennison) v Bradford Districts Clinical Commissioning Group* [2014] EWHC 2552 (Admin).
4 *Booker v NHS Oldham and Direct Line Insurance* [2010] EWHC 2593 (Admin).
5 *R(Grogan) v Bexley NHS Care Trust* [2006] EWHC 44 (Admin).
6 *R(Dennison) v Bradford Districts Clinical Commissioning Group* [2014] EWHC 2552 (Admin).
7 *R(Coughlan) v North and East Devon Health Authority* [2001] Q.B. 213, para 41.

including taking medication, and in dealing with her aggressive and sometimes self-harming behaviour.

The court stated:

> As to the challenge on the ground that the panel's decision was irrational, given the expertise of the panel this was not arguable. They considered that PE's care was unusual, not unique; and that the complexity resulted from the breakdown of her relationship with the council rather than something intrinsic in her care needs. The panel's decision was consistent and reflected the overall recommendation of the multi-disciplinary team. It was also consistent with the views of other bodies and experts.[1]

---

1 *St Helens Borough Council v Manchester Primary Care Trust* [2008] EWCA Civ 931, paras 3, 8.

L

Learning disability

Learning disability has been a major battleground in relation to NHS Continuing Healthcare (CHC) eligibility, not least because of the high cost of care packages for some people with complex needs, in particular, though not only, involving difficult behaviour. See **Challenging behaviour**.

It would therefore appear to be no accident that the guidance singles out learning disability for particular note, something it does not do for any other condition.

The National Framework makes clear that the CHC eligibility rules apply to people – including those with learning disability – irrespective of their client group/diagnosis: 'The question is not whether learning disability is a health need, but rather whether the individual concerned, whatever client group he or she may come from, has a "primary health need".'[1]

The section of guidance on learning disability refers particularly to the need to complete equality monitoring forms, to guard against possible discrimination.[2]

Learning disability: legacy payments

Uncertainty sometimes surrounds 'legacy payments', known also as dowry payments, for people with learning disabilities. These were payments made to local authorities, when long-stay hospitals or campuses were closed by the NHS, to enable them to meet the needs of people with learning disability in the community.

The guidance effectively states that CHC eligibility may still arise:

- **Legacy or dowry payments and implications for CHC.**

    There may be an existing agreement to fund ongoing care for individuals following the closure of long-stay hospitals or campuses. These responsibilities arise independently of a CCG's [clinical commissioning group's] responsibility to provide NHS

---

1   National Framework Practice Guidance 2018, paras 35.1–35.6.
2   National Framework Practice Guidance 2018, para 36.1.1.

Continuing Healthcare, and there should be no assumption that these responsibilities equate to eligibility for NHS Continuing Healthcare or vice versa. Such agreements vary in terms of the commitments they make to fund needs that subsequently arise. Where additional needs do arise, it will be important for the CCG to first check whether there is clarity in such agreements on whether or not they cover responsibilities to meet such needs. If the additional needs fall outside the agreement, CCGs must consider their responsibilities to meet them, in terms both of the CCG's general responsibilities and potential eligibility for NHS Continuing Healthcare.[1]

In other words, one way or another, the CHC rules should apply to people covered by legacy payments, as the original 2008 guidance about these payments also indicated.[2]

Legal cases, see *Indicative cases*

Legal framework

Legal rules about NHS Continuing Healthcare (CHC) sit within a wider legal framework. The precise rules come under regulations made under the National Health Service Act 2006; this NHS legislation itself is part of a bigger picture, which includes the following:

- **Main CHC rules**: NHS Commissioning Board and Clinical Commissioning Groups (Responsibilities and Standing Rules) Regulations 2012. Also, statutory guidance: National Framework for NHS Continuing Healthcare; Decision Support Tool; Checklist; Fast Track Pathway Tool

- **Provision of health services**: National Health Service Act 2006

- **Social care provision and prohibition on local authorities from providing certain health services, including CHC and registered nursing care**: Care Act 2014

---

1 National Framework 2018, para 305.
2 Department of Health (Gateway reference 9906). *Valuing people now: transfer of the responsibility for the commissioning of social care for adults with a learning disability from the NHS to local government and transfer of the appropriate funding.* London: DH, August 2008, para 12.

- **Home adaptations, including for people with CHC needs**: Housing Grants, Construction and Regeneration Act 1996

- **Decision-making under above legislation consistent with human rights**: Decisions made by the NHS and local authorities in relation to CHC must be consistent with the Human Rights Act 1998, which incorporates the European Convention on Human Rights into United Kingdom law

- **Decision-making under above legislation free from discrimination**: Equality Act 2010

- **Health and care providers' duties to meet needs, including needs of people who are CHC-eligible**: Health and Social Care Act (Regulated Activities) Regulations 2014

- **Mental capacity**: Best interests decisions taken under the Mental Capacity Act 2005 in respect of people lacking the relevant mental capacity, although the CHC rules apply equally, whether or not a person has mental capacity.

Legal remedies, see *Disputes between a person and the NHS*

Local authorities, see *Social services*

Local Government and Social Care Ombudsman

Under the Local Government Act 1974, the Local Government and Social Care Ombudsman (LGSCO) independently investigates complaints against local authorities. Normally, under section 26 of the Act, the complainant must have first gone through the local authority's own complaints process.

The LGSCO is not a court of law and ombudsman recommendations are not binding on local authorities; nonetheless, most of the time local authorities comply. Going to the ombudsman is likely to be easier than attempting to bring a judicial review legal challenge.

Although eligibility for NHS Continuing Healthcare (CHC) is ultimately the responsibility of the NHS, and not of the local authority, LGSCO investigations can be relevant to CHC decisions. This is because social services have legal duties which relate to CHC under the Care Act 2014. See *Care Act 2014*.

A number of cases relating to CHC involving adverse findings against local authorities are included in this book. A few key points relating to the LGSCO are as follows:

- **Maladministration and failure in service**. The ombudsman investigates maladministration, failure in a service which it was a local authority's function to provide, or failure to provide such a service. Maladministration is a wide concept, not defined in the Act, but it does not include questioning the merits of professional judgement.

- **Joint investigation against local authority and independent social care provider**. The ombudsman might combine the separate powers to investigate the local authority or to investigate a care provider into one investigation against both, if the local authority has commissioned the service from the provider.[1]

- **Limits to jurisdiction to investigate NHS**. In the context of health and social care, the LGSCO is limited to investigating local authorities or independent care providers. Investigating the NHS is outside of the LGSCO's jurisdiction. So, in a case involving CHC, in which both a local authority and the NHS clinical commissioning group's actions are being challenged, a complaint to both would be advised, opening up the possibility of a joint investigation by both the LGSCO and the Health Service Ombudsman (see immediately below).

    If a complaint relating to a decision about CHC is made against the local authority only, not the NHS, the LGSCO might simply decline to investigate.[2]

- **Joint investigation with the Health Service Ombudsman**. With increased joint working and integration involving health and social care, the LGSCO can investigate local authorities and NHS bodies jointly with the Health Service Ombudsman.[3] This then avoids the problem of limits to jurisdiction outlined immediately above.

- **Recommendations**. The LGSCO makes recommendations by way of remedy. These might relate, for example, to providing a

---

1 e.g. Local Government Ombudsman. *Investigation into complaints against Oxfordshire County Council and Caring Homes Healthcare Group Ltd*, 2015 (15 007 968 and 15 006 620).
2 LGSCO, *Torbay Council*, 2018 (18 000 658).
3 Local Government Act 1974, ss. 33ZA.

service, changing a policy or paying financial compensation. The recommendations are not legally binding (although findings of fact are).[1] If local authorities do not comply, the ombudsman can force the authority to make a statement in local newspapers about the case.[2] As a matter of practice, most ombudsman recommendations are complied with. A rejection of the ombudsman's findings of fact (legally binding) – as opposed to rejection of the ombudsman's recommendations (not legally binding) – might mean it is acting unlawfully.[3]

---

[1] *R(Gallagher) v Basildon District Council* [2010] EWHC 2824 (Admin).
[2] Local Government Act 1974, s.31.
[3] Local Government Ombudsman. *Maladministration causing injustice by Tameside Metropolitan Borough Council statement of non-compliance with ombudsman's recommendations*, 2015, p.2.

M

Means-testing

Under section 1 of the National Health Service Act 2006, provision must be free of charge to patients, other than a few exceptions such as prescription charges and certain hospital appliances. This means that NHS Continuing Healthcare must be provided free of charge by the NHS. An NHS commissioning group therefore cannot conduct a financial means-test either with a view to refusing to provide services altogether, on the basis of a person's finances, or with a view to providing but making a financial charge.[1]

Notwithstanding these rules, it appears that sometimes the NHS does interrogate people about their finances[2] by, for instance, wrongly making even partial continuing care funding dependent on whether the patient receives income support.[3]

This contrasts starkly with the position of social care under the Care Act 2014, which gives local authorities the power to means-test, and therefore charge, for most (but not all) social care provision.

Meeting need

Not only are NHS clinical commissioning groups (CCGs) legally responsible for making an eligibility decision about NHS Continuing Healthcare, but also for deciding how to meet a person's needs.

Guidance notes, therefore, that the package of care is determined by what the CCG considers 'appropriate to meet all of the individual's assessed health and associated care and support needs'. The CCG should have due regard to the person's wishes and preferred outcomes and place importance on any previous local authority assessment; however, the CCG is bound by neither.[4]

---

1 *Booker v NHS Oldham and Direct Line Insurance* [2010] EWHC 2593 (Admin).
2 All Party Parliamentary Group on Parkinson's. *Failing to care: NHS continuing care in England.* London: Parkinson's UK, 2013, p.23.
3 *North Cheshire Health Authority 1996* (E.672/94–95). In: Health Service Commissioner. *Investigations of complaints about long term NHS care.* London: HMSO, 1996.
4 National Framework 2018, para 172.

Mental capacity

It is beyond the scope of this book to include detail about the Mental Capacity Act 2005. In short, however, the rules about NHS Continuing Healthcare (CHC) apply equally to people with, and without, the relevant mental capacity, including the situation in which people eligible for CHC are 'deprived of their liberty' under the 2005 Act.

If a person lacks the capacity to consent or refuse assessment or provision of a service, then a decision must be made in their best interests, as defined in section 4 of the Mental Capacity Act 2005. This decision may be made by practitioners involved in assessment, sharing of information and provision related to CHC, or alternatively by a person who has lasting power of attorney or deputyship (covering health and welfare matters) who can give a form of 'substitute consent', albeit still in the person's best interests.[1]

Although the term 'best interests' might suggest that the optimum arrangements have to be agreed, in fact this is not necessarily the case. See *Cost-effectiveness*.

A best interests decision made by a practitioner or a judge under the Mental Capacity Act 2005 can only consider 'available options'. In the context of this book, those options will be what the NHS is prepared to offer to meet a person's needs under the National Health Service Act 2006, or in the case of social care, what a local authority is prepared to offer by way of discharging its duties under the Care Act 2014.

For instance, in best interests cases involving CHC provision, an NHS clinical commissioning group may limit the options available on grounds of cost or on clinical grounds whilst still offering to meet the person's needs.[2]

Mental Health Act 1983, see *Mental health aftercare*

Mental health aftercare

Some patients have a statutory entitlement to mental health aftercare services under section 117 of the Mental Health Act 1983. In summary, this entitlement arises when they have been detained under particular sections of the Act (e.g. section 3) and are discharged from hospital. Aftercare services must have the purpose of meeting a person's needs arising from or related

---

1 See e.g. National Framework 2018, para 77.
2 *N v ACCG* [2017] UKSC 22 (cost). And: *Harrow CCG v IPJ* [2018] EWCOP 44, para 18.

to the mental disorder, and of reducing the risk of deterioration, thereby reducing the risk of readmission to hospital.

There is no legal power to charge financially for services. The duty under section 117 is a joint responsibility shared between the local NHS clinical commissioning group (CCG) and the local authority.

Mental health aftercare: relationship to NHS Continuing Healthcare
There is sometimes confusion about how provision of mental health aftercare relates to NHS Continuing Healthcare (CHC). Guidance attempts to clarify this, stating that in relation to the mental disorder, section 117 takes precedence and CHC assessment is unnecessary, but that if a person also has physical needs unrelated to the mental disorder, a CHC assessment might be required for those physical needs.

In such circumstances a person might then benefit from section 117 services and CHC services concurrently, respectively to meet the person's mental health needs under the Mental Health Act 1983 and the physical needs under the National Health Service Act 2006.

It would appear that in practice this rule is sometimes disregarded when, for example, CCGs apply a blanket policy not to do CHC assessments for anybody on section 117, even if the assessment is required for physical needs unrelated to the mental disorder (e.g. physical needs in relation to basic daily living arising from a broken hip, a stroke, incontinence, diabetes, etc.). This must legally be an ill-conceived approach for at least the following reasons.

First, the National Framework guidance in which this rule is expounded is statutory guidance and so cannot simply be disregarded.[1]

Second, in any case, the rule explained in the guidance is based on the legal effect of section 117 itself, which as noted above is limited to meeting needs in relation to a person's mental disorder and therefore cannot be used to meet unrelated physical needs. The ombudsman has therefore found fault, when a CCG has wrongly refused to assess.

CCG wrongly refusing to assess for CHC in the case of a person receiving section 117 aftercare services. A CCG refused to consider assessing eligibility for CHC in the case of a woman who received section 117 services; originally, she had been detained under the Mental Health Act 1983 for psychotic depression.

---

1 National Framework 2018, paras 313–317.

> She now needed to be in a care home, but this was because of physical and cognitive deterioration.
> The NHS and social services argued that the care home placement was not related to the reason for her original detention. The ombudsman took a different view, stating that the care home was still meeting significant needs arising from her mental disorder and the CCG should have done a CHC assessment in relation to any other needs.[1]

Mental health aftercare: funding split

As noted above, the section 117 duty is shared by the NHS and social services. However, neither legislation nor guidance prescribes a formula for splitting the funding. Guidance states that it is therefore up to local authorities and CCGs locally to decide to use a particular model or tool. If, when applying such a local tool, the NHS agrees fully to fund the services required in any particular case, this does not mean it is a CHC case.[2] It would simply be section 117 provision, albeit 100 per cent funded by the NHS.

Similarly, if for convenience the CHC Checklist and Decision Support Tool are used to determine the split in section 117 funding, this does not mean that the CHC rules apply either. It is just that the CHC rules will have been borrowed and used to determine the split of funding under section 117. This of course can lead to further confusion if care is not taken. In one case, the CHC rules were used to determine section 117 provision, but were in any case misapplied. The ombudsman duly found fault with an NHS Trust, the CCG and the local authority, a finding based on lack of effective joint working, on poor understanding and on poor communication.[3]

Mobility, see *Decision Support Tool*

Multi-disciplinary team

Regulations state that if an assessment of eligibility for NHS Continuing Healthcare (CHC) is being done, the Decision Support Tool (DST) must be used and completed by a multi-disciplinary team (MDT) – other than in

---

1 LGSCO, *Oxfordshire County Council*, 2018 (16 017 505), paras 21–22.
2 National Framework 2018, para 317.
3 LGSCO, *Leicester City Council*, 2017 (16 000 552), paras 59–68.

end of life cases when the Fast Track Pathway Tool is used, to be completed instead by an appropriate clinician.[1]

Multi-disciplinary team: make-up

The regulations define the MDT as a team consisting of at least two professionals from different health care professions – or one health care professional and one person responsible for assessing care and support needs under section 9 of the Care Act 2014.[2] The local authority has a duty, when requested, to cooperate with the NHS clinical commissioning group (CCG) in arranging for one or more staff to participate in the MDT.[3]

The definition of the MDT is therefore not, at its bare legal minimum, as expansive as it might sound. However, guidance confirms that this is a minimum requirement and that the MDT should 'usually include both health and social care professionals, who are knowledgeable about the individual's health and social care needs and, where possible, have recently been involved in the assessment, treatment or care of the individual'.[4]

These professionals could include, for example, nurse assessors, social care practitioners, physiotherapists, occupational therapists, dieticians and nutritionists, medical practitioners (GPs and consultants), community psychiatric nurses, ward nurses, care provider staff, community nurses, specialist nurses, community matrons and discharge nurses.[5] The person being assessed, or their representative, cannot be a member of the MDT but should be given 'every opportunity' to contribute; this would include recording their views within the DST.[6]

Multi-disciplinary team: role

The role of the MDT is 'to collate and review the relevant information on the individual's health and social care needs. The MDT uses this information to help clarify individual needs through the completion of the DST, and then works collectively to make a professional judgement about eligibility for CHC, which will be reflected in its recommendation.'[7] If the MDT fails to make a recommendation, the ombudsman may find fault.[8]

---

1   NHS Responsibilities Regulations 2012, r.21(5).
2   NHS Responsibilities Regulations 2012, r.21(5).
3   Care and Support (Provision of Health Services) Regulations 2014, r.3(2).
4   National Framework 2018, para 121.
5   National Framework Practice Guidance 2018, para 24.4.
6   National Framework Practice Guidance 2018, paras 24.1–24.2.
7   National Framework 2018, para 123.
8   PSOW, *Carmarthenshire Local Health Board*, 2010 (200801759), para 70.

If an assessment of needs has been completed recently, this can be used to inform the completion of the DST, but that assessment must be an accurate reflection of current need.[1]

Statutory guidance to the effect that the professionals involved should be knowledgeable is not necessarily followed in practice; where it is not, it could be challenged. The Public Accounts Committee in 2018 noted evidence that 60 per cent of healthcare professionals doing CHC assessments lacked sufficient specialist knowledge of the medical condition that they are looking at.[2]

> **No involvement of Parkinson's nurse.** The All Parliamentary Group on Parkinson's reported that a particular concern of a number of organisations was the lack of involvement of expert or relevant health or social care professionals in assessments. People affected by Parkinson's described how they had secured the support of their Parkinson's nurse to provide evidence supporting applications for NHS continuing care. However, the Parkinson's nurse was not involved in the specific assessment, nor was their advice sought, despite being noted as someone involved in the individual's care and treatment.[3]

Given the clear pointer in the National Framework, it is arguably a breach of the statutory guidance if a CCG starts to apply a blanket rule, sometimes reported, that the professionals involved should not know the patient (so they are not tempted to reach a biased decision).

This would appear to represent an anti-clinical, anti-therapeutic mindset, never mind being in breach of the guidance; it is also a neat example of how CHC is not a clinical but an administrative and legal category, something which patients and their families may understandably find difficult to grasp. See *Expertise of assessors, and knowledge of the patient*.

Guidance states a number of approaches could be used – face-to-face, video/teleconferencing – for arranging MDT assessments 'in order to ensure active participation of all members as far as is possible'. However, it goes on

---

1   Decision Support Tool 2018, para 2.
2   House of Commons Public Accounts Committee. *NHS Continuing Healthcare funding*. London: TSO, 2018, p.6.
3   All Party Parliamentary Group on Parkinson's. *Failing to care: NHS continuing care in England*. London: Parkinson's UK, 2013, p.18.

to say that normally there should be a face-to-face meeting.[1] The ombudsman has held that a meeting is required, not just a virtual meeting.[2]

The ombudsman has found fault with the decision-making process of an MDT if the above rules are not complied with. See the example below.

> **Failings of MDT: professional qualifications, make-up of team, extent of evidence, reasoning.** An MDT process was criticised by the ombudsman on a number of grounds. These included:
>
> - lack of knowledge of what professional qualifications the two coordinators had
>
> - lack of an MDT truly representative of Mrs C's health care needs
>
> - the decision to be taken on her eligibility being discussed with the family before the two people had scrutinised the assessments and reports
>
> - lack of an up-to-date nursing assessment
>
> - not taking into consideration the request by the social work assessor that a nursing assessment and a psychiatric report were required
>
> - absolute lack of any recorded minutes of the discussion or of how these two people reached their decision.[3]

---

1 National Framework 2018, paras 121, 26.2.
2 PSOW, *Carmarthenshire Local Health Board*, 2010 (200801759), paras 65, 70.
3 PSOW, *Carmarthenshire Local Health Board*, 2010 (200802583), paras 65, 68.

N

National Framework on NHS Continuing Healthcare

The National Framework on NHS Continuing Healthcare is a large piece of statutory guidance, which should not be departed from without good reason. See *Guidance*.

The National Framework itself does not state that it is statutory guidance; this is unhelpful because most such guidance does contain such a statement, so that its status is clear from the outset. Compare the Care Act guidance, which is actually entitled *Care and support statutory guidance*.[1]

Notwithstanding, the National Framework clearly is, in effect, statutory guidance because NHS regulations stipulate that clinical commissioning groups (CCGs) are required to have regard to it in relation to assessment of eligibility for NHS Continuing Healthcare (CHC), dispute resolution and responding to the recommendations of an independent review panel.[2]

Likewise, local authorities must have regard to the National Framework in relation to referring people to the NHS who might have CHC needs and to dispute resolution – and, by implication, when cooperating in terms of multi-disciplinary assessment to determine CHC eligibility.[3] It sits alongside other statutory guidance, including the Checklist, the Decision Support Tool and the Fast Track Pathway Tool, all of which are referred to also by the NHS regulations.

The courts have stated that the power to establish the National Framework derives ultimately from section 2 of the National Health Service Act 2006, which empowers the Secretary of State to do anything 'whatsoever which is calculated to facilitate, or is conducive or incidental to, the discharge' of duties under the Act, and that the interpretation of the National Framework is 'ultimately a matter for the court having regard to its development, statutory context and purpose'. Therefore, CCGs must take the National Framework into account and can be challenged in judicial review 'for failing to consider it or misconstruing or misapplying it'.[4]

---

1 Department of Health. *Care and support statutory guidance*. London: DH, 2016, para 7.22.
2 NHS Responsibilities Regulations 2012, rr.21(5), 22(2), 23(9).
3 Care and Support (Provision of Health Services) Regulations 2014, rr.3, 4.
4 *R(Whapples) v Birmingham Crosscity Clinical Commissioning Group* [2015] EWCA Civ 435, para 25.

The above notwithstanding, in the *Gossip* case the court noted that the Framework, even if it cannot be ignored, was 'a relevant factor in the process and no more than that'. It did not amount to a 'direction' (which would have to be complied with) and departure from it, even without reasons being given, was not necessarily unlawful.[1]

National Health Service Act 2006

The process for assessment of NHS Continuing Healthcare (CHC) must take place under the NHS Commissioning Board and Clinical Commissioning Groups (Responsibilities and Standing Rules) Regulations 2012. Provision of services to meet CHC needs takes place, overall, under the National Health Service Act 2006:

- **Comprehensive health service.**

    The Secretary of State must continue the promotion in England of a comprehensive health service designed to secure improvement: (a) in the physical and mental health of the people of England, and (b) in the prevention, diagnosis and treatment of physical and mental illness. (s.1)

- **Services free of charge.**

    The services provided as part of the health service in England must be free of charge except in so far as the making and recovery of charges is expressly provided for by or under any enactment, whenever passed. (s.1)

- **NHS provision of services.**

    A clinical commissioning group [CCG] must arrange for the provision of the following to such extent as it considers necessary to meet the reasonable requirements of the persons for whom it has responsibility –

    a. hospital accommodation,

    b. other accommodation for the purpose of any service provided under this Act,

---

1 *R(Gossip) v NHS Surrey Downs Clinical Commissioning Group* [2019] EWHC 3411 (Admin), notably paras 27, 77, 94, 97.

c. medical, dental, ophthalmic, nursing and ambulance services,

d. such other services or facilities for the care of pregnant women, women who are breastfeeding and young children as the [CCG] considers are appropriate as part of the health service,

e. such other services or facilities for the prevention of illness, the care of persons suffering from illness and the after-care of persons who have suffered from illness as the group considers are appropriate as part of the health service,

f. such other services or facilities as are required for the diagnosis and treatment of illness. (s.3)

Guidance states that 'CCGs must exercise these functions consistently with the duty to promote a comprehensive health service. NHS Continuing Healthcare is provided as part of these functions.'[1]

As far as CHC goes, any accommodation provided would fall under paragraphs a) and b) immediately above, whilst other services would come under c) and e). The duties in sections 1 and 3 have in the past been characterised as general 'target' duties, not readily enforceable by individuals, and sufficiently vague to allow the rationing of health care.

The courts have noted that the duty in section 1 is not to provide a comprehensive service, but merely to promote one: not at all the same thing. This is important because 'a comprehensive health service may never, for human, financial and other resource reasons, be achievable'.[2]

National Health Service Act 2006: rationing and CHC

NHS rationing is nothing new. It has occurred ever since the NHS came into being in 1948. Legally, the scope for it is further facilitated because the duties in section 3 are subject to the proviso that provision is restricted to the extent the CCG considers necessary.

In the case of paragraph e), highly relevant to the continuing care of CHC patients, there is a further proviso, that the CCG consider any particular provision as appropriate as part of the health service. So, it is clear that section 3(1) of the National Health Service Act 'does not impose an absolute duty to provide the specified services. The Secretary of State is entitled to

---

1 National Framework 2018, para 41.
2 R(Coughlan) v North and East Devon Health Authority [2001] Q.B. 213, paras 22–25.

have regard to the resources made available to him under current government economic policy.'[1]

However, there is something distinctly peculiar about rationing in relation to CHC. Most rationing involves determining which health care needs, and treatments for them, should be prioritised. For example, the commissioning of hip replacement and cataract surgery seem often to be expendable when CCGs come under pressure.[2] Nobody claims that these are not health care needs, merely that they have to be rationed.

In the case of CHC, however, something qualitatively different is happening; quite obviously health-care-based needs are being re-categorised – through what is effectively administrative and quasi-legal subterfuge – as social care needs. In that way central government attempts to avoid the contentious allegation that it is denying health care at least to some people who, on any reasoned view, have high-level health care needs. This is explained more fully in Chapter 3 of this book.

National Health Service Act 2006: strength of legal duty to meet CHC needs, once assessed

There is a further issue arising from the loose nature of sections 1 and 3 of the National Health Service Act 2006. Namely, whether once a person has been assessed as eligible for CHC, the CCG is obliged to meet the person's needs, despite the person's falling into the legal category of CHC eligibility. There are several issues to consider.

First, the courts have held that provision of services under section 3 of the National Health Service Act 2006 is a target duty only, as already noted above. This enables the Secretary of State for Health, or CCGs at local level, normally to decide which categories of health condition will be eligible for provision and in what circumstances. Thus, the courts have stated that the NHS can prioritise categories of need, choosing not to meet some, albeit that any such decisions must be 'rationally based upon a proper consideration of the facts', including that the NHS has weighed up the nature and seriousness of conditions, and the effectiveness of treatments on offer.[3]

However, in the case of CHC, CCGs cannot decide that CHC needs, as a category, are not eligible needs, because NHS regulations state that they are.

---

1 *R v Secretary of State for Social Services, ex parte Hincks* [1980] 1 BMLR 93.
2 Donnelly, L. 'More than half of NHS authorities rationing cataract operations.' *Daily Telegraph*, 20 March 2019. And: Donnelly, L. 'Hip operations only for those in so much pain they can't sleep under new NHS rationing plans.' *Daily Telegraph*, 26 January 2017.
3 *R v North West Lancashire Health Authority, ex p A* [2000] 1 WLR 977.

Second, in the case of an individual patient eligible for CHC, could the CCG plead lack of resources and decline altogether to meet the person's needs? This might seem an odd question, but the NHS in fact does deny access generally to NHS services on a daily basis to people who are clearly in need, including significant, even urgent, need.

For example, a baby might be accepted as in serious need of, and therefore eligible for, heart surgery but be continually denied on the grounds of lack of resources.[1] Similarly, patients might wait years for orthopaedic surgery and the courts decline to find legal grounds for intervening,[2] and potentially lifesaving treatment for leukaemia might be lawfully denied to a 10-year-old girl.[3]

Third, the courts have stated that provision of CHC is a target duty only:

> the duties relating to the provision of health services and social services is not between two duties that are enforceable by individuals. This is because the duties of the local authority are so enforceable but the relevant duties of the Secretary of State for Health in respect of the NHS are target duties.[4]

It is possible that a target duty may 'crystallise' into a specific, enforceable duty because of human rights considerations.[5] However, the courts have noted that the European Convention on Human Rights 'does not give the applicants rights to free healthcare in general... Even [were there] such a right it would be qualified by the authority's right to determine healthcare priorities in the light of its limited resources'. And even with human rights in mind, 'decisions about the allocation of limited resources may well be justified as necessary in the interests of the economic well-being of the country'.[6]

Fourth, this question arguably remains somewhat open because, on the face of the legislation, it is not clear that a finding of eligibility for CHC means that there is an absolute duty to meet the need in every case in all circumstances, no matter the resources at issue.

---

1   *R v Central Birmingham Health Authority, ex p Collier* (1988) unreported, Court of Appeal. And: *R v Central Birmingham Health Authority, ex p Walker* [1987] 3 BMLR 32, Court of Appeal.
2   *R v Secretary of State for Social Services, ex parte Hincks* [1980] 1 BMLR 93.
3   *R v Cambridge Health Authority, ex p B* [1995] 6 MLR 250, Court of Appeal.
4   *R(Grogan) v Bexley NHS Care Trust* [2006] EWHC 44 (Admin), para 37.
5   *R(T) v London Borough of Haringey* [2005] EWHC 2235 (Admin), para 142.
6   *N v ACCG* [2017] UKSC 22, paras 37, 44.

> **Denying provision for those eligible for CHC?** In one legal case, the NHS was found to have acted unlawfully by denying a person CHC provision on the grounds of the person's own financial resources (in the form of a personal injury compensation payment). However, the judge suggested that had the CCG been denying provision not just for him, but 'for everyone who is otherwise eligible to receive [CHC provision], because it does not have the funds to do so', then the position would have been different.[1]

So, the question seems to be whether the special and detailed rules about establishing eligibility for CHC displace the discretion which the NHS otherwise and normally has to decide about use of its resources on the basis of weighing up clinical factors and priorities.[2]

Fifth, once eligibility for CHC has been established, and the CCG has agreed to meet the needs, then a question may arise as to what the provision will look like. The courts have established that it is for the CCG to decide the level of provision[3] and that it is obliged only to meet needs in the most cost-effective way[4] as the National Framework guidance sets out at some length. Nevertheless, the basic need must be met. For example, when insufficient provision was made to meet a person's CHC needs, despite the clear recommendations by the multi-disciplinary team of what would be required, the ombudsman found fault.[5] See **Cost-effectiveness**.

Nature

The word 'nature' in relation to NHS Continuing Healthcare (CHC) derives originally from legal case law and refers to the 'quality' of care a person requires.[6] It is directly relevant to deciding whether a person has CHC needs or not. It complements the term 'incidental or ancillary' which refers to the 'quantity' of care required. Various legal considerations are attached to both these terms, which occur in both NHS regulations and section 22 of the Care Act 2014.[7] See *Incidental or ancillary or of a nature beyond social services*.

---

1   *Booker v NHS Oldham and Direct Line Insurance* [2010] EWHC 2593 (Admin), para 29.
2   See e.g. *R(Condliff) v North Staffordshire Primary Care Trust* [2011] EWCA Civ 910, para 36.
3   *R(T) v London Borough of Haringey* [2005] EWHC 2235 (Admin), para 145.
4   *N v ACCG* [2017] UKSC 22, paras 37, 44.
5   PSOW, *Carmarthenshire Local Health Board*, 2009 (200800779), paras 131–132.
6   *R(Coughlan) v North and East Devon Health Authority* [2001] Q.B. 213, para 30.
7   NHS Responsibilities Regulations 2012, r.21(7).

Guidance goes on to elaborate that nature is one of the four characteristics of a person's needs that, alone or in combination, may demonstrate the existence of a primary health need, requiring CHC services. The decision about this will follow on from completion of the Decision Support Tool (DST). Thus, nature represents 25 per cent of the possibilities *set out in the guidance* and can, alone, form the basis of a primary health need, even without the presence of the other three characteristics (intensity, complexity and unpredictability).

This would in any case follow from the effect of the NHS regulations, noted immediately above, since under the legislation itself the nature of a person's needs, alone, can legally indicate a primary health need. For patients, families and practitioners, therefore, reference to nature – and the definition of it set out in guidance – is of great importance. Points made in the guidance include:

- **Nature and Decision Support Tool**. If a primary health need is strongly indicated when the DST is completed, guidance implies that detailed reference to the nature of the needs will be less necessary. On the other hand, if there is less certainty from completion of the DST as to the existence of a primary health need, then 'careful consideration must be given to the four key characteristics of nature, intensity, complexity or unpredictability of the individual's needs'.[1]

- **Nature: overall effect of needs and quality of intervention**. Guidance states that nature is about:

    > the particular characteristics of an individual's needs (which can include physical, mental health or psychological needs) and the type of those needs. This also describes the overall effect of those needs on the individual, including the type (quality) of interventions required to manage them.[2]

NHS-employed staff

Guidance states that eligibility for NHS Continuing Healthcare (CHC) does not depend on the use (or not) of NHS-employed staff to provide care, nor on the need for or presence of 'specialist staff' (NHS or otherwise) in care delivery.[3]

---

1   Decision Support Tool 2018, para 38.
2   National Framework 2018, para 59; Decision Support Tool 2018, p.43.
3   National Framework 2018, paras 65–66.

This principle was illustrated in the *Pointon* case, in which a spouse was doing most of the caring (expertly, given her husband's level of needs). She was not employed by the NHS, nor was she a paid nurse or other specialist worker. Yet her husband was clearly eligible for CHC, and she had developed skills and expertise.[1]

Likewise, in another ombudsman case, when the reasons why eligibility was wrongly denied included the fact that a person's needs were met by a nursing home with minimal involvement of NHS staff.[2] See also ***Specialist staff***.

NHS England

NHS England is a public body to which NHS functions are delegated under the National Health Service Act 2006. It describes itself as leading the NHS in England, setting priorities, allocating more than £100 billion in funds and commissioning some health services itself, but mainly 'supporting' local NHS clinical commissioning groups (CCGs) to commission the bulk of NHS hospital, community and ambulance services.[3]

In respect of NHS Continuing Healthcare (CHC), therefore, its main role lies in 'supporting' CCGs. In limited circumstances NHS England itself has a direct responsibility for commissioning CHC services for prisoners and for serving military personnel and their families.[4] In this book, reference to CCG responsibility for CHC should be read as referring also to NHS England in these limited circumstances. NHS England also has a legal duty to appoint members of, and has the legal power to arrange, independent review panels.[5]

The predecessors to NHS England came in the form of 14 regional health authorities (1974–1996); the NHS Executive with eight regional offices (1996–2002); and 28, reduced to 10, strategic health authorities (2002–2013). Meanwhile, NHS England, in existence since 2013, began life with 27 regional teams, now reduced to 12.

The wider role of NHS England and its comparable predecessors in relation to CHC is considered in Chapter 3 of this book.

---

1   *Cambridgeshire Health Authority* (E.22/02–03). In: Health Service Ombudsman. HC 704. *Selected investigations completed October 2003–March 2004*. London: TSO, 2004.
2   PSOW, *Cardiff Local Health Board*, 2008 (200700482), paras 16, 40–49.
3   NHS England. *What does NHS England do?* Accessed on 20 February, 2019 at: www.england.nhs.uk/about/about-nhs-england
4   NHS Responsibilities Regulations 2012, r.20(2).
5   NHS Responsibilities Regulations 2012, r.23.

Northern Ireland

This book does not extend to coverage of NHS Continuing Healthcare in Northern Ireland. In summary, 'Continuing Healthcare' is meant to be available in Northern Ireland through Health and Social Care Trusts (HSCTs). Guidance states loosely only that:

> it is for clinicians, together with other health and social care professional colleagues and in consultation with the service user, his/her family and carers to determine through a comprehensive assessment of need whether an individual's primary need is for healthcare.[1]

In this case an HSCT would then fully fund the care package.

In 2014, Age Northern Ireland published a report arguing that people were being denied access to, and award of, Continuing Healthcare.[2] HSCTs confirmed that, between 2011 and 2016, only 43 people only were assessed as eligible for Continuing Healthcare, a very low number. In 2017, a consultation was held by the Department of Health of Northern Ireland, but no action has been taken since.[3]

Nurse assessors

Guidance makes fleeting reference to 'nurse assessors', stating merely that they might be part of the multi-disciplinary team (MDT) applying the Decision Support Tool (DST), and might require training.[4]

In practice, NHS clinical commissioning groups (CCGs) employ and train staff often known as nurse assessors with special responsibility for carrying out assessments for NHS Continuing Healthcare (CHC) eligibility and also for funded nursing care (FNC) eligibility. They may play a prominent part in ensuring that assessments and eligibility recommendations are carried out properly and according to the rules. Given the complexity and counter-intuitiveness of these rules, together with the defects and contradictions within them (see Chapter 3), this is arguably a demanding and difficult role.

However, because of their sometimes-pivotal role in CHC decision-making, such assessors are sometimes exposed by CCGs to legal pitfalls

---

1 Powell, T. and Mackley, A. *NHS Continuing Healthcare in England*. Standard note: SN/SP/6128. London: House of Commons Library, 2018, pp.23–25. And: Department of Health, Social Services and Public Safety. *Care management, provision of services and charging guidance*. Circular HSC (ECCU) 1/2010. Belfast: DHSSPS, 2010, p.5.
2 Age Northern Ireland. *The denial of NHS Continuing Health in Northern Ireland*. Belfast: Age NI, 2014.
3 Northern Ireland Department of Health. *Continuing Healthcare in Northern Ireland: introducing a transparent and fair system: consultation document*. Belfast: NIDH, June 2017, pp.4–5.
4 National Framework Practice Guidance 2018, paras 1.7, 24.4.

– which, if fallen into, could form the basis of a challenge against a CCG. Problems may arise, for example, if assessors are inadequately trained about the rules, or are encouraged or pressurised by CCGs to adopt practices and take decisions inconsistent with those rules.

> **Practitioner: completing Checklist at wrong time and providing no evidence or reasoning.** A 'nurse case manager' completed a CHC Checklist only after a determination had first been made about the Registered Nursing Care Contribution (now FNC) for the resident of a nursing home. This was in the wrong order; it should have been the other way around. Second, completion of the Checklist resulted in a negative outcome, reached in the most cursory way; every category of need was simply ringed with the word 'no' without any comment, explanation or evidence. Consequently, the CCG was held to have behaved irrationally, unreasonably and therefore unlawfully.[1]

A further practice can unwittingly undermine the MDT requirement in NHS regulations for completion of the DST.

> **Undermining the multi-disciplinary team requirement.** A nurse assessor might carry out the assessment alone, and simply send a completed DST for signing by a social worker. This is hardly what would be implied by the word 'team' in the regulations[2] and is contrary to guidance which states that 'it is crucial to have a genuine and meaningful multi-disciplinary discussion about the correct recommendation to be made. This should normally involve a face-to-face MDT meeting (including the individual and/or their representative).'[3] The ombudsman has stated that an actual face-to-face meeting is required.[4]

Because nurse assessors may be asked by CCGs to complete many assessments, with just a social worker in addition, they may neither know the patient nor be knowledgeable about the person's particular health condition. This, too, may be inconsistent with National Framework guidance:

---

1   *R(Dennison) v Bradford Districts Clinical Commissioning Group* [2014] EWHC 2552 (Admin), paras 12, 13, 17.
2   NHS Responsibilities Regulations 2012, r.21(5).
3   National Framework Practice Guidance 2018, para 26.2.
4   PSOW, *Carmarthenshire Local Health Board*, 2010 (200801759), paras 65, 70.

Whilst as a minimum requirement an MDT can comprise two professionals from different healthcare professions, the MDT should usually include both health and social care professionals, who are knowledgeable about the individual's health and social care needs and, where possible, have recently been involved in the assessment, treatment or care of the individual.[1]

Nurse assessors: further pitfalls to be avoided

At an extreme, perhaps because of the difficult role into which they have been propelled, nurse assessors are sometimes perceived to take a rigid and unforgiving approach, not always in accordance with the rules, and to risk undermining evidence about a person's needs. This can sometimes be challenged.

> **Confrontational, aggressive approach: CHC eligibility wrongly denied.** A woman had a massive stroke, which left her paralysed down one side, with severe dementia and half blind. She was also in a lot of pain. Her daughter, a former magistrate, asked for a CHC assessment but was told there was no point. She insisted. An assessment was carried out and the evidence was downplayed: paralysis was described as weakness and dementia as her being a bit muddled or 'wandersome'.
>
> The daughter requested another assessment. She described one of the assessors as aggressive, confrontational, shouting, jumping up and saying, 'If you speak again, I will close this meeting down and you won't have any chance of being heard then.' The daughter replied, 'That's not fair if you don't let us talk.' The answer came back, 'It's not about what's fair.'
>
> As a result, palliative care could not be provided at home, and the mother had to go into a care home, where she was neglected, losing a stone in weight, suffering a burn and developing infections. The daughter rescued her from the home, but the mother then died a 'hideous death', in a 'shocking state'. The daughter retrospectively appealed the CCG's decision, saying she would bring a solicitor to the hearing. Within two days, the CCG conceded and agreed to refund the care fees.[2]

---

1 National Framework 2018, para 121.
2 Deith, J. 'Continuing healthcare: the secret fund.' BBC Radio 4 *File on 4*, 23 November 2014. Accessed on 18 July 2019 at: www.bbc.co.uk/programmes/b04p86c4

The following ombudsman case is worth summarising in some detail in order to indicate the questionable practices that can sometimes creep into CHC decision-making. These included confrontation, unprofessional behaviour and the making of 'false claims' by a nurse assessor in order to discredit the family and its evidence.

> **Breaching the guidance, excluding the family, making false claims, contrived evidence.** A man had dementia, advanced kidney disease (now terminal) and other medical conditions. In hospital, a full DST assessment was carried out with a ward nurse, a CHC coordinator, the social worker and two members of the family. The meeting ended after three hours without agreement. He was then discharged to an interim placement, funded by the NHS. A different nurse took over as CHC coordinator.
>
> At a second CHC assessment meeting, the professionals' scores were recorded as severe in two domains (cognition and the 12th domain), moderate in five domains, low in three domains and no needs in two domains. The nurse decided the recommendation would be FNC, not CHC, despite the fact that two assessments of 'severe' normally indicate CHC eligibility and that in the 12th domain it was noted that he had aggressive cancer, needed palliative care and his life expectancy was months at most.
>
> The family complained, and this triggered a third assessment meeting, for which the CCG had instructed the nurse to complete a third DST. However, the nurse stated simply that the man would not receive a further DST assessment because she had already completed another Checklist (without the family's involvement) and he was no longer eligible for even a full assessment, let alone a finding of CHC eligibility.
>
> The nurse said the professionals had the factual evidence but the family did not because they had not 'spoken to anybody'. She said that, according to the care home staff, his cognition had improved, although the care home staff subsequently denied this. The nurse also said she had spoken to both of the man's GPs, who had reportedly said he was not in the terminal phase of his illness. The family said that two months earlier the man's consultant had told them he had a maximum of six months to live. The nurse claimed the consultant denied this.
>
> The family stated that at the meeting the nurse had acted as both CHC coordinator and expert, contrary to the guidance; she had dominated the meeting, said the family was not acting in Mr D's best interests, raised inappropriate topics about Mr D's resuscitation status and treatment, and inappropriately discussed his finances. And, the family maintained, according

to the professional assessment the MDT should have recommended that Mr D was eligible for funding, but it did not. Furthermore, both GPs denied having given the nurse the information which she claimed to have received.

Confrontational and unprofessional manner of nurse, making false claims, discrediting the family. The ombudsman made the following findings: that it was more likely than not that the nurse: had failed to carry out her role in accordance with the National Framework; had raised inappropriate and irrelevant matters at the meeting of 31 July, and acted in an inappropriately confrontational and unprofessional manner; had recommended that the man was not eligible for CHC following the meeting when based on her assessment she should have recommended eligibility; had deliberately failed to follow the CCG's instruction to complete another DST at the third meeting; and had inappropriately completed another Checklist without involving the family, contrary to the guidance in the National Framework.

In addition, the nurse had falsely claimed to the family that the man was no longer eligible for a DST, based on a contrived account of the evidence about his condition, including falsely claiming to have received information from his GPs, in order to obstruct the CHC application; had made knowingly false claims to the CCG about what the family said and had done so to discredit the family; and had caused the family significant distress, frustration and inconvenience at an already difficult and distressing time. The CCG was therefore at fault.[1]

This is clearly just one case but, added to evidence recounted above (and in Chapter 3), may represent more than just an outlier. Fittingly, such an ombudsman case, or even judicial review legal case, is taken against the organisation and not the individual practitioner. This is appropriate because, in many circumstances, all roads lead back to the employer in terms of workplace culture, training, supervision, performance targets and pressures placed upon practitioners.

However, practitioners themselves should be wary of the point at which individual professional conduct may come into question and avoid being pushed across lines which professionally should not be crossed.

For example, in another context, of Personal Independence Payment assessments, a number of referrals have been made of nurses to the Nursing and Midwifery Council (NMC). The basis for some of these referrals has

---

1   LGSCO, *Lancashire County Council*, 2017 (16 000 404), para 43.

included ignoring evidence and not accurately recording assessments,[1] the very type of criticism sometimes made about CHC assessments. The NMC has been seriously criticised by the Professional Standards Authority for, hitherto, not investigating these complaints.[2]

Nutrition, see *Decision Support Tool*

---

1 Pring, J. 'PIP investigation: assessment complaints rise by 880 per cent…in just one year.' *Disability News Service*, 26 October 2017. Accessed on 26 June 2019 at: www.disabilitynewsservice.com/pip-investigation-assessment-complaints-rise-by-880-per-cent-in-just-one-year
2 Professional Standards Authority. *Nursing and Midwifery Council: annual review of performance 2017/18*. London: PSA, 2019, paras 6.51–6.62.

P

Panels

Clinical commissioning groups (CCGs) often subject recommendations for NHS Continuing Healthcare eligibility to a local panel. There is no duty to have a panel, equally no rule prohibiting this practice. However, the functioning of a panel is subject to the overall rules on decision-making by the CCG imposed in law by regulations,[1] as well as by the statutory guidance setting out how decision-making should proceed, for example ensuring that panels are not being utilised to introduce delay.[2] See *Clinical commissioning groups*.

Paying privately, see *Private top-up care*

People's own homes

Guidance confirms that eligibility for NHS Continuing Healthcare (CHC) is to be considered irrespective of setting, and it includes the meeting of both health and social care needs.[3] The care package must be funded and arranged solely by the NHS.[4]

It follows, therefore, that in a person's own home, for example, a range of social care as well as health care needs must be met under CHC. Guidance elaborates, stating that this responsibility for assessed health and social care needs could include items such as equipment provision, routine and incontinence laundry, daily domestic tasks such as food preparation, shopping, washing up, bed-making and support to access community facilities (including additional support needs for the individual whilst the carer has a break).

---

1 NHS Responsibilities Regulations 2012, rr.21–23.
2 National Framework Practice Guidance 2018, para 38.3.
3 National Framework 2018, paras 4, 63.
4 NHS Responsibilities Regulations 2012, r.20.

The guidance notes, however, that the NHS is not responsible for basic costs such as rent, food, normal utility bills, clothing and other normal household items. This is because a range of everyday household items are expected to be covered by personal income or through welfare benefits (e.g. food, rent/mortgage interest, fuel, clothing and other normal household items).[1]

> **Motor vehicle fuel costs.** The courts have held that the exclusion in the guidance of fuel costs from CHC provision refers to household fuel and does not refer to fuel for transport, and that if petrol costs, otherwise funded by the patient, are essential to the provision of the package of care, then they could, depending on the circumstances, fall to the NHS to fund.[2]

The guidance refers also to additional support needs that might still come under the Care Act 2014 and within the remit of local authorities, including support with essential parenting activities, deputyship or appointeeship services, safeguarding concerns, and carer support or services required to enable an informal carer to maintain his or her caring responsibilities.[3] This reference to carers' issues under the Care Act 2014 is distinct from clinical commissioning group responsibilities under the National Health Service Act 2006 to provide carers with a break (respite) or other direct help with caring responsibilities. See **Carers**.

Person and family involvement

Guidance states consistently that the person being assessed, together with representatives or family, should be involved in the decision-making process. Given how difficult it is to understand NHS Continuing Healthcare (CHC), this is particularly important.

Without family involvement it becomes easier for the clinical commissioning group (CCG), or sometimes a local authority which is involved, to ignore what could be crucial evidence as to the degree and type of need,[4] or to discredit families and in some cases wilfully to misrepresent them.[5]

---

1 National Framework 2018, paras 291–292.
2 *R(MH) v National Health Service* [2015] EWHC 4243 (Admin), paras 26–27.
3 National Framework 2018, para 294.
4 *R(Goldsmith) v Wandsworth London Borough Council* [2004] EWCA Civ 1170, Court of Appeal, para 79.
5 LGSCO, *Lancashire County Council*, 2017 (16 000 404), para 43.

The guidance states that CHC assessments and assessments for NHS funded nursing care should be carried out so that the 'individual being assessed and their representative understand the process and receive advice and information that will maximise their ability to participate in the process in an informed way. Decisions and rationales that relate to eligibility should be transparent from the outset to individuals, carers, family and staff alike.'[1]

A person-centred approach should include full and direct involvement, taking account of views and wishes, addressing communication and language needs, obtaining consent to assessment and sharing of information, openness about risk, and keeping the individual or their representative fully informed.[2]

In terms of involvement in the decision-making process, the individual 'should normally be given the opportunity to be present at the completion of the Checklist, together with any representative they may have', and likewise in relation to the full assessment process involving the Decision Support Tool (DST):

- **Individual involvement in assessment and completion of the DST.**

  The individual should be invited to be present or represented wherever practicable. The individual and their representative(s) should be given reasonable notice of completion of the DST to enable them to arrange for a family member or other person to be present, taking into account their personal circumstances. If it is not practicable for the individual (or their representative) to be present, their views should be obtained and actively considered in the completion of the DST. Those completing the DST should record how the individual (or their representative) contributed to the assessment of their needs, and if they were not involved why this was.[3]

A lack of information, in advance of assessments and meetings, may simply mean, as the ombudsman noted, that the family member is overwhelmed and does not understand the terminology being used.[4] In the following cases, the ombudsman found lack of clear information and communication.

---

1   National Framework 2018, para 70.
2   National Framework 2018, para 68.
3   Decision Support Tool 2018, para 14.
4   LGSCO, *Norfolk County Council,* 2018 (17 007 590), para 38.

Absence of information about process and incomplete documentation. A woman had suffered a stroke, was admitted to hospital and then discharged to a nursing home. She had insulin-dependent diabetes and had been left immobile and unable to speak. Prior to her discharge, a feeding tube was removed. She was assessed as ineligible for continuing care.

The Health Service Ombudsman criticised the decision on the grounds that the assessment documentation was incomplete and that the family had neither been given information about the eligibility criteria nor been involved properly in the discharge process. The health authority's criteria had been reviewed in the light of the *Coughlan* judgment, but the support documentation for assessment had not been. This led to inconsistency and a lack of clarity.[1]

Poor communication with family. A woman complained in relation to her mother's assessment for CHC. She alleged, amongst other things, that the Trust did not invite her to attend her mother's CHC assessment, and that the assessment and its conclusion, that the mother was eligible for funded nursing care but not CHC, were flawed.

The daughter believed that, as a result of this decision, her mother had had to pay for residential care which should have been fully funded through CHC; the CCG did not tell her of the outcome of her mother's CHC assessment, despite her holding financial power of attorney. This meant she could not appeal the decision. The person doing a later assessment told her that her mother should have been eligible for CHC when first assessed.

The NHS accepted that its communication with the daughter was flawed, a concession which the ombudsman considered appropriate.[2]

The ombudsman has also found fault, in relation to communication and information, when CHC assessment was not explained on hospital discharge;[3] when the difference between CHC and funded nursing care was not explained, and information was not provided about how to appeal a decision;[4] and when, during the process of seeking a review of a decision, a family had letters not responded to, experienced delays in receiving other responses and was provided with incorrect information about the review.[5]

---

1   *Gloucestershire Health Authority* (E.112/02–03). In: Health Service Ombudsman. HC 119. *Selected investigations completed April–September 2003*. London: TSO, 2003.
2   LGSCO, *Cumbria County Council*, 2018 (17 011 029).
3   PSOW, *Powys Teaching Health Board*, 2019 (201805845).
4   PSOW, *Abertawe Bro Morgannwg University Health Board*, 2019 (201806180).
5   PSOW, *Betsi Cadwaladr University Health Board*, 2017 (201605725).

The ombudsman has also stated that family attendance at a local continuing care panel is not necessarily required in order to achieve involvement, so long as they participated in the multi-disciplinary team assessment process. In that case, however, the local panel should consider whether the family had in fact been sufficiently involved in the process.[1]

The ongoing lack of a system to involve family members has also been criticised, especially when the NHS then takes no steps to improve matters.

> **Bypassing the family.** A nurse assessor visited Mr R in spring 2013 and completed an NHS continuing care assessment. Mr R was found not eligible for funding. Ms J (one of Mr R's representatives) later found out that this assessment had happened. She complained that the NHS had not involved his representatives and had not told them about the outcome. The NHS acknowledged that the systems in place for inviting representatives were not as robust as they should have been. But the ombudsman saw no evidence that it had taken action to prevent the same problems happening again. This was fault.[2]

Personal health budgets

NHS regulations provide that clinical commissioning groups (CCGs) must allocate a personal health budget for NHS Continuing Healthcare (CHC) on request, unless such a budget would not be an appropriate way of meeting the person's needs. A personal budget is an amount of money allocated by the CCG to meet a person's CHC needs.

The way in which the budget is used can include the CCG managing the budget, management of it by a third party or a direct payment to the person themselves so they can purchase their own care. For a request to be made for a personal budget, people need to know about the existence of personal budgets. Accordingly, the regulations go on to state that CCGs must publicise and promote personal health budgets and give information, advice and support to people to help them decide whether to request a budget.[3] See also ***Direct payments.***

---

1 PSOW, *Gwynedd Local Health Board*, 2010 (200802454), para 67.
2 HSO, Trust did not involve representatives in continuing care assessment. Summary 553, October 2014. In: HSO. *Report on selected summaries of investigations by the Parliamentary and Health Service Ombudsman October to November 2014.* London: HSO, 2015.
3 NHS Responsibilities Regulations 2012, r.32A–32B; National Framework 2018, paras 296–298.

Personal injury compensation

The fact that a person has a personal injury compensation payment does not affect their eligibility for provision of NHS Continuing Healthcare services. Whether a person has private wealth, medical insurance, personal injury compensation or financial resources from any other source does not affect the principle that the NHS is a non-means-tested service available to all, subject to clinical priorities and available resources for that class of patient and of patient need.[1]

Pointon case

The *Pointon* case was a landmark Health Service Ombudsman investigation.[2] It is one of those cases in which the ombudsman found that the person was clearly eligible for NHS Continuing Healthcare (CHC). The patient had dementia, confused behaviour and a range of associated needs. See **Indicative cases**.

This finding of eligibility was notable because it related both to a person in his own home and to that person being cared for largely by an informal carer, his wife (who had become expert in his care), without the regular input of nurses or care workers. The case is a counter to those NHS commissioning groups which might sometimes attempt wrongly to deny eligibility for CHC on the basis that an informal carer is carrying out caring responsibilities. In fact, such an approach also contradicts the National Framework guidance.[3]

Predictable unpredictability

Guidance states that simply because an unpredictable need becomes known does not mean that it therefore becomes predictable, in effect 'predictably unpredictable'.[4] The 2018 guidance refers to this because predictable unpredictability has become a widespread term used wrongly by NHS commissioning groups (CCGs) to deny eligibility.

---

1 *Booker v NHS Oldham and Direct Line Insurance* [2010] EWHC 2593 (Admin), para 29.
2 *Cambridgeshire Health Authority* (E.22/02–03). In: Health Service Ombudsman. HC 704. *Selected investigations completed October 2003–March 2004*. London: TSO, 2004.
3 National Framework 2018, paras 65–66.
4 National Framework Practice Guidance 2018, para 3.6.

Parkinson's disease and fluctuation.

> Submissions received from people affected by Parkinson's highlighted [that] the fluctuating nature of the condition was often not taken into account by the assessors. Several people told us of examples where they highlighted the unpredictable nature of the individual's needs, suggesting that this should increase their scoring in certain domains of the decision support tool (and thus the likelihood of receiving continuing care funding), only to be told by the assessors that the individual's needs were seen as 'predictably unpredictable' and therefore warranted a lower score.[1]

Brain injury: banging, hitting, lashing out: 'predictable unpredictability'. An 83-year-old woman became ill with viral encephalitis, leaving her with substantial brain damage and unable to care for herself. Her behaviour became manic, banging on windows, hitting her husband, pulling plugs out of the sockets in the hospital ward. She was denied eligibility for NHS Continuing Healthcare (CHC) because the CCG claimed the unpredictable behaviour could be anticipated.[2]

The implications of this approach taken by some CCGs can lead to absurdity. The National Framework states that four characteristics of a person's need may indicate, alone or in combination, the existence of a primary health need.[3] One of these is unpredictability; the other three are nature, intensity and complexity.

This means that, according to the guidance, unpredictability represents 25 per cent of the indicators relating to eligibility for CHC. Yet, arguing that unpredictability, once known, becomes predictable – and, if not known, clearly remains unknown – risks effectively removing 25 per cent of the eligibility possibilities in direct contradiction of the National Framework guidance. See *Unpredictability*.

Primary decision maker

As a matter of law, the primary decision maker in determining eligibility for NHS Continuing Healthcare (CHC) is clearly the NHS in the form of the local clinical commissioning group (CCG). This means that in relation to a CHC decision, the National Health Service Act 2006 is 'dominant not in

---

1   All Party Parliamentary Group on Parkinson's. *Failing to care: NHS continuing care in England*. London: Parkinson's UK, 2013, p.18.
2   Phillips, N. (Victoria Derbyshire programme). 'Our life savings are spent on care that should be free.' *BBC News*, 11 June 2019. Accessed on 18 July 2019 at: www.bbc.co.uk/news/health-48555199
3   National Framework 2018, para 60.

the sense that a decision under that Act will trump any decision of the local authority, but that it is to that Act which the court must go to determine what are health care needs'.[1]

This was stated in a legal case involving a local authority's challenge to an NHS decision about CHC. The statements made in the case have sometimes reportedly led CCGs to believing that they 'can do what they want' in relation to CHC, that local authorities have no say and must therefore pick up whatever the NHS chooses not to do.

This is not legally correct, since the National Health Service Act 2006 does not determine the legal duties of a local authority and the limits to its legal powers; these limits are to be found in section 22 of the Care Act 2014. Therefore, local authorities are not simply a default health provider of last resort.[2]

Primary health need

Primary health need is a legal term; regulations state that the purpose of an eligibility assessment for NHS Continuing Healthcare (CHC) is to determine whether a person has a primary health need. If so, then they are eligible for CHC, which is defined as a package of care arranged and funded solely by the NHS.[3] This then means that 'the NHS will be responsible for providing for all of that individual's assessed health and associated social care needs, including accommodation, if that is part of the overall need'.[4]

Primary health need is not directly defined in legislation. Instead, guidance states that:

> [it] is a concept developed by the Secretary of State for Health to assist in deciding when an individual's primary need is for healthcare (which it is appropriate for the NHS to provide under the 2006 Act) rather than social care (which the Local Authority may provide under the Care Act 2014).[5]

Primary health need can therefore be viewed as the apex, the summit of a pyramid of decision-making, with layers of decision-making further down. This is set out and explained in Chapter 2 of this book. Failure to demonstrate that a decision is taken in line with the primary health need

---

1   *St Helens Borough Council v Manchester Primary Care Trust* [2008] EWCA Civ 931, paras 33, 37.
2   *R(T) v London Borough of Haringey* [2005] EWHC 2235 (Admin), para 70.
3   NHS Responsibilities Regulations 2012, rr.20, 21(5), (6), (7).
4   National Framework 2018, para 54.
5   National Framework 2018, para 10.

test is unlawful, as stated in the *Grogan* case.[1] The key legal indicator relates to the quantity and quality of care required. See **Incidental or ancillary or of a nature beyond social services**.

A common pitfall is for NHS clinical commissioning groups to consider whether a person's needs can be met by a nursing home, with perhaps only occasional input from NHS professionals; if so, funded nursing care (FNC) is awarded, but the primary health need test is not applied. It must be, and indeed it must be applied before FNC is considered.[2] For instance, the ombudsman found fault in the following case.

> **Primary health need test wrongly not followed because a nursing home was meeting a woman's needs.** A woman in a nursing home required help with all personal care, assessment and management of dietary intake, continence and bowel management, and prevention of pressure areas by registered nurses. She was not mobile and had difficulty in expressing her needs. She was at risk of unstable blood sugars, which required close monitoring and management by a registered nurse. There were elements of unpredictability, instability, complexity and risk of harm. Her needs could be met by the care home staff with some input, not great, from NHS staff. Her needs were therefore being managed. The NHS denied CHC eligibility.
>
> The ombudsman found fault because the primary health need test had not been applied, involving the incidental/ancillary and nature questions. Instead the NHS had relied wrongly on the argument that this was a case of well-managed need requiring minimal intervention from NHS staff. This was fault.[3]

Private top-up care

Sometimes in health or social care a person and/or their family are not happy with the provision being offered and would like alternative provision which would be more expensive. In adult social care there are explicit provisions for this to happen in the case of care home, shared lives or supported living placements.

The rules stipulate, however, that any 'top-up' funding must normally be paid by a third party (typically family), not by the person themselves; and this top-up funding must be agreed, and payable to, the local authority, which would remain responsible for the whole of the placement and the

---
1 *R(Grogan) v Bexley NHS Care Trust* [2006] EWHC 44 (Admin), para 51.
2 NHS Responsibilities Regulations 2012, r.21(3).
3 PSOW, *Cardiff Local Health Board*, 2008 (200700482), paras 16, 40–49.

overall fee, including the top-up element.[1] For care in a person's own home arranged by a local authority, there are no explicit rules one way or the other about 'top-up' funding being made either by the person themselves or by a third party.

However, under NHS legislation, which applies to NHS Continuing Healthcare, the position is different, with key points, summarised by guidance, as follows:

- **Review of current package of NHS care.** If the person believes the current care package is insufficient to meet their needs, the NHS clinical commissioning group should offer a review.
- **No NHS subsidy of private care.** The NHS should never subsidise private care with public money.
- **Not paying for NHS care.** Patients should never be charged for their NHS care, or be allowed to pay towards an NHS service (except where specific legislation is in place to allow this).
- **Separation between NHS care and private care.** There should be as clear a separation as possible between NHS and private care. If a person is in a care home, it might not be possible for privately funded care to be provided at a time separate to NHS-funded care. However, in such circumstances, the private care should be delivered by different staff, and they should not be delivering treatment, care or support identified within the care plan as being part of the NHS-funded service.
- **No downgrading of NHS services to take account of private care.** NHS-funded services must never be reduced or downgraded to take account of privately funded care.[2]

Process, see *Decision-making process*

---

1   Care Act 2014, s.30. And: SI 2014/2670. Care and Support and After-care (Choice of Accommodation) Regulations 2014.
2   National Framework 2018, paras 274–278.

Professional judgement

A key part of deciding about eligibility for NHS Continuing Healthcare (CHC) involves professional and clinical judgement required for completion of the Decision Support Tool or the Fast Track Pathway Tool.

The courts are likely to shy away from considering the professional substance or merits of a decision and confine themselves to analysing the decision-making process in CHC cases – taking the 'orthodox judicial review' approach and not considering and ruling on 'a fully-fledged substantive challenge'. They do not, generally, want to get involved in 'adjudicating complicated questions of fact and judgment whose resolution would depend in large measure on the evaluation of expert opinion'.[1]

The Health Service Ombudsman, too, often takes this approach, although she or he does have the power to consider directly the merits of clinical decisions and does so on some occasions. See **Health Service Ombudsman**.

This does not mean that the courts and the ombudsman can never make a substantive decision as to whether a person is eligible for CHC. The *Coughlan* case in which the Court of Appeal confirmed that Pamela Coughlan was eligible for CHC was a substantive decision about her eligibility but arguably not an interference with professional judgement about her needs; the court was merely considering the legal implications of those needs, which had already been established and were not contested.[2]

Prohibitions

Eligibility for NHS Continuing Healthcare (CHC) is determined as much by what social services is legally prohibited from providing as by what the NHS clinical commissioning group is obliged to provide. This is because section 22 of the Care Act 2014 contains explicit prohibitions in relation to both CHC and registered nursing care. See **Care Act 2014**.

The prohibitions themselves derive from legal case law.[3]

Psychological and emotional needs, see *Decision Support Tool*

---

1 *St Helens Borough Council v Manchester Primary Care Trust* [2008] EWCA Civ 931, paras 30, 33.
2 *R(Coughlan) v North and East Devon Health Authority* [2001] Q.B. 213.
3 *R(Coughlan) v North and East Devon Health Authority* [2001] Q.B. 213. As emphasised in: National Framework 2018, para 44.

Public Service Ombudsman for Wales

This book does not extend its coverage to Wales. However, the framework of law and guidance is very similar to England. For that reason, a number of reports from the Public Service Ombudsman for Wales (PSOW) cases have been included in the book.[1] See ***Wales***.

---

1   Some of the older PSOW cases were tracked down through the references provided in: Clements, L. *et al. Community care and the law.* 7th edition. London: Legal Action Group, 2019, Chapter 13.

Q

Quality of care, see *Nature*

Quantity of care, see *Incidental or ancillary or of a nature beyond social services*

R

Referral for NHS Continuing Healthcare

When a local authority is assessing a person under the Care Act 2014, it must make a referral to the NHS clinical commissioning group (CCG) if it appears to the local authority that the person may be eligible for NHS Continuing Healthcare (CHC).[1] The duty is an important one, since a failure to perform it can affect adversely a person's chances of being assessed for, and awarded, CHC.

This duty of course dovetails with the prohibition on social services from doing anything under the Care Act that the NHS is required to do.[2] CHC is an obvious example.

Local authorities have an incentive to make such referrals for CHC assessment in terms of (a) complying with the legal duty to do so, (b) avoiding the possibility of acting unlawfully by funding care which they are prohibited from providing, (c) ensuring that the person receives the health services they require, (d) saving money (either their own or that of the adult in need) since CHC is funded by the NHS free of charge, and (e) avoiding complaints and adverse findings by the ombudsman.

Referral for NHS Continuing Healthcare: strength of duty and pitfalls

The duty to refer depends merely on an appearance of possible need, thus being triggered at a low threshold.[3] This means that local authorities should make referrals even if there is no certainty, or even likelihood, that the person will be found to be eligible.

If the referral is in the form of an already completed Checklist, then the CCG should normally decide about CHC eligibility within 28 days.[4] Otherwise, it is expected that the CCG will arrange for a completed Checklist

---

1 Care and Support (Assessment) Regulations 2014, r.7.
2 Care Act 2014, s.22.
3 *R v Bristol City Council, ex p Penfold* [1998] 1 CCLR 315, High Court. In which a similar phrase was legally scrutinised, in relation to a local authority's duty of assessment.
4 National Framework 2018, Annex E, para 8.

within 14 days – likewise if a referral to the CCG comes from elsewhere, including a request by the person themselves.[1]

The duty to refer is not necessarily a one-off; if a person's needs change, whether in a care home setting or in their own home, the local authority must reconsider whether to submit a new referral, for example in the form of a further Checklist. The ombudsman might find fault if this is not done.[2]

Similarly, delay without good reason, for instance of a month or two in making the referral to the NHS for consideration of CHC, may be fault in the view of the ombudsman.[3] This may be all the more so when, having agreed that it needed to complete a Checklist for a care home resident, the local authority then unaccountably delayed doing so for eight months.[4]

Local authorities sometimes fail to make such referrals, which is odd, since – as already noted – legal, financial and patient welfare matters depend upon referral. And local authorities may find themselves investigated by the local ombudsman, as in the following case when tens of thousands of pounds had to be repaid by the local authority (and the NHS) for care home fees, due to the failure of a social worker to make a referral for CHC.

> **Failure of local authority to refer a person for CHC assessment.** A man suffering from Alzheimer's disease, leading to major memory impairment and agitated behaviour, was admitted as a voluntary patient to a psychogeriatric hospital. On discharge, his wife understood the social worker was applying for CHC. In fact, he wasn't and had not made the referral to the NHS, even though the NHS subsequently confirmed to the ombudsman that they would have awarded CHC. By the time the complaint came to the ombudsman, the man had paid £26,000 in nursing home fees.
>
> The ombudsman found fault with the local authority and recommended that the local authority repay the money. In response, the local authority and the health authority jointly agreed to reimburse the nursing home costs in full, a sum of £26,055.50, and pay interest on this sum at the County Court rate. In addition, the local authority agreed to pay his wife £250 to compensate her for her time and trouble in bringing the complaint.[5]

---

1 National Framework Practice Guidance 2018, para 14.1.
2 LGSCO, *South Tyneside Metropolitan Borough Council*, 2018 (18 011 508), para 16.
3 LGSCO, *London Borough of Bromley*, 2018 (17 011 664), paras 28, 59.
4 LGSCO, *London Borough of Wandsworth*, 2019 (18 007 020), para 34.
5 LGO, *Hertfordshire County Council*, 2003 (00/B/16833), paras 29–32.

In another case, the local authority delayed for some six weeks, without good reason, in informing the CCG once a care home placement had become permanent, despite the CCG having requested this information. This meant that the CHC assessment and finding of eligibility were in turn delayed (although backdating was forthcoming in this case). Financial reasons alone make such delay puzzling, since in such a case, the local authority, as well as the person whose care home placement it was, was incurring avoidable expenditure.[1] Similarly, a delay in three months in sending information to the CCG was fault.[2]

If a person's needs are recognised to have increased, but the local authority both fails to increase provision of the current social care package, and to make a referral for assessment for CHC, then the person's needs will not be met and the ombudsman may find fault.[3] In the following case, it was an elderly man's daughter who had to find out about, and then raise the issue of, CHC; the local authority had omitted to do so.

> **Person denied CHC funding for years because of local authority failure to help get a CHC assessment.** A man left an NHS mental health unit and entered a care home in July 2009. The NHS assessed him for CHC but found him not eligible. In December 2013, he moved to a nursing home. His daughter contacted the NHS in October 2015, having been told by a friend about CHC; the NHS asked the Council to complete a Checklist in November 2015. In February 2016, the NHS awarded him CHC backdated to December 2015. In July 2016, following an appeal, the NHS agreed to backdate its funding to April 2012.
>
> The local authority accepted it was at fault for not helping the daughter get a CHC assessment for her father; had it done so, it was likely the NHS would have been funding her father's care from April 2012 much sooner. This would have saved the daughter distress, time and trouble, for which the local authority was to pay her £1500.[4]

Sometimes local authority staff simply don't understand the process for making the referral for CHC; this too will be fault if the ombudsman

---

1 LGSCO, *London Borough of Bromley*, 2018 (17 011 664), paras 58–62.
2 LGSCO, *Telford and Wrekin Council*, 2017 (15 019 906), para 14.
3 LGSCO, *Staffordshire County Council*, 2018 (16 015 050), paras 101–102.
4 LGSCO, *Suffolk County Council*, 2018 (17 013 410).

investigates.[1] For instance, when staff didn't know how to complete the Checklist, they simply relied on information provided by a carer; as a result the Checklist had subsequently to be completed all over again. This was fault.[2]

Similarly, a senior social worker visited to review, and to complete a Checklist for, a woman with multiple sclerosis and dementia, with complex care needs, and who was dependent on others for all her needs. He did neither; consequently, she was not assessed as eligible for CHC until some months later. The local authority was at fault.[3]

Registered nursing

The provision of registered nursing care is relevant to NHS Continuing Healthcare (CHC) in various ways, including the following.

First, local authorities are prohibited, under section 22 of the Care Act 2014, from providing it. See **Care Act 2014**.

This is why even if a local authority places a person in a care home when the person is not eligible for CHC, it is still the NHS clinical commissioning group that has to fund the registered nursing care element of that placement. See **Funded nursing care**.

Second, a need for that funded nursing care in a nursing home must be determined only after a CHC consideration in the form of a Checklist or Decision Support Tool (or Fast Track Pathway Tool).

Third, even if a person's needs can be met by registered nursing alone, without additional nursing or health input, this does not in itself preclude eligibility for CHC.[4]

Rehabilitation and recovery

Guidance states that one reason for deferring completion of a Checklist (and possibly Decision Support Tool), especially in relation to discharge from acute hospital care, is because a person might within a few weeks make some degree of recovery or might benefit from rehabilitation.

In this case, deferred screening and assessment would provide a more accurate picture of a person's ongoing needs. It would also mean that the NHS would in many cases be responsible for arranging and funding interim

---

1 LGSCO, *West Sussex County Council*, 2017 (16 017 324).
2 LGO, *Kirklees Metropolitan Borough Council*, 2016 (15 017 848), paras 34–35.
3 LGSCO, *Kent County Council*, 2018 (18 003 112), paras 20, 26, 36.
4 *R(Grogan) v Bexley NHS Care Trust* [2006] EWHC 44 (Admin), para 51.

care and services following hospital discharge but before consideration of NHS Continuing Healthcare (CHC).[1] See ***Hospital discharge***.

Hospital discharge aside, NHS clinical commissioning groups sometimes deny eligibility for CHC, not on the grounds that the person does not meet the criteria, but that there might be treatment, care or some form of therapy available to which the person might respond in due course.

This would seem a legally questionable approach, since assessment of eligibility is about current, not future, need. In general, if a person currently meets the CHC criteria, they should be eligible. If months or a year later they have improved as a result of other treatment, care or therapy, then a review should take place, if necessary, to revise eligibility. It is one thing to defer a decision for a few weeks, as in the case of hospital discharge; it is quite another to defer potentially for months or even years, on the off-chance that a person's condition might eventually improve.

Reimbursement

Guidance provides a framework for reimbursement by NHS clinical commissioning groups (CCGs) of money owing either to local authorities or to individuals. This is for periods of care which should have been identified as NHS Continuing Healthcare (CHC) but were not.

If the CCG has taken longer than 28 days, unjustifiably, in deciding CHC eligibility following a completed Checklist, then reimbursement from day 29 is due if the person is subsequently found to have CHC needs – unless the CCG can demonstrate that the delay was 'due to circumstances beyond the CCG's control'.[2] Such circumstances could include delay by a third party in providing essential evidence, delay in responding by the individual or their representative, or delay in convening the multi-disciplinary team because of the absence of a non-CCG practitioner whose attendance is essential.

Reimbursement to a local authority would be under section 256 of the National Health Service Act 2006; to an individual who had self-funded, it would be an ex-gratia payment, explained in guidance called *Managing public money*.[3]

---

1 National Framework Practice Guidance 2018, para 18.4; National Framework 2018, para 112.
2 National Framework 2018, Annex E. And: HM Treasury. *Managing public money*. London: HMT, 2018, para 4.7.4.
3 National Framework 2018, Annex E. And: HM Treasury. *Managing public money*. London: HMT, 2018, para 4.7.4.

(In one case investigated by the Health Service Ombudsman, the CCG agreed to refund a local authority for care home fees it had paid. However, during the dispute the family had incurred solicitors' costs in their attempt to avoid paying care home fees during the dispute. Because of the CCG's delay in resolving the case and in finding CHC eligibility, the ombudsman unusually recommended that the CCG also reimburse the family for the legal fees of £250.)[1]

Reimbursement: retrospective reviews

Sometimes challenges are made about denial of CHC to patients who have since died. Long periods of care may sometimes be an issue. Equally, some challenges are about long-term funding for a person who is still alive, and involve looking back at when a decision was first made that the person was not eligible for CHC.

In such cases, disputes can sometimes drag on for many years and sometimes result in large retrospective payments being made by CCGs. In one such protracted case investigated by the ombudsman, the claim had been made in 2010, but remained unresolved in 2017, by which time the dispute was still ongoing but the patient dead. The NHS admitted 'administrative failings'.[2]

Remedies, see *Disputes between a person and the NHS*

Resources

At the heart of NHS Continuing Healthcare (CHC) policy and practice lies the question of who is going to pay to meet a person's needs: the NHS, the local authority or the person themselves (if the latter is judged as having primarily social care needs rather than a primary health need).

Patients, families and practitioners would be well advised to be aware of this because financial pressures can undermine lawful decision-making and cause prolonged conflict. The following case was a telling illustration of how the NHS or social services may strive to avoid responsibility for care.

---

1 HSO, Mistakes in continuing care funding decision. Summary 490, October 2014. In: HSO. *Report on selected summaries of investigations by the Parliamentary and Health Service Ombudsman October to November 2014*. London: HSO, 2015.
2 PSOW, *Powys Teaching Health Board and Betsi Cadwaladr University Health Board*, 2018 (201702490 and 201703074).

> **A tale of financial resources and legal conflict.** Two legal cases were brought by St Helens Borough Council. The first lay against Manchester Primary Care Trust and sought, as it happens unsuccessfully, to establish that a woman with mental health needs should have been assessed as having a primary health need, and that therefore the NHS should have funded her care.
>
> Having lost this first case, the second case involved a dispute with another local authority, with St Helens arguing that if her needs were indeed social care in nature, then she was the responsibility of Manchester City Council, rather than St Helens, on the basis of rules about her 'ordinary residence'. This time St Helens was successful in shunting the cost of her care elsewhere. The reason why it was so eager, perhaps desperate, to do this was simple: her annual care package, at home, cost £675,000 and was thought to be one of the most expensive care packages in the country.[1]

The reason why the National Framework guidance warns off NHS clinical commissioning groups from financial gatekeeping when making CHC eligibility decisions is simple;[2] it is precisely because it appears to be such a common occurrence.

Respite care

Sometimes family carers need a break from caring for people eligible for NHS Continuing Healthcare, in which case responsibility for the substitute care required falls to the NHS. See *Carers*.

Responsible commissioner, see *Clinical commissioning groups*

Review of decision about CHC, see *Disputes between a person and the NHS*

---

1 *St Helens Borough Council v Manchester Primary Care Trust* [2008] EWCA Civ 931. And: *R(Manchester City Council) v St Helens Borough Council* [2009] EWCA Civ 1348.
2 National Framework 2018, para 156.

Reviewing a care package

Reviewing a person already receiving NHS Continuing Healthcare (CHC) is a way of checking that the care being provided continues to meet need and, on occasion, if a person has improved significantly, to consider withdrawal of CHC funding. However, in practice, NHS clinical commissioning groups (CCGs) sometimes appear to use reviews regularly, improperly and persistently to shed responsibility for meeting a person's needs. This tendency has been referred to generally in Chapter 3 of this book.

The National Framework guidance states that a person receiving CHC services should be reviewed within three months and thereafter at least annually, unless more frequent review is required because of their clinical needs.[1] Guidance makes the following key points about review:[2]

- **Proportionality**. Reviews should be proportionate in frequency, format and attendance.

- **Primarily about appropriateness of care plan and not about revisiting eligibility**.

    Reviews should primarily focus on whether the care plan or arrangements remain appropriate to meet the individual's needs. It is expected that in the majority of cases there will be no need to reassess for eligibility.

- **Change in needs**. A change in need should trigger a full reassessment of eligibility for CHC, including the requirement of a multi-disciplinary team using and completing a Decision Support Tool.

- **Well-managed needs**.

    When undertaking NHS Continuing Healthcare reviews, care must be taken not to misinterpret a situation where the individual's care needs are being well-managed as being a reduction in their actual day-to-day care needs. This may be particularly relevant where the individual has a progressive illness or condition, although it is recognised that with some progressive conditions care needs can reduce over time. (See ***Well-managed needs***.)

---

1   National Framework 2018, para 181.
2   National Framework 2018, paras 182–190.

- **Unilateral withdrawal following review.**

    It is a core principle that neither a CCG nor a local authority should unilaterally withdraw from an existing funding arrangement without a joint reassessment of the individual, and without first consulting one another and the individual about the proposed change of arrangement.

The points listed above are notable, since in practice they may sometimes be disregarded.

First, on proportionality, some people with progressive conditions, which are not going to improve, are subjected to disproportionately frequent reviews of eligibility. This can be anxiety provoking and distressing,[1] all the more so if eligibility is then withdrawn, despite a deteriorating condition.[2]

> **Dementia, diabetes, then leg amputation: CHC withdrawn as health needs became greater.** A person with dementia and type 1 diabetes received NHS funding only to have it withdrawn following a leg amputation, even though the dementia was worsening. Nothing much had changed: she still had intense needs, had now lost a leg, still had dementia, still had type 1 diabetes, still could not do her own injections nor administer her own medication. To the daughter, it seemed like a case of the NHS chopping off her mother's leg and, as a consequence, cutting the funding.[3]
>
> **Taking away CHC four times from a person with dementia who couldn't walk, stand, talk or feed herself.** A 77-year-old nursing home resident suffered from dementia. She received CHC, but three times she was reviewed, three times CHC was removed, and on each occasion, following persistent argument by her 78-year-old husband, it was reinstated, before being removed again several weeks before she died. By that time, she couldn't walk, stand, talk or feed herself. The husband was faced with having to pay for those last few weeks of care.[4]

---

1   Continuing Care Alliance. *Continuing to care: is NHS Continuing Healthcare supporting the people who need it in England?* London: CCA, 2016, p.21.
2   All Party Parliamentary Group on Parkinson's. *Failing to care: NHS continuing care in England.* London: Parkinson's UK, 2013, p.22.
3   BBC *Panorama*. 'The national homes swindle: a growing scandal.' Broadcast 23 July 2006. Transcript accessed on 27 June 2019 at: http://news.bbc.co.uk/1/hi/programmes/panorama/5216252.stm
4   Taylor, J. and Rigby, N. '"Medical opinions ignored" by NHS payment assessor, workers say.' *BBC News* (BBC East), 10 September 2017. Accessed on 17 July 2019 at: www.bbc.co.uk/news/uk-england-41187615

Second, in practice, reviews frequently focus on whether eligibility can be revoked rather than on the appropriateness of the care package. This is contrary to the National Framework guidance of 2018. It is notable that, in the context of Personal Independence Payments, the reassessment of people with lifelong and severe conditions has been stopped.[1] The CHC guidance on review seems now to advocate a similar approach.

Third, revocation of eligibility might sometimes, wrongly, occur without a full reassessment of eligibility.

Fourth, the grounds for removal of eligibility are frequently given as 'well-managed needs', despite the fact that the guidance expressly states that this is not a justification for such removal.

Fifth, CCGs sometimes inform local authorities unilaterally about withdrawal of CHC, again contrary not just to the guidance but also to the regulations, which stipulate that the Decision Support Tool and multi-disciplinary team are required for a reassessment of eligibility, as well as consultation with social services.[2] See **Withdrawal of care**.

---

1   Rudd, A. 'Closing the gap between intention and experience.' Speech, 5 March 2019. Accessed on 13 August 2019 at: www.gov.uk/government/speeches/closing-the-gap-between-intention-and-experience
2   NHS Responsibilities Regulations 2012, r.21(2).

S

Safeguarding

If safeguarding issues concerning abuse or neglect arise in respect of a person eligible for NHS Continuing Healthcare, then guidance outlines the NHS clinical commissioning group's (CCG's) direct responsibility to address them, as well as its duty to cooperate with social services.[1]

Social services have responsibilities to make safeguarding enquiries under section 42 of the Care Act 2014, in case of suspected abuse or neglect. Duties of cooperation, including around safeguarding, between NHS bodies and social services are under sections 6 and 7 of the Care Act.

Social services, in some circumstances, have a duty to appoint an independent advocate under section 68 of the Care Act in relation to safeguarding. In addition, if a CCG has commissioned care from an independent care provider, that provider also has its own duty to protect service users from abuse, neglect, ill treatment and improper treatment under regulation 13 of the Health and Social Care Act (Regulated Activities) Regulations 2014.

Scotland

This book focuses on England only. In Scotland, however, the policy about NHS Continuing Healthcare (CHC) is in principle the clearest in the United Kingdom. In 2015, the Scottish government took the step of trying to achieve clarity about CHC by confining it to hospital-based care.[2]

How consistent this guidance is with the *Coughlan* case, which stated that the NHS could not simply confine eligibility for CHC to hospitals, is not entirely clear.[3] This is because the NHS (Scotland) Act 1978 is based on the same principles as the National Health Service Act 2006 in England.

---

1 National Framework 2018, para 170.
2 Scottish Government. DL (2015) 11. Hospital based complex clinical care.
3 *R(Coughlan) v North and East Devon Health Authority* [2001] Q.B. 213, paras 41–42.

However, the implications of reclassifying people out of hospital as having predominantly social care rather than health care needs are different in Scotland from England. For those in the community in Scotland who consequently receive personal care (as social care rather than health care), it is free of charge to people aged 65 or over and to those under 65 who have a degenerative condition.[1] People still have to pay, following a means-test, for care home accommodation (as opposed to the care provided within it). And Scottish local authorities spend considerably more on adult social care than is the case in England: 43 per cent more.[2]

Screening, see *Checklist*

Section 117, Mental Health Act, see *Mental health aftercare*

Setting

Guidance states that:

> NHS Continuing Healthcare [CHC] may be provided in any setting (including, but not limited to, a care home, hospice or the person's own home). Eligibility for [CHC] is, therefore, not determined or influenced either by the setting where the care is provided or by the characteristics of the person who delivers the care.[3]

At times, the NHS has in the past tried to limit the availability of CHC in settings other than hospital:

> **Wrongly equating continuing care with hospital care only.** The local eligibility criteria for CHC were being applied such that if a person could be cared for in a nursing home rather than an NHS facility, an assumption was made that the

---

1 Community Care (Personal Care and Nursing Care) (Scotland) Regulations 2002, as amended.
2 Triggle, N. 'English "short-changed on care funding".' *BBC News*, 29 May 2019. Accessed on 28 May 2019 at: www.bbc.co.uk/news/health-48438132. And: Charlesworth, A. and Watt, T. 'The real cost of a fair adult social care system.' *Health Foundation*, 29 May 2019. Accessed on 30 May 2019 at: www.health.org.uk/news-and-comment/blogs/the-real-cost-of-a-fair-adult-social-care-system
3 National Framework 2018, para 63.

person would not be of Continuing Healthcare status. The ombudsman criticised this, notwithstanding that the criteria did in principle allow for exceptions, but in practice this aspect of the criteria was 'likely to be missed by those interpreting the policy'.[1]

Undue emphasis on hospital care. A health authority stated that people in specialist nursing home care could be eligible for continuing care funding. However, the criteria went on to state that this would only be where there was constant availability of on-site specialist medical expertise 24 hours a day, or of highly complex or specialist medical equipment to maintain life. In reality, this was only possible in hospital; thus, the issue of whether a person needed hospital medical provision was overly significant in the decision about eligibility for continuing care.[2]

No scope for CHC funding in nursing homes. A health authority's criteria, leaving no scope for the NHS to fund the full cost of care in a nursing home, were defective and over-restrictive, since such an approach might raise questions about quality of life (a person might be better off elsewhere than in a hospital) and, in any case, many authorities would have insufficient hospital beds available to sustain such a policy but still properly fund CHC.[3]

Respite care available only as an NHS inpatient. The ombudsman criticised the fact that continuing care funding would be available for respite care only if the person concerned became an NHS inpatient, but would not be available for him in his own home, so as to give his main carer, his wife, a break.[4]

No continuing care for younger, highly dependent patients, other than in hospital. The health authority had decided, as a matter of policy, not to contract for private nursing home places for continuing care needs. Yet the allocated 24 long-stay hospital beds for continuing care were insufficient for that purpose. In order to manage this shortfall, the authority's policy simply excluded NHS funding for the continuing care of younger, highly dependent patients not in need of hospital

---

1   *Dorset Health Authority* (E.208/99–00). In: Health Service Ombudsman. *NHS funding for long term care.* London: TSO, 2003.
2   *Berkshire Health Authority* (E.814/00–01). In: Health Service Ombudsman. *NHS funding for long term care.* London: TSO, 2003.
3   *Shropshire Health Authority* (E.2119/01–02). In: Health Service Ombudsman. HC 787. *Selected investigations completed December 2002–March 2003.* London: TSO, 2003.
4   *Cambridgeshire Health Authority* (E.22/02–03). In: Health Service Ombudsman. HC 704. *Selected investigations completed October 2003–March 2004.* London: TSO, 2004.

> inpatient treatment. The Health Service Ombudsman found this to be a failure to provide a service that it was a function of the health authority to provide.[1]

One legal case examined whether if a person already had CHC provision in the community and then entered hospital, a CHC package should continue if the basic hospital care were not sufficient to meet the person's needs. The court took the view that the assumption would be that hospital care would be sufficient; were it not, then the NHS clinical commissioning group would have to take steps to remedy this.[2]

Skin, see *Decision Support Tool*

Social care

Social care is meant, legally, to be distinct from health care. Hence the great divide in principle between the National Health Service Act 2006 and the Care Act 2014. However, the boundary is far from clear and tends to shift over time. Guidance attempts, vaguely, to distinguish them. See ***Health care needs***.

Adult social care is the remit of local social services authorities. See ***Social services***.

Social services

Social services in England are part of unitary, metropolitan or county councils (local authorities) with social services functions. These functions are discharged primarily under the Care Act 2014 for adults – and under the Children Act 1989 and Chronically Sick and Disabled Persons Act 1970 for children.

For the purposes of this book, the term 'social services' is used interchangeably with the term 'local authority'. Local authorities play a key role in NHS Continuing Healthcare (CHC) in terms both of what they should be doing (such as making referrals for CHC) but also what they are legally prohibited from doing, including, importantly, the meeting of CHC needs. See ***Care Act 2014***.

---

1 *North Worcestershire Health Authority* (E.264/94–95). In: Health Service Commissioner. HC 11. *Selected investigations completed April to September 1995*. London: HMSO, 1995.
2 *R (by her litigation friend RW) v NHS Sheffield Clinical Commissioning Group* [2014] EWHC 1345 (Admin), paras 3, 49.

Local authorities find themselves sometimes in a difficult position, caught between legal duties (and prohibitions) and working cooperatively with the NHS. Unfortunately, undue acquiescence or even servility can have unfortunate consequences, including (a) local authorities acting unlawfully by meeting CHC needs which they are prohibited from doing, (b) commissioning care at a level that is inadequate to meet the person's health care needs with resulting detriment to a person's health and welfare, (c) spending scarce public money inappropriately, and (d) means-testing and financially charging people for care which should be provided by the NHS.

The ombudsman has found fault when social services just 'goes along' with NHS decision-making. For instance, in one case, a nurse assessor had flouted the CHC assessment rules, undermined a family's evidence and made false statements. The ombudsman found fault with the NHS clinical commissioning group but also with the local authority since, at both practitioner and managerial level, the local authority had supported the nurse assessor as a matter of course but without grounds for doing so.[1]

Specialist staff

Guidance states that eligibility for NHS Continuing Healthcare (CHC) is not dependent on, amongst other things, whether NHS or specialist staff are required to provide care.[2] This reflects the following ombudsman case, the *Pointon* case, involving the care by his wife, rather than specialist (NHS or otherwise) staff, of a man with dementia in his own home.

> **Eligibility for continuing care without input by a registered nurse.** The case involved the care at home by a woman (and personal assistants funded by social services) of her husband, who had Alzheimer's disease. One of the grounds on which the NHS had held that he was not eligible for CHC was that he did not receive regular care from registered nurses.
>
> Two of the senior staff involved in the decision (both nurses) stated that the wife was not providing nursing care, since nursing qualifications and skills could not be self-taught and took many years to acquire. Therefore, the care being given by the wife could not be highly professional and thus could not indicate CHC eligibility.

---

1 LGSCO, *Lancashire County Council*, 2017 (16 000 404), paras 45–51.
2 National Framework 2018, paras 65–66.

> Yet both an independent medical consultant and a consultant psychiatrist disagreed with this view; they said that the severity of the man's condition meant he had health care needs 'well beyond' anything that the average care worker was competent to deal with. The consultant psychiatrist also gave the view that the care was being provided in a professional manner, and was equal, if not superior, to the care the husband would have received on an NHS dementia ward. Indeed, the 'atmosphere was not one that could be replicated in a continuing care ward'.[1]

---

1 *Cambridgeshire Health Authority* (E.22/02–03). In: Health Service Ombudsman. HC 704. *Selected investigations completed October 2003–March 2004*. London: TSO, 2004.

T

Timescales, see *Delay*

Topping up, see *Private top-up care*

Training

Guidance states that NHS clinical commissioning groups (CCGs) and local authorities should ensure practitioners in health and social care receive high-quality joint training which gives consistent messages about the correct application of the National Framework for NHS Continuing Healthcare.[1] It seems far from clear, in practice, to what degree CCGs are achieving this. For example, in 2018, the Public Accounts Committee of the House of Commons reported on poor training of staff.[2]

There is an incentive for CCGs to ensure that understanding of NHS Continuing Healthcare (CHC) remains poor. If few practitioners understand it, they are not in a position to help patients and families by way of information and advice about what CHC is and what steps to take.

In some areas, it appears that CCGs have taken to exerting significant pressure on local authorities not to have independent legal training for their own staff, as opposed to training delivered and controlled by the CCG.[3] For one organisation to seek to limit another organisation's access to independent training about national legislation and guidance is, on the face of it, extraordinary.

---

1   National Framework 2018, para 208.
2   House of Commons Public Accounts Committee. *NHS Continuing Healthcare funding*. London: TSO, 2018, pp.6, 11.
3   Personal communications with the author, by local authority managers, about this matter.

Transition

Guidance refers to a transition process for children who have continuing care needs as children but then need to be considered for adult NHS Continuing Healthcare (CHC) when they reach the age of 18. Guidance points out that eligibility for children's continuing care does not presuppose eligibility for CHC.[1]

One reason for this is the difference between the definition of continuing care for adults and the definition for children. See **Children**.

Therefore, the transition process at age 18 may be significant in terms of the person's entitlement and how their needs will, or won't, be met. The guidance contains an outline of how transition should be managed, including the following points:[2]

- **Timely clarification**.

    The needs of a young person, and any future entitlement to adult NHS Continuing Healthcare should be clarified as early as possible in the transition planning process, especially if the young person's needs are likely to remain at a similar level until adulthood.

- **Aged 14**.

    Children's services should identify those young people for whom it is likely that adult NHS Continuing Healthcare will be necessary and should notify whichever CCG [clinical commissioning group] will have responsibility for them as adults. This should occur when a young person reaches the age of 14.

- **Aged 16**.

    This should be followed up by a formal referral for screening to the adult NHS Continuing Healthcare team at the relevant CCG, when the child or young person is 16.

- **Aged 17**.

    As soon as practicable after the young person's 17th birthday, eligibility for adult NHS Continuing Healthcare should be determined in principle by the relevant CCG, so that, wherever applicable, effective packages of care can be commissioned in time

---

1   National Framework 2018, para 34.
2   National Framework 2018, paras 338–344.

for the individual's 18th birthday. In order to do this staff from adult services (who are familiar with the adult NHS Continuing Healthcare National Framework) will need to be involved in both the assessment and care planning to ensure smooth transition to adult services. If needs are likely to change, it may be appropriate to make a provisional decision, and then to recheck it by repeating the process as adulthood approaches.

- **Aged 18.**

    Any entitlement that is identified by means of these processes before a young person reaches adulthood will come into effect on their 18th birthday, subject to any change in their needs. The first review for NHS Continuing Healthcare would then normally take place three months after the person's 18th birthday and thereafter at least annually.

- **Right to review as for adults.**

    If a young person who receives children's continuing care has been determined by the relevant CCG not to be eligible for a package of adult NHS Continuing Healthcare in respect of when they reach the age of 18, then they and their parents or guardians – or in the case of looked after children their social worker and Independent Reviewing Officer – should be advised of their non-eligibility and of their right to request an independent review, on the same basis as NHS Continuing Healthcare eligibility decisions regarding adults.[1]

---

1   National Framework 2018, paras 331–344.

U

Unpredictability

According to guidance, unpredictability is one of the four characteristics of a person's needs – characteristics that, alone or in combination, may demonstrate the existence of a primary health need, and therefore eligibility for NHS Continuing Healthcare (CHC). The decision about this will follow on from completion of the Decision Support Tool (DST).

Therefore, unpredictability represents 25 per cent of the possibilities at this stage of the decision-making process and can, alone, form the basis of a primary health need, even without the presence of the other three characteristics (nature, intensity and complexity).

These four characteristics are to enable the NHS clinical commissioning group (CCG) to determine the quality and quantity of care that the person needs. The question of quality and quantity derives from legal case law. See ***Incidental or ancillary or of a nature beyond social services***.

For patients, families and practitioners, therefore, reference to unpredictability – and the definition of it set out in guidance – can assume considerable importance. Key points about it include the following:

- **Unpredictability: overall effect of needs and quality of intervention**. Guidance states that unpredictability is about:

    > the degree to which needs fluctuate and thereby create challenges in managing them. It also relates to the level of risk to the individual's health if adequate and timely care is not provided. An individual with an unpredictable healthcare need is likely to have either a fluctuating, unstable or rapidly deteriorating condition.[1]

- **Unpredictability: questions to ask**. Guidance goes on to set out questions that may help the consideration of unpredictability. These relate to whether the individual or others supporting him or her can anticipate when needs may arise, whether the level of need changes frequently and at short notice, whether the condition is unstable,

---

1 National Framework 2018, para 59; Decision Support Tool 2018, p.43.

what happens if the need is not met when it arises and how significant the consequences are, to what extent professional knowledge and skill are needed to respond appropriately and spontaneously, and what level of monitoring and review is required.[1]

- **Predictable unpredictability**. Guidance states that:

    the identification of unpredictable needs does not, of itself, make the needs 'predictable' (i.e. predictably unpredictable) and they should therefore be considered as part of this key indicator.[2] (See *Predictable unpredictability*.)

As noted above, unpredictability is one of the four characteristics to be considered at this stage of the decision-making process; any one of these, alone or in combination, can indicate eligibility for CHC. Thus, grammatically and legally, the conjunction between these words is effectively 'or' (whereas the word 'and' would require all four).

Nevertheless, CCGs may sometimes act inconsistently with the National Framework guidance, insisting that CHC eligibility is not possible unless there is unpredictability. Beyond the grammar of the guidance, key legal and ombudsman cases have in any case involved patients with essentially stable, if complex, nursing needs.[3] The following account suggests just such misguided insistence, even when there were clearly complex and intense needs.

> **Multiple needs: scored very highly by the multi-disciplinary team (MDT), but the nurse assessor denies eligibility because unpredictability is not present.**
>
> When we do attend assessments, it can be extremely hard to make the nurse assessors understand why someone has complex health needs. I was recently working with a gentleman who had PSP [progressive supranuclear palsy]. He couldn't move and needed hoisting everywhere. His condition meant he often didn't remember this limitation so he would often try to stand and then fall over. He had awful swallowing problems, where he had so much saliva it got into his lungs. This meant his mouth was constantly having to be cleared. He was fed through a tube eight times a day. His wife was providing all his essential care.

---

1 National Framework Practice Guidance 2018, para 3.6.
2 National Framework Practice Guidance 2018, para 3.6.
3 See range of cases summarised under *Indicative cases*.

> I was part of the MDT that graded him at the highest level for nearly half of the categories in the DST, which should have meant he qualified for NHS CHC. When the case was reviewed the nurse assessor said he wasn't eligible. We couldn't believe it. They said they disagreed with how unpredictable his needs were. His application was rejected. We appealed the decision but he passed away two months later.[1]

---

[1] Continuing Care Alliance. *Continuing to care: is NHS Continuing Healthcare supporting the people who need it in England?* London: CCA, 2016, p.10.

W

Wales

The NHS Continuing Healthcare (CHC) rules in Wales are similar to those in England.[1] Whilst the NHS in Wales has tried to limit its responsibilities for CHC in similar vein to England, nonetheless the implications and consequences are not financially quite so stark when people are reclassified as having social care rather than health care needs. *First*, Welsh local authorities spend considerably more on adult social care than is the case in England: 33 per cent more.[2] *Second*, in Wales, a maximum of £90 per week for personal care is payable if a person is in their own home. If in a care home, then a person will pay only if their resources exceed £50,000, compared to £23,250 in England.[3]

Well-managed needs

National Framework guidance states that just because a person's needs are being well managed does not, in itself, mean that the person ceases to be eligible for NHS Continuing Healthcare (CHC). It all depends on why the needs appear to be well managed.

Nevertheless, NHS clinical commissioning groups (CCGs) sometimes use this very reason – contrary to the guidance and therefore challengeable – to withdraw CHC provision or indeed deny it in the first place. The consequences can be not just arguably unlawful but also detrimental to the service user, as well as leading to social services undertaking to meet needs which they are legally prohibited from meeting. In trying to counter and challenge suspect decisions, the following key points are relevant:

---

1 Welsh Government. *Continuing NHS Healthcare: national framework for implementation in Wales.* Cardiff: WG, 2014.
2 Triggle, N. 'English "short-changed on care funding".' *BBC News*, 29 May 2019. Accessed on 28 May 2019 at: www.bbc.co.uk/news/health-48438132. And: Charlesworth, A. and Watt, T. 'The real cost of a fair adult social care system.' *Health Foundation*, 29 May 2019. Accessed on 30 May 2019 at: www.health.org.uk/news-and-comment/blogs/the-real-cost-of-a-fair-adult-social-care-system
3 Care and Support (Charging) (Wales) Regulations 2015, as amended.

- **Well-managed needs are still needs**. Guidance states that:

    The decision-making rationale should not marginalise a need just because it is successfully managed: well-managed needs are still needs. Only where the successful management of a healthcare need has permanently reduced or removed an ongoing need, such that the active management of this need is reduced or no longer required, will this have a bearing on NHS Continuing Healthcare eligibility.[1]

- **Well-managed needs, behaviour, no recorded incidents**. Guidance states that:

    An example of the application of the well-managed needs principle might occur in the context of the behaviour domain where an individual's support plan includes support/interventions to manage challenging behaviour, which is successful in that there are no recorded incidents which indicate a risk to themselves, others or property. In this situation, the individual may have needs that are well-managed and if so, these should be recorded and taken into account in the eligibility decision.[2]

- **Well-managed needs: obtaining evidence**. Guidance states that:

    Specialist care providers may not routinely produce detailed recording of the extent to which a need is managed. It may be necessary to ask the provider to complete a detailed diary over a suitable period of time to demonstrate the nature and frequency of the needs and interventions, and their effectiveness.[3]

- **Well-managed needs: environment**. Guidance states that:

    Sometimes needs may appear to be exacerbated because the individual is currently in an inappropriate environment rather than because they require a particular type or level of support – if they move to a different environment and their needs reduce this does not necessarily mean that the need is now 'well-managed', the need may actually be reduced or no longer exist.

---

1   National Framework 2018, para 142.
2   National Framework 2018, para 143.
3   National Framework 2018, para 144.

For example, in an acute hospital setting, an individual might feel disoriented or have difficulty sleeping and consequently exhibit more challenging behaviour, but as soon as they are in a care home environment, or their own home, their behaviour may improve without requiring any particular support around these issues.[1]

- **Well-controlled conditions: medication.** Guidance states that:

    It is not intended that this principle should be applied in such a way that well-controlled conditions should be recorded as if medication or other routine care or support was not present... The multi-disciplinary team should give due regard to well-controlled conditions when considering the four characteristics of need and making an eligibility recommendation on primary health need.[2]

The ombudsman has found fault when eligibility is denied on the basis that a patient's needs are being currently well met, since the relevant question is about the level of need, not whether it is being met.

Needs currently being met at home: wrong basis for decision. A woman, living at home with her husband, had Alzheimer's disease, was immobile and was unable to communicate. Her needs were met by her husband, paid carers and district nurses. She was denied eligibility.

The ombudsman stated:

I would also like to express my concern about the level of detail in the minutes of the first MDT [multi-disciplinary team] meeting in January 2009 and the reasons given for the decision that Mrs F was ineligible for CHC funding. The minutes state that Mrs F's 'needs are currently being met' as part of its reasoning why Mrs F was not eligible for CHC. This is not the test. The eligibility test relates solely to the level of someone's needs, not whether those needs are being met or not. The minutes do not show any consideration of Mrs F's needs against the factors for eligibility.[3]

---

1 National Framework Practice Guidance 2018, para 23.1.
2 National Framework 2018, para 146.
3 PSOW, *Aneurin Bevan Health Board and Caerphilly County Borough Council*, 2012 (201001820 and 201002050), para 29.

Similarly, this misconceived approach to well-managed need undermined the primary health need legal test when, despite having complex and intense needs in a nursing home, a woman was wrongfully denied CHC – on the grounds that the nursing home was meeting her needs with minimum involvement of NHS staff.[1]

Despite the law and such ombudsman cases, well-managed need seems to be a common ground for withdrawal, typically through repeated use of reviews, as evidenced by the Continuing Care Alliance.

> **Withdrawing CHC from people with continuing needs.**
>
> From our survey results, of the people successfully awarded NHS CHC, 44 per cent had gone through at least one reassessment. Most local areas insist on reassessing people at least annually. Our FOI [Freedom of Information Act request] found that between April 2015 and March 2016 one CCG withdrew funding from 241 people following a reassessment. There are occasions where withdrawing NHS CHC can be justified (if a person's health needs have reduced). However, many people being reassessed are in the advanced stage of their condition, and often near the end of their life with little room for improvement.
>
> Many people who have been reassessed shared their feelings of concern and distress with the alliance. Having NHS CHC funding withdrawn can mean care packages are reduced or removed altogether. With many people unable to afford equivalent care packages themselves, the person in need of care can be put at risk. People with dementia are commonly reassessed regularly. Despite having a progressive condition, funding is often removed when someone goes from having problem behaviour to being more withdrawn or moves from being at risk of falls to being bed bound. This is despite other health needs emerging as a result of these changing circumstances.[2]

Such reviews may be counter to common sense, as well as law.

---

1   PSOW, *Cardiff Local Health Board*, 2008 (200700482), paras 16, 40–49.
2   Continuing Care Alliance. *Continuing to care: is NHS Continuing Healthcare supporting the people who need it in England?* London: CCA, 2016, p.21.

> **Deteriorating condition, but cessation of CHC.**
>
> Since the previous assessment, the individual's mobility had deteriorated to the extent that they were now permanently bed bound. The use of the DST [Decision Support Tool] then gave the individual a lower score in the mobility category because they were at a reduced risk of falling. This subsequently rendered the individual ineligible for NHS continuing care. While it is logical to assume that someone who is bedbound is less likely to fall over, it is completely illogical to then deduce that this means their overall health needs have lessened.[1]

In addition, wrongful withdrawal of eligibility for CHC, on the ground of well-managed need (or indeed on any other doubtful ground), can have detrimental consequences for the person, financially and in terms of health and welfare.

> **Detrimental effect of withdrawal of CHC.** Eligibility was withdrawn (doubtfully on the reported facts in the case) from a man with dementia, challenging behaviour and various physical needs, seemingly because the care home was doing a good job caring for him – thus suggesting a well-managed need. The local authority seemed not to object. Instead, it accepted responsibility, but insisted on a cheaper placement elsewhere in which the man's condition, physical and mental, deteriorated in such a way as to harm him and trigger a safeguarding enquiry.[2]

Likewise, in the following Court of Protection case, doubtful withdrawal of CHC eligibility (commented on but not ruled upon by the judge) led to an unfortunate chain of events.

> **Doubtful withdrawal of CHC, leading to a reduction in care from the local authority, safeguarding concerns and an attempt to remove a wife from her husband.** A woman who had dementia, had suffered a stroke and had various physical needs was assessed as eligible for CHC needs. Following a second

---

1   All Party Parliamentary Group on Parkinson's. *Failing to care: NHS continuing care in England.* London: Parkinson's UK, 2013, p.22.
2   LGO, *Worcestershire County Council*, 2014 (12 004 137).

> stroke, eligibility was removed, highly questionably – although because of the nature of the legal proceedings (Court of Protection), the judge was unable to rule on this.
>
> The local authority subsequently reduced the number of hours of home care from 63 hours, provided previously by the NHS, to 49 hours. It also applied a rigid policy that it would not provide more than three hours respite for her husband who was trying to care for her at home. The judge could find no evidence that this level of respite was adequate.
>
> The judge found that this low level of assistance had placed the husband under great strain and that much of his conduct, objected to by the local authority, could be attributed to this lack of respite care. The local authority sought to argue in court that the wife's best interests would be served by removing her from her husband and by depriving her of her liberty in a nursing home; the judge, ultimately, took a contrary view.[1]

Withdrawal of care

Regulations refer to the importance of continuity in the context of assessments of eligibility and disputes between NHS commissioning groups (CCGs) and local authorities.[2] They also refer to a duty on the part of the CCG, as far 'as is reasonably practicable…to consult with the relevant social services authority before making a decision about a person's eligibility for NHS Continuing Healthcare (CHC), including any decision that a person receiving CHC is no longer eligible to do so'.[3]

Guidance elaborates by making clear that there should not be unilateral withdrawal of care, either by the local authority or CCG, without consultation and a joint reassessment.[4] Unilateral withdrawal may therefore underpin a finding of fault by the ombudsman.

> **Unilateral withdrawal and poor communication.** A CCG notified the local authority that the latter should take over funding but did not follow this up. The local authority did not respond, a muddle ensued and the care home was left £64,000 out of pocket, a detriment the ombudsman recommended the local authority should remedy.[5]

---

1 *A London Local Authority v JH* [2011] EWHC 2420 (COP).
2 NHS Responsibilities Regulations 2012, r.22(3); Care and Support (Provision of Health Services) Regulations 2014, r.3(4).
3 NHS Responsibilities Regulations 2012, r.22(1).
4 National Framework 2018, para 190.
5 LGO, *London Borough of Enfield*, 2016 (15 018 745).

Unilateral withdrawal with informing social services. A health board withdrew funding, after several years of provision, from a person with an acquired brain injury. There was no liaison with social services, who felt obliged to pick up the funding. No multi-disciplinary team reassessment had recommended that he was no longer eligible, and no formal, challengeable decision had been shared with the patient's representatives. The ombudsman found fault with the health board and took the view that it was 'attempting to unload its own financial obligations onto the Council'.[1]

The ombudsman has also criticised unilateral reduction (as opposed to complete withdrawal) of care by a CCG.[2]

---

1 PSOW, *Anglesey Local Health Board*, 2009 (200800349), para 97.
2 LGSCO, *South Tyneside Metropolitan Borough Council*, 2018 (16 018 767), para 29.